NAKED
AT THE
FEAST

NAKED
AT THE
FEAST

A Biography of
Josephine Baker

BY LYNN HANEY

Illustrated with Photographs

DODD, MEAD & COMPANY

NEW YORK

Acknowledgment is made to the following for their kind permission to reprint the following material from copyright:

Excerpt from *Been Here and Gone* by Frederic Ramsey, Jr. Copyright © 1960 by Rutgers, The State University. Reprinted by permission of Rutgers University Press.

Excerpt from *His Eye Is on the Sparrow* by Ethel Waters, with Charles Samuels. Copyright 1950, 1951 by Ethel Waters and Charles Samuels. Reprinted by permission of Doubleday & Company, Inc.

Excerpt from "The Last Time I Saw Paris," by Jerome Kern & Oscar Hammerstein, II. Copyright © 1940 T. B. Harms Company. Copyright renewed. ℅ The Welk Music Group, Santa Monica, CA. 90401. International copyright secured. All rights reserved.

Excerpt from *Paris Was Yesterday* by Janet Flanner, published by The Viking Press, Inc. Reprinted by permission of The Viking Press, Inc.

Excerpt from "J'ai Deux Amours" by Vincent Scotto, H. Varna and George Koger. Copyright © 1930, renewed 1958 Francis Salabert. Copyright © 1931, renewed 1959 Miller Music Corporation. All rights for the U.S.A. controlled by Miller Music Corporation. All rights reserved.

Excerpt from "I'm Just Wild About Harry" by Noble Sissle and Eubie Blake. © 1921 Warner Brothers, Inc. Copyright renewed.

Excerpt from "Bye, Bye, Blackbird" by Mort Dixon and Ray Henderson. Reprinted by permission of Warner Brothers, Inc.

Excerpts from "Harlem on My Mind." Copyright © 1933 by Irving Berlin. Copyright renewed 1960 by Irving Berlin.

Excerpt from *Papa Hemingway* by A. E. Hotchner. Reprinted by permission of International Creative Management. Copyright © 1955, 1959, 1966 by A. E. Hotchner.

1 2 3 4 5 6 7 8 9 10   83531

Library of Congress Cataloging in Publication Data

Haney, Lynn.
  Naked at the feast.

  Bibliography: p.
  Includes index.
  1. Baker, Josephine, 1906–1975. 2. Dancers—
France—Biography. I. Title.
GV1785.B3H36   793.3′092′4 [B]   80-18973
ISBN 0-396-07900-8

For
Ulla Gross

Acknowledgments

Six years ago my friend Hugh Beeson Jr. said to me, "Why don't you write a book about Josephine Baker?"

"Who is Josephine Baker?" I asked, as one might say, Tell me about Sarah Bernhardt or Isadora Duncan. I had a vague notion of a mirthful vamp cavorting about Paris in the razzle-dazzle Twenties. And I knew her to be, in the joyous extreme, an original. But who was she? Where did she come from? I began collecting stories about Josephine, tantalized by each new discovery. Then, more questions. The lovers. The husbands. Such an outrageous smorgasbord of souls. And so many! Could such a shameless exhibitionist experience genuine love and pain? Was there anything beneath the glittering facade? Or was Josephine just a bewitching feat of stagecraft? But if this were true, how in the world did she summon up such courage in North Africa during World War II and in the American South in the McCarthy era?

And so my friend's casual suggestion, "Why don't you write a book about Josephine Baker?" started me on the most exciting project of my life.

As I excavated Josephine's past, I realized that many of the myths surrounding her were just that: myths. Breathtaking sagas created by public relations agents, by Josephine herself, and by her sycophants.

While I was gathering my initial data and preparing to interview her, Josephine died. Fact now began to intrude upon the legend as many of those who had hesitated to talk openly about Josephine before at last felt free to reveal sad and amusing stories.

During the course of writing this book I talked to 416 people, many of whom knew Josephine intimately and were willing to share their candid impressions. In trying to thank so many persons, it is hard to know where to begin. Some gave bits and tatters; others loaned me their diaries, notes, and letters. A few, such as Josephine's brother Richard Martin who had never been interviewed before, contributed a wealth of family details.

Bricktop, Janet Flanner, and Anita Loos made Josephine's golden years in Paris come alive for me by dipping back into their personal recollections. Eubie Blake, ninety-six and still going strong, gave me a wonderful report on Josephine as the obstreperous chorus girl in *Shuffle Along.* Caroline Dudley, now in her eighties and tending a vineyard in south central France, produced scrapbooks and reminisced about bringing Josephine to Europe. Dr. Henri Comte, who performed a hysterectomy on Josephine in Casablanca, told me of the patient he almost lost. Poster artist Paul Colin, who still keeps an atelier off the Champs-Elysées where he proudly displays his 1925 poster for *La Revue Nègre,* described their first night together in Paris and refuted many a romanticized tale. Robert Ganshaw, a former agent of Josephine's whom I encountered at Nathan's Famous on Broadway, gave me the benefit of his vast network of theatrical sources. Hubert Dilworth, manager of Leontyne Price, introduced me to several pivotal personalities in Josephine's life. And two of Josephine's confidantes, Marie Spiers of Paris and Florence Dixon of New York, shared their private memories, while her perspicacious secretary Carolyn Carruthers gave me the "inside scoop" on Juan Perón.

Researching La Bakaire's sixty-eight years was a picaresque adventure. "I'm writing a biography of Josephine Baker" proved such a successful opener that I even tried calling her friend Fidel Castro, Paris to Havana, but couldn't get through.

Jean-Claude Baker, the director of *Téléfrance U.S.A.,* offered intimate glimpses of his foster mother and supplied a constant flow of names and telephone numbers as well as his beautiful Paris pied-à-terre nestled in the shadow of Sacré-Coeur. Jocelyn Augustus Bingham, still known as "Frisco" and still a Paris bon vivant, guided me through cellar jazz clubs and out-of-the-way *boîtes,* searching for old musicians who had known Josephine in those early days when she first arrived in Paris. Lisette Malidor, the lovely black headliner at the Moulin Rouge now touted on the boulevards as the new Josephine, permitted me to witness the activity of a Paris music hall backstage.

During my three trips to France, four newspaper articles appeared, telling of my quest for material; an extensive piece in *Nice-Matin* by Arlette Sayac proved enormously helpful. I also spoke on Radio Française, asking listeners who could help me to call. The response was electric. People of every description came forward: cabaret owners and domestics, retired newspapermen, actors, box-office personnel, producers, trollops, and gangsters.

Visiting the places in France where Josephine had lived, I knocked on the doors of neighboring houses. In Le Vésinet, Hélène Guignery permitted me to photograph stacks of letters from Josephine. In the Dordogne, Andrée Choqueteau, Josephine's private secretary during the Sixties, supplied me with crucial information, as did Merle Trijoulet, Josephine's accountant at the castle. On the Riviera, several of Josephine's children were helpful, particularly Jari and Luis. In Nice, Marcel Sauvage, who collaborated on three of Josephine's autobiographies, carved days from his schedule to fill me in on many personal moments in her life. And, yes, a bouquet to Margaret Wallace, Josephine's sister, who is stylishly ensconced at the Continental Hotel in Monte Carlo, where she works as a cleaning woman for a Russian princess.

In all my far-flung wanderings, no encounter was happier or more instantly rewarding than my meeting with Ellen Sweets, then a reporter for the *St. Louis Post-Dispatch*. When I arrived unannounced at the newspaper's office and asked to be introduced to someone who could put me in touch with key members of the black community, out came Ellen, a barefoot Brenda Starr in dashiki garb. She called throughout the city, tracking down members of Josephine's family, childhood friends, and people who knew and remembered Josephine's father, Eddie Carson. Three other sources in St. Louis proved especially useful: Richard Martin Jr., Josephine's nephew; Red Bernett, a gentleman of ninety-five who in 1919, as manager of the Booker T. Washington Theatre, took Josephine off the street and gave her her first professional job; and Judge Nathan B. Young, the foremost historian of black St. Louis, who provided me with a gold mine of historical lore.

To the following I should also like to express my gratitude for their help and cooperation: Henri Astric, C. Howard Burney, Robert Caro, Bruno Coquatrix, Dorothy Crayder, Mary Dicceco, Robert Frisch, Margaret Frith, Marie-Joli Gomi, Michael Gyarmarthy, Jimmy Hall, Frank Hartmann, Jack Haney, Kay Haney, Shirley Herz, Jack Jordan, Donna Lawson, Rosette Le Noire, Robert Newman, Patrick O'Higgins, Frederic Rey, Marie Rochas, Howard Saunders, Bobby Short, Jacqueline

Stone, John Streeter, Margarethe Thomas, Frank van Brakle, and Freddie Washington. As well as the Authors Guild, the Authors League, and the PEN-American Center.

Since Josephine's career was a lengthy one, her ups-and-downs, ins-and-outs, and comings-and-goings were documented extensively by the press. She was sometimes wreathed with orchids and, at others, with onions, by the following publications, all of which gave me access to their files: the *Boston Globe, Chicago Tribune, New York Daily News, International Herald Tribune, L'Intransigeant, Le Figaro, New York Times, Nice-Matin, Paris-Match, Paris Soir, St. Louis Post-Dispatch,* Paris Bureau of UPI, and *Vanity Fair.* And I wish to acknowledge the valuable information gleaned from six black publications: the *Amsterdam News, Chicago Defender, Ebony, Jet, Pittsburgh Courier,* and *St. Louis Argus.*

Also, thanks are due to the Boston Public Library; the Missouri Historical Society; Marta Luchisin of the Dance Collection and Paul Myers of the Theatre Collection of the New York Public Library at Lincoln Center, the Astor, Lenox and Tilden Foundation; La Bibliothèque Nationale in Paris; La Bibliothèque Municipal in Perigueux; Ruth Ann Stewart and Ernest Kaiser of the Schomburg Center for Research in Black Culture; the St. Louis Public Library; the Sterling Library at Yale University; and Betty Kepple, Henrietta Myer, and Valerie Fidrych of the Stonington Free Library of Stonington, Connecticut.

A potpourri of praise goes to my agent Hy Cohen and to those at my publisher Dodd, Mead & Company who were most generous with their time and talents.

In addition, another group willingly gave of themselves, helping shape both the content and form of the biography, offering sound advice during its development and progression, and editing as well as proofreading the manuscript. They are Hugh Beeson Jr., Lindsay Bradford, Peter Burchard, Henri Ghent, Royce Gross, and Louise Pittaway. Finally, a gold medal should be struck for Ulla Gross. Its inscription should read: *Primus inter pares.*

Lynn Haney
September 18, 1980

Prologue

"Elle est morte. Elle est immortelle."

—A voice in the crowd.

It was April 15, 1975. In the dove-gray light of a rainy Paris morning, seven thousand mourners stood waiting in the Place de la Madeleine. The funeral cortege inched its way through the mob to the steps of the great pillared church. Josephine Baker was dead.

She gave her last show without moving a muscle, but as always, the audience was hers. Here and there an hysterical or a fainting believer heightened the tension. Hundreds of gendarmes locked arms to restrain the crush of people.

In the midst of the melee, an old woman in a tattered overcoat sat on a folding chair next to the flower stall at the bottom of the church steps. She smiled in anticipation. "Ah, le bel enterrement!"

From the cobblestoned square, Josephine's fans flung bouquets onto the hearse, already a bower of flowers. "The little people of France were her real followers," says Arlette Sayac, a reporter for *Nice-Matin*. "Josephine didn't have the petty faults they know about, the stinginess, the rudeness and sniping. Her faults were on a grand scale—megalomania, unbridled egotism and wild squandering—faults that are beyond the imagination of le petit bourgeois. So they only saw the good things about Josephine. To them, she was a goddess."

Finally the police barred the 20-foot-tall iron doors of the church and fought those trying to get inside. The church was already packed, with some mourners even sitting on top of the rickety wooden confessionals to get a better view.

This was a finale Josephine would have adored. Her catafalque was draped in the tricolor and placed between two rows of flags representing the various branches of the military. Her war medals, the Légion d'Honneur and the Médaille de la Résistance, lay on a white satin pillow. Princess Grace of Monaco was in tears. An old friend, musician Pierre Spiers, played Mozart's Requiem on the Madeleine's majestic organ, then drifted into Josephine's theme song, "J'ai Deux Amours" . . . "My Country and Paris."

Josephine, who had defied all laws but gravity, would now ascend to Valhalla, that wing of heaven reserved for warriors who die in battle. What could be more appropriate for a departing deity of the Folies-Bergère?

How fitting that all this should take place at the Church of the Madeleine, a massive model of a Greek temple distinctly reminiscent of the Parthenon. Parisians consider the Madeleine très chic for funerals, situated as it is in the fashionable 8th Arrondissement, brimming with glittering shops—including Fauchon's—and with sumptuous restaurants, just a few strides from the Ritz.

Napoleon originally built the Madeleine as a "Temple of Glory" to keep alive the memory of his victories. Despite such pagan origins, it became a church, named for Mary Magdalene, the harlot whom Christ forgave. And later, in 1849, Chopin's Funeral March was performed here for the first time at the modestly attended services for its composer.

Josephine, by contrast, received a twenty-one-gun salute, an honor usually reserved for statesmen and reigning monarchs. Throughout the nation, French families gathered in front of their television sets to watch her funeral. The Madeleine's curate, Dean Thorel, gave a stirring eulogy praising her rare courage and genuine commitment to the dust of life. In a touch of Gallic politesse, he did not mention that Josephine was once an international symbol of Parisian wickedness.

Josephine had always liked to visit the Madeleine and to light a votive candle before the statue of the Virgin, asking help with the many favors she was seeking from the Almighty. Her belief in God, and in all the saints of heaven, was unshakable. She wore her religion like her skin. Although christened a Baptist, immersed in the muddy waters of the Mississippi at the age of ten, she claimed to be a Catholic, a Jew or a Moslem, depending on where she was. But as much as she tried to adopt more polished faiths in her aching hunger to belong, Josephine was, at heart, a Holy Roller.

She was a down-home shouter, a yeller, a hollerer. The fire in her soul was ignited by the power and magic of the spirituals, the sorrow songs of bondage she learned as a frightened child.

> *Precious Lawd, take my hand.*
> *Lead me on. Let me stand.*
> *I'm tired. I'm weak. I'm worn.*
>
> *Through the storm, through the night.*
> *Lead me on, to the light.*
> *Precious Lawd, take my hand.*
> *Lead me on. . . .*

Leaving the Madeleine after a visit, Josephine would look downhill along the rue Royale, toward the Obelisk of the Place de la Concorde, to the Seine, the Palais-Bourbon and the dome of the Invalides. This was her city, the city she, Josephine Baker, conquered—not once, but twice.

ONE

"She was a tiger lily out of a scum pond."

—Judge Nathan B. Young, City Court No. 2,
St. Louis, Missouri

Josephine was born in St. Louis on June 3, 1906. The earliest photograph of her, taken when she was about eighteen months old, shows Josephine seated on a bare, straight-backed wooden chair, wearing a long white dress trimmed with lace. Her abundant dark hair, brushed away from the forehead, forms a halo over a full round face that would look almost cherubic were it not for the petulant curve of the lower lip and the challenge in the eyes, glorious dark eyes that stare unflinchingly into the camera.

The child looks like an infant empress, the distillation of generations of royalty. In another incarnation Josephine might have been the daughter of a sultan or a maharajah, but in this life her origins were humble.

Josephine was the out-of-wedlock daughter of Carrie McDonald, a domestic, the descendant of Negro and Apalachee Indian slaves who worked on cotton plantations in South Carolina. She was born when Carrie was twenty-one.

Carrie arrived in St. Louis with her mother and her aunt in 1904, two years before Josephine's birth. It was the year of the Louisiana Purchase Exposition, also called the St. Louis World's Fair, the largest and gaudiest show Americans had seen since the Philadelphia Centennial Exposition of 1876.

1

St. Louis lies along a crescent-shaped bend of the Mississippi, a river of dreams and wild romance. The city founded as an eighteenth-century French trading post soon thrived and became a sporting town, with a reputation for graft and sin. The ethnic mix of the new metropolis produced a livelier, more cosmopolitan place than other Midwestern centers. Italians, Ukrainians, Greeks, Syrians, Austrians, and large numbers of Germans settled in and around St. Louis, drawn by the fertile Missouri soil and the rich underground resources.

For the black man, St. Louis was better than most Southern cities. Blacks came with the early French and Spanish settlers, and others came later when slave owners and traders moved across the Mississippi River from America's Southland. One of the largest slave-trading markets in America was conducted on the east steps of the old St. Louis courthouse, which now faces the Gateway Arch. Nearby on Locust Street between 4th and 5th streets was Lynch's infamous slave pen, where those to be auctioned at the courthouse were kept.

At a time when Chicago was still a cow pasture, there were five thousand blacks in the city of St. Louis, many of whom were property owners. These men had purchased their freedom or had had it bought for them by free black men. The tone of race relations in St. Louis had been set by the French when they settled the city. A gentleman, by a Frenchman's standards, was judged by the refinement of his servants. A Frenchman's slaves were often educated people. Some made trips to Europe with their masters, learning continental ways. Following the Civil War these educated, privileged freedmen became the upper crust of St. Louis black society. During the golden riverboat days, they were the artisans, the leading barbers of the city, the caterers, the stewards, the highly paid servants. They settled on the South Side, living in substantial houses, and even though segregation was the rule, their children attended both public and parochial schools with the children of whites.

German immigrants, who came to St. Louis after the abortive revolutions in Northern Europe in 1848, fleeing the oppression of their Fatherland, had no quarrel with black Americans. Many Germans, in fact, held antislavery sentiments. Some mar-

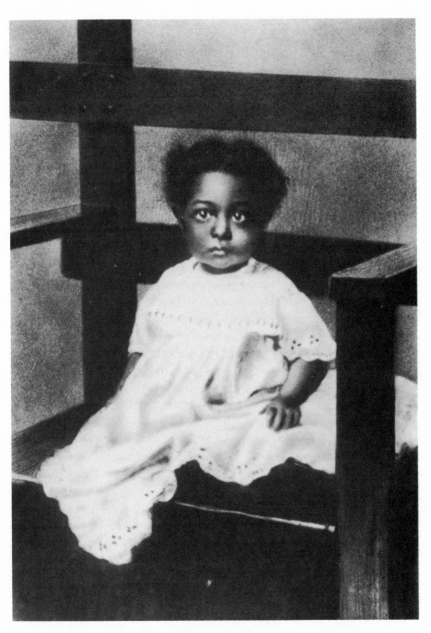

Josephine as a baby.

ried blacks. Many Negro musicians studied under Germans and learned the German language.

Following the Civil War, up from the plantations and bayous of Mississippi and Louisiana came other Afro-Americans, field hands, domestics, blacksmiths and roustabouts.

The St. Louis levee was an apron of industry. The steamboats from the Mississippi Delta brought not only workers to St. Louis, but delivered a supply of beautiful women, many of them octoroons. This vital era was in full flower at the time of the city's World's Fair, the culmination of a prosperous decade. Nothing was impossible in a place where Pianolas tinkled "Meet Me in St. Louis," and people from everywhere rushed to do so.

The Fair introduced such outrageous inventions as vacuum cleaners, electrical hearing aids and ice cream cones. Two years and $40 million went into converting Forest Park into a fairyland of shimmering lagoons traversed by Venetian gondolas, waterfalls and formal gardens. In block-long plaster palaces, visitors saw such wonders of modern technology as dial telephones and wireless telegraphy. A constant flow of celebrities and dignitaries kept the city's hostesses busy. The need heightened for domestic service: black maids and cooks, butlers and porters. Carrie McDonald had no trouble finding daywork.

The McDonalds rented a small apartment on Lucas Avenue, in the heart of the ghetto. The tenements were set in an industrial slum, tucked between factories belching foul-smelling smoke while producing the city's many products—shoes, drugs, stoves, streetcars, saddles, coffins, carpets, buggies and, of course, beer.

A tall, dark-skinned girl with an aristocratic nose, high cheekbones and a steady graceful posture, Carrie was anxious to join in the excitement of this rambunctious city. She had no trouble gaining entree, for she was not only remarkably pretty but had a beautiful body. This extraordinary physical endowment would be passed on to Josephine. It was not just a question of intriguing proportions, a genius of biology or chemistry set her apart.

Though lacking the panache of a born performer, Carrie showed a flair for music and dancing, and also acted in amateur theatricals in downtown St. Louis. She met Josephine's father,

Eddie Carson, Josephine's father.

Eddie Carson, at the Gaiety Theatre when both were cast as natives in *A Trip to Africa*.

Eddie Carson was a drummer who played on the Mississippi riverboats as well as in local parades, at picnics and funerals, and in the saloons, brothels and vaudeville houses of St. Louis's notorious Chestnut Valley. The Valley was a red-light district near Union Station that covered twelve blocks in the heart of downtown. This twilight zone was known as the Valley because its two arteries, Chestnut and Market streets, started on a slight hill, dipped a little and rose again.

The Valley was a rowdy wonderland, a magnet for the hard-muscled roustabouts who worked on the Mississippi steamboats and levees and for the well-heeled cattlemen and pleasure-starved Babbitts in town on business. Chestnut and Market streets were honeycombed with honky-tonks, barrel houses serving nickel shots of liquor, gambling halls featuring faro and chuck-a-luck, and brothels boasting beautiful octo-

roons, making St. Louis an inland rival of New York's Tenderloin and San Francisco's Barbary Coast. There was an almost
wholesome air about the place. Girls solicited on bicycles, riding
the streets in broad daylight, advertising their charms by letting
the wind sweep up their skirts. On warm summer nights
women in short translucent dresses stood in doorways, singing
the blues. Under the hot red lights the haunting voices of
whorehouse divas penetrated the sultry air. "Backwater blues
done cause me to pack my things and go. . ."

Eddie Carson was a character. A short, vivid man with
medium-brown skin and vast reserves of nervous energy, he
was an immaculate dresser who liked flaming colors. He wore a
broad-brimmed hat with a bright vermilion hatband, a boxback
coat and cloth-topped patent leather shoes with bright pearl
buttons. He hung out at pool halls and chattery jam-packed
bars on Market Street, where he bandied quips with "sweetback
papas" and their women in low-cut dresses.

Despite his love of the sporting life, Eddie was a notch above
most musicians in the Valley. His formal education ended when
he finished fifth grade at Alexandre Dumas, one of St. Louis's
segregated schools, yet Eddie never stopped trying to better
himself, to stretch his abilities to their limits in the narrow arena
of black St. Louis. Eddie wanted to sing and dance as well as
play his drums.

Ed McKinney, a friend of Carson's who also came of age in
the District, remembered Eddie's eagerness to master new
skills. "He used to hang out at Professor Julius Caesar Lucky's
Dance Academy to practice new steps. Eddie didn't have the
money for lessons, so he would play drums at Lucky's Friday
night socials to pay for instruction. He became so proficient that
Lucky hired him as a dance teacher." Eddie taught all the popular dances of the day—the Grand Square, the Imperial, the
Parisian, lancers, schottisches, the waltz and the cakewalk.

In addition to playing nightclubs and vaudeville houses,
Eddie was a snare drummer for the Pythian Society's Band.
The Pythian Society was a fraternal organization whose band
played for circuses and on holidays. Eddie became a familiar
figure marching down Grand Avenue, one of the widest streets
in St. Louis, with his head erect, his back rigid as a pole, his

drumsticks flying. "He was the best damn parade drummer in town," Ed McKinney recalled.

Eddie loved ceremonies. He gloried in the pomp and excitement of parades. As the band's pacesetter, he revealed a sensitivity at odds with his strident clothes that endeared him to fellow musicians. Whenever he passed a church, he softened his drumbeat, a signal to the rest of the band to pause. That was Eddie's way of showing respect.

A year or so after Eddie met Carrie, Josephine arrived. In looks and in temperament, Josephine favored her father. The small round face, the tipped nose and the prominent teeth all came from Eddie. She also inherited his energy and musical talent. Josephine was a plump baby, prompting Carrie to nickname her Tumpie, a variation of Humpty Dumpty.

After Josephine's birth Carrie continued to live at home with her mother and aunt. At night she carried Josephine around to the winerooms and vaudeville houses in the Valley so she could be with Eddie, who was drumming in a three-piece band.

Though born out of wedlock, dirt poor, in a disease-ridden slum, Josephine was lucky in one respect. St. Louis was musically rich and, from the beginning, she was at the heart of it. An habitué from birth of such legendary shrines of ragtime as the Gilt Edge Bar, an upstairs dive over Pickett's Drugstore, the Rosebud Café at 2220 Market Street and the Four Deuces Saloon across from Union Station, Josephine was the child of a golden age.

Sitting in bars like these, waiting for calls, the bards of Chestnut Street created ballads based on events of the town, then sang them for drinks and tips. Songwriters from Tin Pan Alley came to the District, dropped in at whorehouse parlors, places like Babe Connor's, and cribbed ditties they would turn into hits. When a talented St. Louis musician named Harry Duncan ran afoul of the law and the authorities decided to string him up, he gave concerts in his death cell—limited tickets issued by the sheriff—playing for talent scouts from New York.

Not far from where Josephine was born, at 212 Targee Street, a legend and a song had originated six years earlier when Frankie Baker shot Allen (Johnny) Britt, a handsome eighteen-year-old "mack" who had a way with women. "Frankie and Johnny were lovers," the song goes. "Oh, Lordie, how they could love." That is, until the fateful September night when Frankie saw Johnny at Stolle's Dance Hall with pretty Alice Fry. Then Frankie reached under her kimono for her little pearl-handled .44. She pulled the trigger and the gun went root-atoot-toot. As Frankie turned away, she heard Johnny moan:

> *Oh, my baby, kiss me, once before I go.*
> *Turn me over on my right side, the bullet hurts me so.*
> *I was your man, but I done you wrong.*

For a year Johnny's mother, Nancy Britt, wandered the streets in widow's weeds, lamenting the death of her son. A nameless piano player banged out a few lines of song, and this eventually became part of the lore of St. Louis.

In 1906, the year Josephine was born, St. Louis was the world's capital for some of the happiest, most infectiously lilting music ever heard, ragtime. These tunes originated with black piano players in the free and easy resort towns along the Mississippi. Ragtime was piano music. The left hand thumped a steady march tempo while the right hand performed miracles of syncopation. And in the early 1900s, St. Louis boasted the greatest ragtime piano players: Joe Jordan, Sam Patterson, Joe Young, Gertrude "Sweety" Bell and the best of them all, Tom Turpin, the undisputed King of the Piano.

The stout, somber, seldom-smiling Tom Turpin was the composer of such hits as "Harlem Rag," "Bowery Buck," "St. Louis Rag" and "Nannette Waltz." Scott Joplin, ragtime's foremost composer, a Turpin disciple, spent eight years in St. Louis at the turn of the century before moving to Chicago. His influence on music of the back rooms and brothels of St. Louis lasted a decade or more. His "Maple Leaf Rag" drifted past the swinging doors of the Valley saloons:

> *Oh go 'way man, I can hypnotize dis nation,*
> *I can shake de earth's foundation wid de Maple Leaf Rag!*
> *Oh go 'way man, just hold yo' breath a minit,*
> *For there's not a stunt that's in it, wid de Maple Leaf Rag!*

Carrie and Eddie worked up a song-and-dance routine that they performed in bars and vaudeville houses during their gypsy journeys through the District, sometimes carrying Baby Josephine onstage for the finale. Their act died young. Sixteen months after Josephine was born, Carrie gave birth to a second child, a boy she named Richard.

Like many firstborns, Josephine did not like sharing the spotlight. And she always felt that Carrie loved Richard more than her, bestowing on him the all-forgiving love of mother for son. Years later Josephine was still openly jealous and sometimes bitter: "Richard was a wanted child."

After Richard was born, Eddie's love for Carrie cooled. He drifted off and eventually married someone else. Josephine never forgot the feeling of desertion engendered by Eddie's departure. All her life she would look for protectors, older men who were often her lovers, to shield her from her inner fears. And when she became famous, Josephine invented fantasy daddies to fill the vacancy left by Eddie. There were alternately a "white boy who went to school with Mama," a "Spanish dancer," a "Jewish tailor," or a "Creole from New Orleans," depending on her mood, her need and her audience.

Most often Josephine opted for a Jewish patrimony because she felt a deep identification with the relentless struggle of the Hebrews against oppression. And when she was in a storytelling mood, Carrie's origins were also altered to make the story more dramatic. In 1967 she told Susan Barnes of *The London Sun:* "My father was Jewish. . . . Mother was an African. Her family were slaves from the Sudan. . . . The older I get, the more I feel the Jewish blood and the African blood in me. It's essential for me to return to Israel and put my bare feet in the hot sand near the Wall of Lamentation. I'm always going there when I'm in trouble."

To Carrie, Eddie's departure was a lethal blow, bringing a premature end to her youth. Eddie had been Carrie's window on the gaudy, glittering life of the street. She had fed off his sparks. On her own, she lacked the ability to shine. Having lost the man she loved, locked into motherhood, Carrie used Josephine as her scapegoat. Josephine's physical and temperamental similarity to Eddie was a cruel reminder of happier days. Josephine triggered a sharp animosity in her mother that was terrifying to a child. "Mama said things to me I'm sure she couldn't mean, that she hated me and wished I were dead."

Though Carrie could be grotesquely cruel to Josephine, she loved her and shaped her in her own image. While lacking Eddie Carson's scintillating charm, Carrie possessed the sturdier qualities of resilience and courage. She refused to be vanquished by the many tragic events that marked her life. She marched through them, head held high, bolstered by a deep religious fervor and, despite the degradation of poverty, an innate sense of her own superiority. Carrie was a survivor. That was her great legacy to Josephine. And, in return, Josephine became her lifeline. Josephine would give Carrie the dream she never had.

When Josephine was five years old, Carrie married Arthur Martin. He was a tall, hulking man who had a deep capacity for kindness but a volatile temper that surfaced when life became more than he could bear. Once when Carrie served Arthur some overcooked hot dogs for dinner, he lost control, picked up the wieners and shoved them into her mouth, choking her until she wrestled free.

Arthur adopted Josephine and Richard and treated them as his own. Skipping the formalities of legal adoption, Carrie paid a few dollars to Sister Emma, a neighbor and friend who was a notary public, to stamp a piece of paper stipulating that Arthur was the father of Josephine and Richard.

The children called him Weatherbird or Brother Bird or sometimes just Bird. Richard, who was a baby when Eddie left, accepted Arthur as his father. Josephine liked Bird but never saw him as a father.

An unskilled laborer fighting to survive, Arthur lacked Eddie's charm and flamboyance. In St. Louis common laborers earned seventeen to twenty cents an hour. There was no such thing as job security; workers were fired at the whim of their employers. Arthur spent long hours standing in lines in front of factory gates waiting for a chance to beg for work.

Security seemed within the family's grasp when Arthur found a steady job in a foundry ten miles from their house. Because he worked at night, he often missed the last trolley and had to walk home. He had no boots, and when it snowed he wrapped his shoes in newspapers tied around his ankles. Richard long remembered an injustice to Arthur, a sad part of Martin family legend. "One time his boss underpaid him five cents. When he counted his money and saw he'd been shortchanged, he ran back to the office and punched his boss. The police took him to jail. After his release he was out of a job for a long time. Everybody said he was crazy for beatin' up his boss, but five cents could buy a lot to eat in those days."

Within the next few years Carrie and Arthur had two daughters of their own, Margaret and Willie Mae. Josephine was intensely jealous of Margaret, as she had been of Richard. But for Willie Mae, the baby of the family, she felt only love.

Willie Mae, like Josephine, was spunky, an early talker and a quick learner. Josephine's affection for her baby sister grew deeper when the family dog clawed Willie Mae, leaving her blind in one eye. When the neighborhood kids made fun of Willie Mae, Josephine became her champion. Years later Josephine wrote a fairy tale, *Une Tribu Arc-En-Ciel*, about a one-eyed black hen banished from the barnyard because she is different from the other hens.

The Martins lived like vagabonds, moving from one apartment to another, sometimes evicted for nonpayment of rent. "Sued outdoors" was the local expression. This rootlessness, added to Eddie's earlier desertion, left its mark on Josephine. Home became important to her, a fortress in a hostile world.

Josephine was often sent to stay with her Grandmother McDonald and her Aunt Elvira, who lived together on Lucas Avenue. Elvira, who had strong Indian features, was neurotic, given to wild, unreasoning rages that frightened Josephine. But Grandmother McDonald, a rotund maternal woman with big sad eyes, gave Josephine the unqualified love she missed from her mother.

Grandmother McDonald baked Tumpie cornbread and spread it with jelly. In the afternoons she gathered Josephine on her lap and told her fairy tales—*Little Red Riding Hood, The Three Little Pigs, Snow White*. The story Josephine liked best was *Cinderella*. For Josephine, fairy tales had the shaping influence of religion. Fairy tales gave body to her deepest desires, promised her a happy ending. They were a thread, a motif that ran through her life.

After several moves the Martins settled on Gratiot Street in the poorest, dirtiest part of the ghetto, a street parallel to the two dozen tracks that terminated at Union Station, a place of whistles, bells and smoke, covered by a layer of grit.

Gratiot Street was lined with brick houses built by Germans, mostly during the 1850s. The simple, dignified facades, crumbling during Josephine's time, still retained much of their original beauty. But the rickety back porches were broken and ugly and overlooked filthy, foul-smelling courtyards strung with the laundry of the poor.

The Martins shared a small house with another family. Their apartment consisted of two rooms lit by benzene lamps. For insulation, Arthur covered the walls with newspapers, unintentionally livening the rooms with his black-and-white collage. Water for cooking came from a communal tap in the hall. The toilet was in the backyard, covered by a drafty shed.

Josephine bathed in a laundry tub, in water used by her mother, stepfather, brother and sisters. Carrie and Arthur slept in one room and the children in the other, on a thin and lumpy mattress alive with bedbugs. Twice a year Josephine and Richard dragged the bedsprings into the yard, soaked them with oil and set them afire to burn the eggs of the "chinches." But the rats were the worst. At night their bed, "chinches" and all, was an island of safety.

Whenever they had an empty chili or tomato can, they nailed it over one of the holes in the floor. But the rats bit and clawed their way around the tins, invaded the bedroom and scampered across the floor, heading for the kitchen, looking for food or poking into closets, gathering papers and rags for their nests. Richard, sitting up in bed, tried to pick them off with a slingshot. After Gratiot Street, for the rest of her life, Josephine hated sleeping alone.

The Martin's fight for survival became a series of daily cliff-hangers which, while often frightening, produced an almost welcome excitement.

Every day before dawn, Josephine and Arthur walked two

miles to the Soulard Market, the city's wholesale produce center, to scavenge for food. The farmers, driving their horse-drawn carts filled with vegetables, congregated on the market grounds, on the old commons south of the original village of St. Louis, to greet and gossip with each other.

Soulard, covering half a city block, was a rectangular complex of open-air sheds packed with stalls overflowing with fresh cabbages and squash, broccoli and carrots, a bright mix of garden colors. Here Josephine felt the lifebreath of the city and became a part of a world she was later to love in Les Halles, the great central market of Paris, Zola's "ventre de Paris."

Josephine crawled underneath the stalls to retrieve bruised fruit and vegetables. Like the children of gypsies who play on the sympathy of people they beg from, Josephine was a pet. The vendors, beguiled by her industry and charm, gave her fresh apples and apricots. Mornings when Arthur had change in his pocket, he crossed the street from Soulard to the open-air butcher stalls and bought ham hocks, pig's ears or pig's tails. For the Martins, every meal was a triumph.

Union Station, built at the turn of the century, resembled a huge medieval castle. A landmark of Josephine's youth, its heavy stones, turrets and watchtower loomed like a protective giant above the tenements on Gratiot Street. The yards of Union Station, three acres in all, comprised Josephine's soot-and-cinder playground. Union Station, which saw a constant stream of trains, served more passengers than any other station in the country.

Josephine and Richard watched sleek new trains slide into town: New York Central's *Knickerbocker,* the Baltimore and Ohio's *Diplomat,* the *Rebel* heading for New Orleans, the *Ann Rutledge* bound for Chicago. In *Been Here and Gone,* Frederic Ramsey, Jr., writes about the influences that contributed to black music, the spirituals, blues and jazz. He notes the impact of trains on people who lived alongside the tracks: "Trains were nearly everything. They made men want to pick up and go away. They were powerful, and they moved fast. Trains separated lovers, and brought them back 'someday.' There were glory trains, little black trains, good morning trains, good-bye trains, midnight specials and southbound rattlers. A freight car was a slow rattler; a boxcar, a sidedoor Pullman; an engine, the hog. Trains figured in song as images of despair, desire, escape, success in love, lonesomeness, fear, awe and exasperation; beyond all these, trains offered deliverance through death. Trains took people home, if they had a home; they took people down a long road, if they were looking for a home."

Winters in St. Louis were sometimes mild and sometimes severe, but they all seemed cold to Josephine. "I started to dance to keep warm," she remembered.

With the cunning of the poor, thinking the police would not prosecute children for minor offenses, the people of Josephine's neighborhood dispatched their young to steal coal from the freight cars behind Union Station. Arthur made Josephine and Richard a wagon from discarded pieces of wood. And in the yards the two of them hunted for the nuggets that dropped to the ground from a conveyor loading the cars. As soon as she was strong enough, Josephine climbed to the tops of the hopper cars and threw choice pieces of coal to Richard, a feat no one else dared attempt.

By the time she was six, Josephine was street smart. Using her charms to get what she wanted, she developed almost extrasensory perception. She read people's desires and catered to them. Her memory for faces was extraordinary.

When it was time for Josephine to start first grade, Carrie took her to the Children's Hospital to have a smallpox vaccination. The clinic was staffed by residents, one of whom was young Bordon Veeder who inoculated Josephine.

Fifteen years later, when Veeder was a well-established pediatrician, he visited Paris with some colleagues. The doctors were touring Montmartre one night, walking along the rue Fontaine, when they spotted Chez Joséphine, the cabaret she had started in 1927. The men went in and took a ringside seat. Bordon Veeder was nursing his drink when the dusky young Josephine, long-legged and naked except for a spray of ostrich feathers, burst onstage, dancing to a rollicking piano. All at once Josephine saw Veeder and hurdled the footlights to sit on his lap. Veeder blushed crimson. Josephine lifted an ostrich feather, grasped his hand and ran it along her thigh. Stopping at a coin-shaped depression, the scar of her childhood vaccination, she said, "Look what you did to me!"

Carrie enrolled Josephine in first grade at Lincoln School, a short walk from Gratiot Street across a steel footbridge spanning the tracks. A squat brick building adjoining a small playground, Lincoln served poor and middle-income blacks. Although each class contained at least fifty students, the rooms were equipped with only forty desks; the overflow sat on benches at the sides of the room.

Unable to submit to the slightest restraint, Josephine hated school. She missed the adrenalin-pumping life of the street. She could not sit still. She created a carnival of confusion. "I detested being told to do this and that. I always preferred my liberty. And the teacher tried to get me to stop making faces. The face isn't made for sleeping. Why not make faces?"

Although Carrie would not allow Eddie Carson to visit the children, he sometimes stood outside the rusty fence of the Lincoln schoolyard and watched Josephine during recess. Though wary of him, Josephine accepted the gumdrops and candy canes he slipped through the hole in the fence.

When she was young, Joyce McDuffy, now in her seventies, lived in a house behind the Martins. She was Josephine's classmate and friend. The two girls played together during recess and walked home together across the footbridge. Joycie loved Josephine, but Josephine embarrassed her by constantly getting into scrapes with her teachers and fighting with her fellow students. "Tumpie was always needlin' people. She'd poke the kids and stick out her tongue at them. And Tumpie was dirty. I used to try to get her to clean herself up, but it didn't do no good. She was much too fidgety. She'd wash half her face and forget to wash the other half."

In the tight little world of Lincoln School, Josephine was an underdog, caught in a situation she was powerless to change. She was among the poorest of the poor, often hungry, always shabbily dressed. For a year she wore the same clothes every day, a blue middy dress trimmed in white. She went barefoot or wore ill-fitting shoes. For a while Josephine wore a pair of high-heeled shoes, a present to the family from someone who must have had small feet. Arthur cut down the heels, but the toes of the shoes turned up and Josephine's unsteady gait caused her friends to laugh.

Josephine often played at the McDuffy house with Joycie and Robert McDuffy. Robert was twelve when Josephine was seven. Throughout Josephine's career, numerous producers would claim the distinction of having discovered Josephine Baker, but Robert McDuffy was the first to capitalize on her talent. An enterprising boy, Robert was casting about for a way to earn some spending money. He decided to give show business a try.

The Booker T. Washington Theatre, a small black vaudeville house, had recently opened at 23rd and Market, bringing excitement to the neighborhood. It featured some of the best black talent of the time, including Bessie Smith, Ma Rainey, Ida Cox and Butterbeans and Susie. The theatre ran a new show every week with a different theme—African, cowboy, Egyptian, you name it. The owner, Charlie Turpin, Tom Turpin's brother, held ragtime piano contests for local musicians. Robert McDuffy went to the Booker T. Washington once a week, then came home and copied the professional routines in his basement productions. His acts were called McDuffy's Pin and Penny Poppy Shows.

Robert used orange crates for seats, candles in tin cans for lights, and made a curtain of many colors from cast-off pieces of material. He charged the neighborhood children a penny or a pin, using the pins to hold together his costumes. Josephine and Joycie kicked up their legs in his two-girl chorus line. "He was our flimflam man," Joyce McDuffy remembers. "He was the big producer who put together the acts and collected the money. Tumpie and I didn't get nothin' for bein' in the show, but we loved it. We both kinda had it in our minds to grow up to be dancers."

McDuffy Productions inspired Josephine. She performed for her family, marching down the steps of the Martin's cellar, pretending she was starring in a big-time show. Brother Richard was not impressed by her talent. "She never changed her act. She made the same entrance again and again."

When Josephine was eight, Carrie returned from work one night to announce that she had found a Mrs. Keiser, who would give Josephine room and board in exchange for doing chores around the house. Josepnine never could forget the terror she felt at the thought of being sent away from home to live with a stranger. "I would have loved to run away but I knew it was useless because I was too small."

Though Mrs. Keiser seemed kind when she called for Josephine, though she bought her a pair of shoes and a dress, she was a Simon Legree, determined to extract from the child every ounce of work in her. Josephine was in bondage, forced to perform a ceaseless round of chores.

She soon discovered that Mrs. Keiser was a sadist. "She beat me until I had blisters on my back. She would pull me out of my bed by the ears. She said I used too much soap washing the dishes.

"At night I slept in the cellar with the dog in a large box in the corner, and when I crawled into bed he would make a place for me. He was a good dog and I gave him half my food."

The mutt had been hit by a car, permanently crippling his left hind leg. Josephine named him Three Legs. She lived in fear that the dog catcher would whisk him off to the pound. In the afternoons, returning from school, she announced her arrival at the Keiser's household by calling, "Here, Three Legs. Here, Three Legs."

Josephine had another pet, a young white male chicken named Tiny Tim. For many months Tiny Tim lived in a cage tucked under Josephine's kitchen work table.

Thriving on the scraps Josephine fed him, Tiny Tim burgeoned into a handsome young cock.

"Kill him," said Mrs. Keiser one afternoon. "He's ready to be eaten."

Without saying a word, Josephine did as she was told. She placed Tiny Tim between her legs, held his head low and cut his neck with a pair of scissors.

Josephine watched Tiny Tim squeal and squirm as the blood trickled down her legs. Then she kissed him and plucked him and handed him to Mrs. Keiser.

Josephine was seeing life imitate literature. Like her fairy tale heroine Cinderella, she was forced to dwell among the ashes and to work as a drudge for a woman as malicious as the wickedest of Grimm's stepmothers.

Since, under Missouri law, Mrs. Keiser was obliged to send Josephine to school, the classroom now became a haven, a respite from her oppressor.

History interested Josephine most, particularly stories of the royal families of Europe. When her teacher talked about kings and queens who rode in carriages, wore rubies and sapphires, issued commands and dubbed knights, Josephine imagined herself on a throne. She yearned for the beauty, passion and adventure that seemed to be the stuff of royalty. Her fantasies became a narcotic, obliterating her cruel and ugly life. "All my queens were blond. I could see them walking step after step after step."

Josephine's first period of servitude came to a halt when she let a pot of water on the stove boil over. Mrs. Keiser, enraged, grabbed her arm and plunged her hand into the scalding water. Josephine ran next door, howling in pain, the skin of her hand already peeling. The neighbor took Josephine into her arms and Josephine lost consciousness. The next thing she knew she was lying in a hospital bed surrounded by Carrie, a doctor and a nurse.

Once back home Josephine made forays with her friends across Grand Avenue onto alien turf, the neighborhoods of the whites. There she knocked on doors, drumming up trade by offering to clean stoops, mind people's babies and make trips to the marketplace. Smart and resourceful, she began to make money. "On good days I could make fifty cents. I would give forty-five cents to my family. On days like that, everybody loved me."

Richard remembered her tenderness during those years. "I won't say she tried to make a false appearance. Josephine was always smilin' an' laughin'. But you could see a little bit in her face, the reflection of things down deep in her heart."

Carrie found a steady job working in a laundry run by Arthur's sister. The family moved to 2632 Bernard Street, a bigger house with a full-size kitchen.

But things were no better for Arthur there. Defeated in his struggle to keep a job, he became increasingly depressed, retreating from his family and starting on a solitary journey into madness. As Eddie Carson's departure helped shape

Josephine's mistrust of men, so did Arthur's inability to take hold and survive.

Josephine looked to men for love, for sustenance and sex, but she never relied on them. She relied on herself.

As Arthur's position in the family weakened, Carrie's grew stronger. Josephine saw her mother as the dominant figure in the home. In her weakest moments, exhausted from overwork and crushed by disappointments, Carrie was still a formidable matriarch. And the mantle of breadwinner was being passed onto Josephine, not Brother Richard, because Carrie knew that a black woman, not a black man, would always be in demand as a worker.

Richard, Margaret and Willie Mae thought Josephine was "bossy," but still they turned to her for guidance and relied on her strength. It was Josephine, not Carrie or Arthur, who made Christmas for the family. When she was doing odd jobs, Josephine asked her employers for discarded dolls, bits of chalk for hopscotch and lengths of rope for jumping. She wrapped her presents in discarded paper. "She was like a mother and father to us," Richard remembers.

One Christmas Eve a rich St. Louis woman who had hired Josephine to scrub her floors started telling her about Santa Claus and his fleet of reindeer. "There is no Santa Claus," Josephine snapped. "I'm Santa Claus."

When Josephine was ten, an engaging mountebank drove his horse-drawn gypsy wagon down the cobblestone streets of the District, waving to passersby, urging them to follow him. This pied piper's wagon carried a raggle-taggle band of performers. The Medicine Man set up his stage on a vacant lot in the twenty-seven-hundred block of Clark Avenue, not far from 2632 Bernard Street.

The Medicine Man, selling Kickapoo Snake Oil and other colorful but most often worthless concoctions, was a delightful, rascally, typically Southern gentleman, sporting a Stetson, a gray pointed beard and a Prince Albert coat bedecked with medals given him "by the crowned heads of Europe, Asia, Africa and Australia."

Since legitimate doctoring was much too expensive for the poor and the clinics available to blacks were few, the Medicine

Man did a thriving business diagnosing the ailments of his gullible customers. His remedies were liberally spirited with alcohol. Some contained opium, morphine or cocaine. They were guaranteed to cure everything from tapeworm to lice, venereal disease to menstrual irregularities.

To drum up interest and soften his customers, the Medicine Man sponsored shows of vaudeville artists accompanied by bands of jug blowers, washboard beaters, kazoo players and country-style fiddlers.

As darkness came on, the Medicine Man lit kerosene torches, proclaiming that gaiety, music and song were to be had free of charge. Josephine joined the gathering, staring in delight at the vagabond performers clustered on the little stage.

Toward evening's end a dance contest was announced, and as the jug band pumped out a crude jazz spasm Josephine felt a sense of hot excitement. She jumped to the stage, bucked and winged and stamped her feet. She threw her arms skyward and kicked out her legs in a pulsing, rhythmic exhibition. The audience laughed, clapped and slapped their thighs.

When she finished, the doctor patted her head and handed her a crisp new dollar bill. This was the first time Josephine had ever earned money for anything other than menial labor. She broke away and ran straight home, the dollar crumpled in her hand. "Mama! Mama!" she cried. "I won first prize for dancing."

TWO

"For me, St. Louis represented a city of fear and humiliation."

—Josephine

In 1917, when Josephine was eleven, the East St. Louis race riot ravaged black neighborhoods less than ten miles from her house. Though Josephine was not involved in the massacre, the event took on a symbolic significance for her. Josephine became convinced she was a black Joan of Arc, anointed by God to save her people from oppression.

In its violence and brutality, the East St. Louis race riot was one of the worst in the history of the country. During a day and night of horror, thirty-nine blacks and nine whites died. Property damage totaled half a million dollars; 312 buildings and 44 boxcars were reduced to ashes.

East St. Louis was a vast, abrasive no-man's-land made up of stockyards, meat-packing plants and foundries. Workers crowded together in neighborhoods close to the yards and industrial buildings. A substantial portion of the black population lived in small wooden shacks and derelict boxcars.

During the first two decades of this century, an exodus of blacks from the South tripled East St. Louis's black population. For the first time large numbers of blacks aggressively claimed what they knew were their rights. Blacks, competing with the white labor force, made heavy demands on the limited housing, transportation and recreational facilities.

When factory owners stepped up their hiring of blacks, sabotaging white hopes for better wages, labor agitators spread rumors that blacks armed with guns and knives were invading white neighborhoods bent on theft, rape and murder. Open warfare started on July 2, when bands of armed whites tore into East St. Louis, setting fire to boxcars and shacks. Blacks fleeing their homes were beaten and stoned.

East St. Louis was linked to her sister city by bridges. More than 1500 blacks fled across the Eads Bridge to seek safety in St. Louis. Josephine stood with her neighbors near the end of the bridge watching the pathetic, frightened people cross the Mississippi River. Mothers carried their infants so the men could use baby carriages and wagons to transport the aged and their possessions to safety. Children carried dogs and cats. The burning buildings, the terror of the people, left their mark on Josephine. "We children stood huddled together in bewilderment. We were hiding behind the skirts of grown-ups, frightened to death."

The Red Cross set up a relief center at the Municipal Lodging House on South 12th Street to provide food, clothing and shelter for the refugees. In the melee that followed, it was impossible for Red Cross officials to distinguish the fugitives from St. Louis blacks. Josephine went to the Municipal Lodging House with others from her neighborhood to stand in line for handouts. At the Lodging House she heard lurid stories of atrocities commited by whites against blacks.

For Josephine, the riot would always remain an open wound. She told the story again and again, in such vivid detail that many people listening to her, including reporters and magazine writers, assumed that she had lived in East St. Louis.

The massacre cast a shadow across the Chestnut Valley and the surrounding ghetto. Until its outbreak, race relations in St. Louis had been strained but rarely violent. Now both blacks and whites were prey to the same sort of malicious rumors that had caused the riot.

One story persistently making the rounds on Bernard Street was that medical students at St. Louis University, short of cadavers, were on the prowl for blacks whose bodies they could use in their studies. Handicapped people were said to be favorite targets, giving the students a chance to study abnormalities. If the students could not catch and kill a lame person or a humpback, so the story went, they would take a child. After supper, as her children went out to play, Carrie would caution, "Watch out. The studyin' doctors will get you and take you for experiment."

Josephine was on the threshold of adolescence and was filled with rebellion. Her womanhood was stirring as Carrie's youth was fading. Josephine saw her mother, who had once been lively and pretty with dreams of her own, become worn and gaunt. She saw the light die in her eyes.

The friction between mother and daughter now took a competitive turn. Carrie manipulated Josephine through criticism, ignoring her talent and erratically giving and withholding love so that Josephine was forced to be in a state of needy dependency, trying again and again for her mother's approval.

Josephine resented the power Carrie had over her and feared her mother's anger. Still, she refused to knuckle under to Carrie. Instead, the constant needling acted as a spur to prick and enflame Josephine's daredevil nature. She wanted to show Carrie that she, Josephine, was even sturdier than her bloodline.

Things came to a head one summer night, Richard remembers. "Us kids had a curfew. We had to be in by nine o'clock. We couldn't say we didn't know the time because every night at nine a steam whistle blew at the Liggett and Myers factory. The whistle could be heard for miles around."

Josephine disobeyed the curfew and came home an hour late. Carrie yelled, threatening to send her to reform school. Josephine sassed back. Infuriated, Carrie grabbed Josephine, pulled her pants down and whipped her with a strap.

Josephine was raging mad. She slammed out of the house and ran down the street, resolving never to return. But she did not run far.

The night was hot and the steps were filled with people. A man in his fifties, the owner of an ice cream parlor who knew Josephine, saw the tears and fury in her eyes. He invited her to live with him and work in his shop.

The arrangement lasted a very short time because the neighbors were outraged, complaining to Carrie that a pubescent girl should not share quarters with a middle-aged man. So Josephine moved to Grandmother McDonald's and took a job as a waitress at the Old Chauffeur's Club on Pine Street.

The Old Chauffeur's Club was a hangout for the best jazz musicians in town. As she waited on tables, Josephine kidded with the musicians, imitating the way they sang and danced. Eliah Shaw, a piano player at the club, remembers, "She sure was a fiery young lady. She wouldn't stand still."

Josephine began to change. She looked into the mirror, moistening her fingers with her tongue, then bending her recalcitrant hair into spit curls. Her feverish gait and silly grimaces came into focus. She began to develop a personal style. Brother Richard saw all this. "She was always movin'. It was like the music of the time was in her bones."

Sunday afternoons were Josephine's favorite time of week, for it was then she would walk across to 23rd and Market, to the red brick Booker T. Washington Theatre, and plunk down her nickel at the box office. As the line of chorus girls danced onstage, their legs kicking toward the rafters in mechanical precision, Josephine was transported into a make-believe world. With their gossamer hair and gleaming cocoa-colored skin, the chorines became her goddesses. She imagined herself in the chorus line, responding to the wild applause, dancing, dancing with the others, an object of lust and adoration. Josephine was stagestruck.

The Old Chauffeur's Club was right next door to Pythian Hall, headquarters for Eddie Carson's band. Eddie stopped in at the Chauffeur's Club often, grateful for a chance to see his daughter without running into Carrie. Eddie had not done badly as a drummer. He still played in the District, and he had spent a season touring the country with the Ringling Brothers' Band. Even so, he never had any money to spare.

Josephine was now discovering what money could buy. Every night, waiting on tables, she was exposed to the pampered St. Louis women with their diamond rings and sumptuous clothes. After work Josephine "stepped out" with the boys in the Valley. She resented looking like a ragamuffin. Often when Eddie came to see her she would put the touch on him. One night she asked for a watch.

"I can't, Tumpie," he said. "I'm hard up myself right now."

Josephine refused to listen. After all, Eddie had three step-children who must be siphoning off money that was rightfully hers. Yet Florence Alexander, one of Eddie's stepchildren who is now in her sixties, says she grew up in a foster home, that Eddie never gave much. "Josephine had her opinion, which was wrong, and she never tried to find out differently."

Josephine worked at the Old Chauffeur's Club about eight months. She was thirteen years old and, more or less, support-ing herself. Then without warning she quit her job. She stopped by the house one day and said, "Mama, I'm getting married."

Carrie made no effort to stop her even though nobody, in-cluding Josephine, knew much about the groom. His name was Willie Wells. He was in his late twenties and worked in a foundry. "How she run up on Willie, I don't know," her brother Richard says. "I don't think it was at the restaurant. She had a girlfriend and they used to go to dances in the neighbor-hood. Maybe she met him at one of the dances."

Josephine and Willie were married in the living room of her Aunt Josephine Cooper's apartment. Her aunt had a little money and so could make things nice for the wedding. Josephine wore a long white dress and Willie wore a suit. The minister pronounced them man and wife. The guests ate roast pork and baked macaroni.

The newlyweds moved into a room of their own in Carrie and Arthur's house. When Willie went off to work during the day, Josephine stayed home. Suddenly the firebrand was un-naturally placid.

A month or so after the marriage, Josephine started knitting baby clothes, which she stacked in neat piles on her bureau. She also bought a little wooden bassinet.

Josephine's happiness was short-lived. One evening Carrie and Arthur were sitting downstairs in their kitchen when Willie slammed into the house and bounded up the stairs. He burst into the bedroom where Josephine was, yelling, "Come out here. Le'me break your neck."

Carrie did not move. Arthur did not move. Then they heard loud noises and both ran upstairs. Josephine had a broken bottle in her hand. Willie's face was bleeding from a cut just above the eye. Josephine seemed calm. "I was defendin' myself," she said.

Willie went to the doctor, who stitched the wound. After that he left Josephine.

Richard, who was twelve when the marriage broke up, never knew the cause of Willie's anger. He had never seen his sister as sad as she was in the months following Willie's departure. All the life went out of her face. The baby clothes disappeared. Richard drew a natural conclusion. "She must have had an abortion, 'cause nothin' arrived."

Josephine went back to the Old Chauffeur's Club as if the marriage had never happened. Many of the girls she knew from Lincoln School had gone on to Sumner High. Her friends were just starting to go out on dates. To them, Josephine, who worked in the District, who had been married and separated, was an object of intense curiosity. Joycie McDuffy thought Tumpie was fast.

When asked about her marriage to Willie Wells, Josephine made a joke of it. "Willie? I hardly stayed with him overnight."

While at the Club, Josephine was befriended by members of a ramshackle trio calling itself The Jones Family Band. Old Man Jones, as he was known in the Valley, played a big brass horn, his pretty common-law wife was a trumpet player and their daughter, Doll, a promiscuous girl about Josephine's age, played the fiddle. The Joneses carried their instruments all around the District, performing in front of barber shops, pool halls and any place they could make a little music and pass the hat.

Old Man Jones had seen Josephine's talent, watched her practice her dance steps and heard her sing her songs. He invited her to join his trio.

Josephine quit her job at the Club and roamed with the Jones Family up and down Chestnut and Market streets, singing ragtime ditties, stomping her feet and dancing. The Booker T. Washington Theatre had four shows a day, five when they had a hit, and after Josephine joined the trio she and the Joneses got into the habit of playing on the corner of 23rd and Market, catching the theatre crowd standing in line.

One of those who noticed Josephine was the theatre's stage manager, Red Bernett. Bernett is now well into his nineties and lives alone in a St. Louis row house. Though almost sixty years have passed since the moment he first saw Josephine, he remembers it well. "She was a bitty thing standin' there singin' to the people. She had a lovely voice. An' she kinda' handled herself like Diana Ross. She was just that thrillin'." Bernett made a mental note to take Josephine off the street as soon as an opportunity came. "You could see she was poor. An' tellin' the truth about it, that's one reason I was anxious to put her on the stage."

A troupe called the Dixie Steppers was scheduled for a week's run at the Booker T. Washington. When the troupe arrived, Bob Russell, agent for the Steppers, announced that he was short one act. His husband-and-wife comedy team had had a fight in Kansas City, split up and gone their separate ways. Bernett told Russell about the Jones Family. "I went out that same evenin' and got Old Man Jones and brought him to the theatre. Russell incorporated the whole family in the show."

Josephine was to sing and dance with the band as well as fill in on the Steppers' chorus line. The night before her debut, Bob Russell told her to stand in the wings and study the girls as they ran through their numbers. Seeing her idols close up, under harsh lights, Josephine was stunned. The "girls" ranged from eighteen to thirty-five. They had the firm, athletic bodies of dancers, tight little buttocks, and cancan muscles from doing the high kicks. Their faces were blotched and worn from rugged living. Their eyes were hard.

In her second autobiography, *Une Vie de Toutes Les Couleurs,* published in 1935, Josephine wrote about that moment, the moment when she lost her theatrical innocence. "The cheers, the lust of the men in the audience, the whistles, the laughs, the cries, never seemed to cross the footlights and reach them. They were only dancing because they didn't want to starve." The only place to be, she could see, was at the top.

On the night she opened, Josephine wore a costume made for a much larger woman. The dress fell to her ankles instead of her knees. The tights made wrinkling bands around her legs. She looked like a little girl playing dress up, wearing her mother's monstrous clothes. As she danced onstage, the audience howled. Instead of suffering humiliation, Josephine laughed with them. "Seeing everybody looking at me electrified me." She said she felt as if she had had a slug of gin. She kicked out of the line of hoofers, shaking and shimmying, performing as she had performed on the street, adding a dash of eroticism with a series of bumps and grinds.

Bernett stood in the wings overjoyed that his hunch about Josephine was right. "The minute she hit that stage, she arched her back just like an animal. She'd jut that ass up, like a rooster flipping his tail."

Because of Josephine's success, the Dixie Steppers and the Jones Family were held over a second week. Josephine was rewarded with a "single," a solo dance, and performed in a skit called "Twenty Minutes in Hell," in which she played a prostitute. A man dressed in a devil's costume chased her around the stage yelling, "Away with you, you little imp!"

The Martins were happy with Josephine's success, but proudest of all was Willie Mae. Only nine years old, she came to the show every day after school and hung around backstage. Red Bernett remembers: "That one-eyed girl had a whole lot'a mouth. She wanted everybody to know she was Josephine's sister."

At the end of the second week, Bob Russell invited the Jones Family to join his company touring the South. Josephine and the Joneses left St. Louis on a midnight train, headed first for Tennessee. Josephine always claimed to have run away from home, but Carrie knew she was going and did not try to stop her.

Carrie was like a lioness who thrusts her cub out in the wild yet still keeps an eye on it. Though Josephine was physically free, her mother remained a presence lurking in the distance.

The Dixie Steppers traveled on the Theatre Owners Booking

Association circuit, a vaudeville chain that played exclusively to blacks. T.O.B.A.—Tough On Black Asses, so named because of its pay scale—ranged from New York to Florida, Chicago to New Orleans. Bob Russell paid her ten dollars a week.

Life on the Sawdust Trail was cruel and frightening, romantic and exciting. The performers were brassy, passionate people. Their loves, jealousies, tears and laughter enlivened the sleepy villages in which they played. Their trunks were shabby and their clothes flashy. The men were brightly shirted cockerels. The women were painted, powdered and bejeweled. The life of the troupe was one of constant motion, spent at lunch stands, in boardinghouses and on rickety grit-sifted railroad cars where the hoofers and comedians snatched half an hour's sleep before the conductor called out the next stop. The railroads in the American South surprised even the child of Gratiot Street, the lissome girl who had risen in the shadow of Union Station. The trains rocked and screeched into sun-baked towns, places that had nurtured the Ku Klux Klan, where pink-faced baggage masters stared through the smoky windows of the cars at the row of black faces. Where did those niggers find the money to travel?

The humiliations were constant. The simple act of ordering coffee and a doughnut drew a hostile blue-eyed stare. The only movie show in town carried the warning *For Whites Only,* and ubiquitous signs on latrines proclaimed *White Ladies* and *Colored Women.* The signs were a foolish white man's game, but what Negro was brave enough to laugh at night in a town where ghosts might suddenly appear, men in chalk-white flowing dress riding saddles ornamented with skulls?

The theatres the Dixie Steppers played in made the Booker T. Washington look like a palace. Roofs leaked, the chairs were broken, people sat around on the floors. Though most of the theatres were rickety frame buildings, some were open-air hollows where performers were subjected to the vagaries of the weather.

The cost of admission was twenty-five cents, and that usually included someone walking away with the door prize—usually a coveted gold tooth, occasionally a ham or a turkey.

Theatre owners posted such signs as:

WE KNOW THIS THEATRE IS ROTTEN—HOW'S YOUR SHOW?
and
DON'T BLAME THE ORCHESTRA—THEY ARE TOO BUSY
AT THE FOUNDRY TO REHEARSE.

The acts were a mix of slapstick, hokum and blue humor. Josephine was cast as a topless Cupid, fitted with a harness and suspended by a rope from the ceiling. Two young lovers sat on stage, waiting for the archer's arrow. A muscular stagehand, operating the block and tackle, stared up through the flies at Cupid and gripped the hemp that kept her from falling. Josephine could never forget: "The piano played a long roll. Then I flew like an angel. But as I sailed though the air, my wings got stuck on the bottom of the curtain. When the curtain went up, it took me with it. I swung back and forth, kicking, balanced in the air. . . . I looked out and saw one hundred sets of white teeth laughing at me."

Ethel Waters, who toured the South on the T.O.B.A. circuit at the same time as Josephine, remembered the audiences they faced. "Rugged individualists all, they did whatever they pleased while you were killing yourself on the stage. They ran up and down the aisles, yelling greetings to friends and sometimes having fights. And they brought everything to eat from bananas to yesterday's pork chops.

"But they were also the most appreciative audiences in the world if they liked you. They'd scream, stomp and applaud until the whole building shook. Years later, when I first stepped before a white audience, I thought I was a dead duck because nobody tried to tear the house down. They merely clapped their hands. Such restraint is almost a sneer in the colored vaudeville world."

On the T.O.B.A. trail Josephine shared quarters with the Joneses. They cooked in their bedroom and sometimes slept in one bed. Even for Josephine, who had never led a conventional life, living conditions like this were degrading. Mr. Jones, an ugly shriveled man, was a devotee of voodoo. He cut off lengths of his wife's black hair, rolled them around rusty tenpenny nails and planted them under his side of the mattress. When the spirit moved him, he pricked his fingers and dripped blood into his morning coffee. In lieu of sugar, he sweetened his coffee with pulverized sow bugs. When the Dixie Steppers hit New Orleans, Doll Jones fell for a Bourbon Street dwarf with a penchant for sadomasochism. At unexpected times young Doll's lover would stop by the hotel to whip her. Josephine was only fourteen and lacked love and guidance. The Joneses would provide little of this. "She was like an orphan then," Ethel Waters remembered.

Josephine idolized Clara Smith, the star of the show, a blues singer with a beautiful voice and a repertoire like Sophie Tucker's. Clara was a presence on and off the stage. She wore a bright red wig set off by violet makeup. Her lips, extraordinarily full, surrounded a set of dingy yellow teeth that clenched a corncob pipe. Once when Clara was immobilized by constipation, Josephine sat by her bed, reeling off jokes, telling her stories about the Chestnut Valley. Clara warmed to Josephine's charm and took her under her wing, spending afternoons with her, helping her improve her reading and writing, and buying her licorice, peppermint sticks and sweet potato pie.

The charms of New Orleans, the Vieux Carré, the life of the markets, the riverfront, and the charms of Doll's sadistic lover killed the Joneses' lust for travel. When the Dixie Steppers left, the Joneses stayed.

Josephine went with the Steppers to Chicago. The chill, wintry Windy City was a wide-open town.

Storyville had been closed by the Department of the Navy in 1917 when New Orleans was host to battleships, destroyers and cargo ships carrying troops and weapons. The place was thought of as a danger to the soldiers and sailors. From that time on, jazz musicians began drifting north. The drift had now become an exodus. Chicago was becoming the new jazz center, a place of jam sessions and mad creative flights of fancy. This Golden Age was born and nurtured on Chicago's South Side, a throbbing ghetto that reflected the gathering pace of the city.

With the ragtag Steppers, Josephine made the rounds of South Side dance halls and illicit gin mills, hangouts for mobsters and millionaires.

By the time the Dixie Steppers reached Philadelphia, Josephine was desperately lonely. There she encountered another Willie, William Howard Baker. They met at a house rent party.

House rent parties had a raucous charm all their own. If a family could not pay the rent, they hired a piano player and a drummer. Then they stocked up on cheap hooch and invited all comers to chip in their nickels, dimes and quarters. Invitations were passed out on the street. Usually some enticing lines accompanied the address:

We Got Yellow Girls, We've Got Black and Tan.
Will You Have A Good Time?—YEAH MAN!

These slapdash affairs brought together maids and gangsters, poets and shoeshine boys. Sometimes the parties went on for days. The food was yummy: fried fish, hog maws and black-eyed peas.

Willie was in his mid-twenties, small and wiry, with an easy smile, clear skin and a glint of red in his nappy hair. Though not conventionally good-looking, he was warm and kind.

Willie was a Pullman porter. Before that he worked as a jockey. Like Josephine, he had the trained reflexes of someone who has command of his body.

Willie shared Josephine's taste for excitement and her yen to travel. To Josephine, still a giggly teenager with a puppy's unremitting need for affection, Willie seemed strong and secure. He would be her anchor. And she, in turn, would guarantee him adventure.

Willie's family took a dim view of their son taking up with an underage chorus girl in a third-rate road show. So, in September 1921, the couple eloped to Camden, New Jersey, where they were married by a Justice of the Peace. Josephine was fifteen years old.

Josephine took Willie home to St. Louis. The Martins were surprised but hospitable. Brother Richard says of the second Willie, "He was a jolly guy and seemed glad to meet us, but that was the only time we seen him."

The newlyweds returned to Philadelphia to take up housekeeping at Mom's Charlestons, a theatrical boardinghouse near Broad Street. On Sundays they went to visit Willie's parents. Mrs. Baker felt that Willie had married "down" because Josephine was darker than the Bakers. "If somebody came to the house, Willie's mother would find some excuse to keep me in the kitchen," Josephine confided to a friend.

THREE

"We never thought Josephine would be famous or nothin', but when she got with *Shuffle Along,* Oh Lordie!"

—Brother Richard

Josephine was living in Philadelphia at the time a promising musical was having its tryout. The show, *Shuffle Along,* was soon to be a smash hit, the first all-black musical to make it to Broadway. It was glittering, fast-paced and funny, a drawing card for the best black talent.

The score was crammed with wonderful songs—"Bandana Days," "I'm Just Wild About Harry," "Love Will Find a Way" and "The Gypsy Blues." Trixie Smith sang "He May Be Your Man But He Comes to See Me Sometimes."

Josephine ran over to the Dunbar Theatre to audition. Noble Sissle, who wrote the songs with Eubie Blake, recalled Josephine as a nervous little girl "with big brown eyes like saucers. She stood shivering in the doorway in the cold March rain that was coming in torrents outside."

Flournoy Miller, a partner in the show, took one look at Josephine and drew Sissle aside. "That kid looks awfully young to me."

"I'm fifteen," Josephine interrupted.

Sissle patted her on the back. "There's a New York law prohibiting the use of chorus girls under sixteen years of age. Sorry."

Sissle was undone to see Josephine break down. "Big tears

filled her eyes, and with drooping head looking like a wilted flower she slowly turned, half stumbling down the steps leading to the stage door exit.

"We stood there watching her as she walked down the alleyway leading to the street. We could hear the sobs, first faintly, then bursting forth in a flood of grief. As she stood at the gate, her lithe body seemed to falter slightly. Then without even looking back she disappeared into the rain."

Six months after *Shuffle Along* had opened on Broadway and become a hit, Sissle and Blake organized a road company to play one-nighters.

Josephine could not get *Shuffle Along* out of her mind. She was obsessed with the show. Leaving Willie in Philadelphia, she took the train to New York, hoping somehow to get a part.

She launched a campaign that lasted for weeks, showing up again and again for tryouts, constantly pestering stage manager Al Mayer. (Sissle and Blake were too busy with the New York company to oversee auditions for their second baby.) Once, when she was broke, she spent a night sleeping in Central Park.

When Mayer finally relented and hired her for the road company, he broke an unwritten rule. Josephine's complexion, darker than that of the other girls, made her an exception. And it made her the scapegoat of the cast.

Until recent times, the black ideal, the beautiful prototype, had light brown skin and modified Negro features. Black chorus girls in the 1920s were judged by these criteria as well as for their bodies and dancing ability. Most of the sixteen chorus girls in *Shuffle Along* were "high yallers"; many were quadroons and octoroons. They prided themselves on the lightness of their skin and drew a vicious color line between themselves and Josephine. They called her "the monkey."

These girls were fighting for their lives, pushing upward from ghettos throughout the country. How could they be magnanimous? As entertainer Bobby Short explains, "If you were an ordinary girl, not a rich one, it was your only chance to break out of your poverty and station. You either became a chorus girl or a prostitute or somebody's maid."

Years later, after she became an international star and returned to New York on tour, Josephine encountered old show

Portrait of Josephine at sixteen. Already twice wed, Josephine was attracting a wide following as the comic chorus girl in *Shuffle Along*, a Broadway musical that began the vogue for black singing and dancing that lasted throughout the Twenties.

girls from *Shuffle Along* at parties in Manhattan, and she let them know they were not welcome in her presence unless they were willing to play acolyte to the goddess "Bakair."

As she started on the road in *Shuffle Along*, Josephine refused to be eclipsed. The dance director put her at the end of the chorus line, the traditional comedy spot, and she milked the position for all it was worth. The cast's hostility toward her was considerable.

They played Chicago in winter with the wind lashing in off Lake Michigan. Josephine developed an inflammation of the nasal passages which produced an unpleasant odor. "A lot of the girls shied away from her," recalls Freddie Washington, a dancer in the show. "We all dressed in a large room, and as I was coming into work one night I saw a couple of the girls move her makeup outside the dressing room before Josephine arrived. I put her things back in place and said to the ringleader, 'How can you be so cruel?' "

When the *Shuffle Along* road company landed at a theatre on Fulton Street in Brooklyn, Sissle and Blake heard about Josephine. They were then working on a musical called *Chocolate Dandies* and did not have time to go see her, so they dispatched an old song-and-dance man from their office to look her over.

The veteran hoofer saw Josephine's potential. Eubie Blake remembers how excited he was. "He came runnin' back to us. He said, 'Get that girl. She's the greatest thing I've ever seen. Get her!' So we took her out of the road company and put her in the Broadway show. She kept us in stitches all the time. At rehearsal she used to stand behind me and mimic me when I was directin' the orchestra.

"And the public loved her. Before the show I used to go out in the lobby to get a line on how many tickets we're sellin'. I'd be out there, talkin' to the people, mentally checkin', not writin' anythin' down.

"People who heard about Josephine would come in an' ask, 'Is that cross-eyed girl in the show?' Big-time white people, not medium white people, because they used to pull up in Cadillacs and Duryeas and Rolls Royces.

"They thought Jo was cross-eyed. She wasn't. She worked

that way. And she worked like she didn't know the steps. She could outdance anybody in that line, but she was never in step with the other girls. She was doin' all sorts of gyrations with her legs, trippin', gettin' out of step and catchin' up, playin' marbles with her eyes. She's in step with the music but she's not doin' what the other girls are doin'. People used to be screamin'. They didn't know she was doin' comedy."

Eubie Blake, then an energetic man in his thirties with mischievous eyes and a razor-edged wit, fell under the spell of the sixteen-year-old "enfant terrible." Eubie, whose parents had come up from slavery and were solid, religious, middle-class blacks, started his career at the age of fifteen, banging out ragtime in Baltimore brothels. Before long he was in New York, writing music and cutting his own piano rolls. Now he was Blake of Sissle and Blake, one of the hottest writer-composer teams in the city.

Eubie knew about Josephine's lonely journey up from the slums. He acted as her confidant. "She was a one-man-at-a-time girl. We were together right up until that lady came and took her to France."

Blake saw in Josephine a signal trait. When she wanted something, she reached out and took it. The price be damned. "One Sunday Josephine was walking down Fifth Avenue with two other girls. They passed a candy store on 42nd and 5th Avenue that had a big red box of chocolates in the shape of a heart in the window. It cost thirty-five dollars. Josephine bought it. That's exactly what she was makin' a week. Thirty-five dollars."

Eubie asked her why she had not bought a smaller box. "Because I wanted *that* box of candy." Then she asked Eubie to give her the next week's salary so she could buy a fancy coat. When he refused, she bought it on credit.

When the number-one company of *Shuffle Along* went on tour, Josephine went with it, playing in Boston, Milwaukee, Des Moines, Indianapolis and St. Louis. Her salary jumped to $125 a week, an astronomical sum in those days. The show opened in St. Louis at the American Theatre. It was performed before a mixed audience, but with the blacks relegated to the balcony.

Josephine's return to St. Louis fired her will to succeed. She believed in fame, in its magical power to seal her off forever from the horrors of her childhood.

To her friends on Bernard Street, Josephine was the hometown kid who made good. Brother Richard never forgot her triumphal return. "The whole neighborhood turned out to see her. It was really somethin'." The girls who had snickered at Josephine's hand-me-down clothes at school now paid to see her. And the boys who had played kickball with her and gone with her to the white neighborhoods to shovel snow and take out trash sat up in the balcony and cheered. Mildred Franklin, who taught dancing on the playgrounds and had seen that Josephine was gifted, came to the show. Carrie and Arthur, Richard, Margaret and Willie Mae were also there.

Two people from Josephine's past refused to participate. One was Red Bennett. After Josephine went south with the Dixie Steppers, she never wrote to thank him for giving her that first important break, to let him know how she was doing. He resented being ignored. "She forgot the stone she stepped on." And Joyce McDuffy, too, felt slighted. "I can understand Tumpie's ambition. She wanted to have something, but you would think she'd remember her old friends."

A group of local musicians sponsored a party for the cast at the Old Chauffeur's Club, where Josephine had worked as a waitress. Eddie Carson came, accompanied by his wife and stepdaughter. Though polite to Eddie and his second family, Josephine bolted soon after greeting them and did not come back, apparently wounded by the confrontation with the father she had tried to forget.

But Eddie Carson sought out Eubie Blake and asked to be hired as drummer for the show. He explained that he was Josephine Baker's father and wanted to be in the show with his daughter. Eubie Blake refused. "He begged me to put him in the band. 'I'm sorry,' I told him. 'I already got a drummer.'"

Josephine paid a visit to 2632 Bernard Street. It was a painful homecoming. The house was cold as ice. The laundry tub, where she had taken her baths, stood forlornly in the middle of the kitchen.

Carrie never asked Josephine about her life as a showgirl.

Josephine took her mother's silence as an indictment. Arthur, almost catatonic, was lying on the couch in the living room, too deeply depressed to query the family star.

Willie Mae, eleven then, clung to her sister and, as Josephine was leaving, looked at her with soulful eyes. "Take me with you," she pleaded.

Josephine was torn between the fear of being criticized by the other chorines for dragging her one-eyed sister around the country and the urge to rescue Willie Mae. As the sisters parted, Josephine made a promise. "I'll send you money for clothes, and I'll pay for your schooling."

Josephine made good on her promise. She sent Willie Mae $1500 from Paris to buy a baby grand piano. Willie Mae loved music, and Josephine hoped she would develop her talent.

Willie Mae finished high school, the only one in her family to do so, and planned to go on to teachers' college. But she never made it. Nor did Josephine ever see her sister again. In 1927 Willie Mae died as the result of a self-induced abortion.

After touring with *Shuffle Along,* Josephine joined the company of *Chocolate Dandies,* the next Sissle and Blake hit musical. The show was even more glittering and extravagant than *Shuffle Along,* and Josephine was given several parts including a blackface routine in which she imitated the sounds of a saxophone and the role of a vamp in a clinging white satin dress, a part she loved.

Her career as a comic began to build. Press notices called attention to her goofy looks, mostly the result of makeup and costumes and her gift for pantomime. Ashton Stevens of the *Chicago Herald and Examiner* called Josephine "the comic little chorus girl whose very gaze was syncopation and whose merest movement was a blues."

At the same time, her appearance as a femme fatale drew little attention. Poet e. e. cummings remembered seeing Josephine as the slipjointed clown in *Dandies* and later as the star of the Folies-Bergère. He found the metamorphosis incredible. In *Chocolate Dandies* she "resembled some tall, vital, incomparably fluid nightmare, which crossed its eyes and warped its limbs in a purely unearthly manner—some vision which opened new avenues of fear, which suggested nothing but itself. . . . It may seem preposterous that this terrifying nightmare should have become the most beautiful (and beautiful is what we mean) star of the Parisian stage. Yet such is the case."

Dandies closed in May 1925. Josephine went to work at Sam Slavin's Plantation Club above New York's Winter Garden Theatre at 50th and Broadway. There she shared a dressing room with Ethel Waters, star of the show, and with Bessie Buchanan.

Bessie, a well-bred beauty, was black bourgeois. Her mother was a teacher; her father was the first Negro Red Cap hired at Grand Central Station. Bessie set her sights high, which impressed Josephine. They became best friends, each admiring the spunk of the other. Years later, Bessie entered politics and earned a seat in the New York legislature, the first Negro woman to achieve such an honor.

The Plantation Club was an after-theatre playground for café society. The review, beginning at midnight, was attended by Irving Berlin, David Belasco, Norma Talmadge and other lights of the time. The audience was segregated; blacks were banished to seats at the sides of the room.

Rosetta LeNoir, principal writer of the recent Broadway musical *Bubbling Brown Sugar,* a memoir of Harlem, vividly remembers the harsh prejudice against blacks in the 1920s. "You couldn't try on a bra or a slip at Bloomstein's at 125th Street. Black women couldn't try on hats in stores on Fifth Avenue. You got a white person, a neighbor or somebody in your building, to do it for you."

At the Plantation Josephine was exposed to an insidious form of prejudice, more painful than Jim Crow laws. As a black cabaret dancer, she was expected to make the customers happy in ways other than singing and dancing. She was a "sepia lovely," a vessel for puritanical America's repressed sexuality. Many men considered the black woman not only more sexually adventurous but, as writer James Weldon Johnson put it, "a more beautiful creature than her sallow, songless, lipless, hipless, tired-looking, tired-moving white sister."

In the 1920s whites took a voyeuristic interest in black night life. They were intrigued by the glittering lights and bright sounds of Harlem. Jazz-drunken cabarets—the Plantation, the Cotton Club, Small's Paradise, the Savoy—were filled with handsomely dressed slummers who danced the black bottom and watched risqué reviews that featured "tantalizin' tans" and "hot chocolates."

Nighttime Harlem radiated joy. "It was Disneyland blazing with lights," recalls Anita Loos. "Every window had a Gramophone in it, blaring out into the street. People were dancing in the alleys, hanging out of windows, singing. It was the gayest place that certainly this country ever produced."

Many blacks, needing money, profited from white curiosity. In Harlem cards were distributed advertising "Slumming Hostesses for Inquisitive Nordics."

Places like the Plantation and the Cotton Club, as their names suggest, were rigged to convey an old-time Southern feeling, making whites feel they were being catered to by carefree darkies.

Ethel Waters, in her autobiography *His Eye Is on the Sparrow*, wrote about the difference between Harlem and the white café society world of the Plantation Club. "Uptown a whore was a whore, a faggot was a faggot, a dike was a dike, a mother-hugger was a mother-hugger. Downtown it was different— more complicated. A whore was sometimes a socialite; a pimp could be a man-about-town; a thief could be an executive; a faggot could be a playboy; a dike might be called a deb; mother-hugger was somebody who wasn't adjusted and had problems."

After work one night, Josephine found herself in an odd situation. A white New York actress came to the Plantation review and invited Josephine and three other women in the show to a midnight supper in her Ritz Carlton suite. The actress promised to pay for their company.

Josephine had never seen a hotel like the Ritz. "I'll never forget my first impression of thinking I was walking into a palace."

As they sat at supper, Josephine was dazzled by the woman's diamond bracelet. The actress seemed nervous, almost hysterical, but Josephine did not think much of it until supper was finished. Then the evening took on a bizarre coloration. The actress herded the dancers into the bathroom and handed them each a lace negligee. "Hurry up," she said. "Take off your clothes."

The other chorus girls put on the nightgowns and filed into the bedroom. But Josephine took her time, fidgeting, growing increasingly apprehensive.

When Josephine finally walked into the bedroom, she saw the actress sprawled across the bodies of the other three women, who were stretched out on the bed like sardines. The actress flailed her arms as she worked the dancers over, rising to a frenzy.

At first Josephine was frightened. "Then I started to cry. And then it made me mad."

After dressing rapidly, Josephine headed for the door. Just as she was about to exit, however, she changed course. Displaying the chutzpah that came to be her hallmark, she walked back to ask for her pay. "The woman kicked me out without giving me a cent."

Though Josephine did a specialty number at the Plantation Club, she was not receiving the recognition she felt she deserved. "I longed to be like Ethel Waters, a sexy, sultry blues singer."

In the afternoons Josephine practiced her singing. She tried to modulate her voice, make it sound less like a bird. She hoped with a little polish to land a bigger part in the show.

Ethel Waters saw Josephine as a potential threat. She put her down as a cute, funny kid. "Josephine was a mugger with a great comic sense. She could also play the trombone."

One night Ethel Waters had laryngitis and Sam Slavin asked Josephine to stand in for her. The featured song was "Dinah," an international hit launched and made famous by Ethel Waters. Josephine had a bad case of nerves but went out and sang just the same. Her vitality and brashness won her wild applause.

As the weeks went by, Josephine grew increasingly restless. While she wondered what would happen to her, André Daven, producer of the Champs-Elysées Theatre in Paris, was sitting in his office thinking up new shows for his immense stage.

Daven was in a tight spot. His theatre was running in the red.

Paris audiences, fickle, spoiled beyond measure by the fertile early 1920s, demanded constant innovation. Daven was at his wit's end trying to woo them to his establishment.

Like a flock of swallows, the cognoscenti moved en masse from opening to opening. Bon vivant Gerald Murphy remembered, "Every day was different. There was a tension and an excitement in the air that was almost physical. Always a new exhibition, or a recital of the new music of Les Six, or a Dadaist manifestation, or a costume ball in Montparnasse, or a premiere, or a new play, or one of Etienne de Beaumont's fantastic 'Soirées de Paris' in Montmartre—and you'd go to each one and find everybody else there, too."

Hoping to fill his immense Théâtre des Champs-Elysées, Daven had presented Anna Pavlova in *The Dying Swan* and, with the help of Rolf de Maré, a young Swedish Diaghilev, had introduced the controversial Ballet Suédois. For one production of the Swedish Ballet, Cole Porter wrote "Within the Quota," a witty musical satire about a Swedish immigrant in the United States. But for Daven each production was a leap of faith. Every show must succeed if the theatre was to survive.

Daven's friend, cubist Fernand Léger, had recently seen the magnificent exhibit of African sculpture at the Exposition des Arts Décoratifs. He suggested that Daven produce an all-black show. "Give them the Negroes," Léger said. "Only the Negroes can excite Paris."

A short time after Léger made his suggestion, Caroline Dudley, a peripatetic American, breezed into Daven's office and asked, "Would you be interested in presenting a show of authentic Negro vaudeville?"

"Oui. Bien sûr!" said Daven, not having the slightest idea what such a thing was.

After a remarkably brief discussion, Daven said, "Go back to New York. Cable me if you can find the performers for the show. I'll sent you money to bring thirty people."

Caroline Dudley returned to the States, made the rounds of black nightclubs and cabarets, and spotted Josephine at the end of the chorus line at the Plantation Club. "She stood out like an exclamation point!"

Josephine had already toyed with the idea of going to

Europe. In New Orleans and Chicago, as in New York, she had heard black performers talk about the opportunities abroad. And a French waiter at the Plantation Club, who culled morsels from his customers' plates and presented them to Josephine as love tokens, told her, "In Europe they would adore you. They would see your real worth."

Yet when Caroline Dudley invited Josephine to go to Europe with her troupe, Josephine could not decide. "At first I said, 'Yes, I'll go.' But during the next two days, I changed my mind three times."

Sam Slavin said he would double her Plantation Club salary, raising it to $300 if she would stay. Dudley offered to triple it, but still Josephine hesitated. "After all," said Dudley, "I was not the big producer with the diamond in my tie and the big cigar. I was nobody. This was the first show I ever produced."

There seemed an element of destiny in the meeting of Josephine and Caroline Dudley. A thirty-five-year-old white woman with pretty, birdlike features and vibrant eyes, Caroline Dudley radiated the kind of devil-may-care optimism Josephine had sorely missed in her mother.

Dudley was the daughter of a liberal Chicago physician who often invited blacks to dinner. "I grew up on Booker T. Washington's knee," she liked to boast.

She went with her father to black vaudeville shows on State Street in Chicago and fell in love with the music, the ragtime, the beginnings of jazz and the raunchy humor. This early exposure to black vaudeville gave her the experience, rare among whites, of seeing authentic black entertainment originated by blacks and performed for blacks.

Caroline was one of the celebrated Dudley sisters, a handsome trio renowned for being bright, rich and daffy. John Dos Passos, one of their many fans, wrote of them: "Somehow, out of the impact of French novels read in their teens and of impressionist paintings devoured at the Art Institute, they had invented a certain style. Life must be a *déjeuner sur l'herbe* painted by Renoir on the banks of the Seine. . . . They carried this special style into their conversation and their cookery and their whole way of living."

At the time she met Josephine, Caroline Dudley was the wife

of an American Foreign Service officer about to be transferred to the American Embassy in Paris. Her ardor for her husband had cooled. Casting around for a fresh outlet for her energies, she sensed the time was right for black entertainers in France. "I knew I wanted to take an American Negro show to Paris. I got this idea in my head and I couldn't get it out. I felt I was the only person who could produce this show."

Hoping not to lose his wife, her husband agreed to back *La Revue Nègre*.

Knowing the roots of Josephine's talent, Dudley saw her as a mission. She wanted Josephine to fulfill herself, to be an artist, an exceptional comedian.

Josephine said she needed an evening gown to wear on the boat to Europe, so Caroline Dudley took her to the showroom of a Seventh Avenue designer. As the models entered one by one, parading in front of Josephine, offering expensive creations for her approval, Caroline Dudley was surprised to see that her unschooled protégée was equal to the occasion. Josephine was at home in the opulent setting.

As each dress went by, Josephine said, "No, no," or "That won't do," as if she had been reviewing designers' clothes all her life. Finally a model walked out in a simply cut scarlet-red gown, slashed low in front. Josephine said, "That's it."

Caroline Dudley pulled out her checkbook.

Because Josephine was still a minor, Dudley went to the Passport Office in lower Manhattan, acting as her guardian and assuming responsibility for her.

The clerk read out a question on marital status. "Single?"

"Yes and no," said Josephine.

"Married?"

"Yes and no."

"Divorced?"

"Yes and no."

The man lost patience. "Which is it?" he asked.

Josephine shrugged and flashed a radiant smile. She was still married to Willie Baker and kept his name, but she never talked about him. She had decided to cut Willie out of her life, dropping him as she had dropped Eddie Carson and Willie

Wells. They were excess baggage and Josephine wanted to travel light.

On the evening of September 15, 1925, the S.S. *Berengaria,* bearing the troupe of *La Revue Nègre,* luxuriated at her New York pier, a lighted jewel, streamers rocketing away from her decks. The gangplank quivered and flashbulbs exploded as reporters and photographers hounded pretty flappers and sleek, rich men.

As visitors left, the band struck up a farewell melody and the floating giant eased away from the dock, attended by a bevy of feisty tugs, and steamed down the Hudson to cross the broad expanse of the Bay.

Josephine stood at the rail near the bow, a thousand things racing through her mind. "My life passed in review before me. I saw Bernard Street and my raggedy playmates. . . . When the Statue of Liberty disappeared over the horizon, I knew I was free."

The Brunhilde-like *Berengaria* was a war orphan. The ship had been taken from the Germans in 1918 and thereafter sailed under American colors. Clumsy, Teutonic, loud and splashy, the "Big B" was a gaudy ferryboat, exuding the spirit of the age. She and her clientele deserved each other. The Sultan of Jahore, Lord Duveen, the Earl of Warwick, and rich Americans—Cortlandts, Vanderbilts and Swopes—walked the sundecks, looking like drawings from *Vanity Fair.* Said one ship's officer, "Everybody on the *Berengaria,* even the dogs, were 'socially prominent.' " But the *Berengaria* was also as rigidly segregated as any topflight American hotel.

To help cover travel expenses, Caroline Dudley agreed to put on a show for the first-class passengers. Since there was no script for these shipboard performances, rehearsals were needed. Josephine refused to participate. "I know just what I'm gonna' do," she said.

"Tant mieux," said Caroline Dudley.

Josephine wanted to appear as a sultry, elegant beauty who sang nostalgic melodies. Remembering her evening as Ethel Waters's stand-in, she decided to sing the blues.

Wearing the scarlet low-cut dress Caroline Dudley had bought her, Josephine walked on stage alone. The band played an introduction and Josephine sang "Brown Eyes." The acoustics were bad. This was nothing like the Plantation Club. Her birdlike voice seemed thin; she had not yet been trained to project it.

"She was a flop, a dead duck," remembers Caroline Dudley. "I knew she would be, but I let her go ahead. I wanted her to realize that her forte was comedy."

Josephine turned on Caroline Dudley, blaming her, venting irrational rage. Her sponsor had let her make a fool of herself. As Caroline Dudley left the first-class lounge, Josephine followed her, filling the companionway with accusations. "You're fixin' t'kill me," Josephine said. "I'm finished. I'm leavin' tomorrow."

Caroline Dudley had written glowing letters to André Daven about Josephine's talent, hoping he would give her a special part, but Dudley did not show her feelings. "Do just as you like, but you can't leave tomorrow. We're in the middle of the ocean."

The following morning Caroline Dudley heard a soft knock on her door. Josephine stood in the companionway, shy and frightened. "Miz Dudley," she said. "Why you choose me? Why you want me to come?"

Caroline Dudley, who had never thought of Josephine as a beauty, smiled and put her arm around her. "Because you are beautiful and chic and you can dance."

FOUR

"In the beginning Josephine was *très sauvage.* She ate spaghetti with her hands."

—Michael Gyarmarthy, Directeur
Artistique des Folies-Bergère

At ten o'clock on the morning of September 22, 1925, André Daven, with two of his assistants from the Théâtre des Champs-Elysées, stood at the Gare St. Lazare, the great railroad station named for Lazarus of the Scriptures, watching the Le Havre-Paris boat train roll in. The engine hissed and wheezed to a stop.

Rain swept across the buildings of Paris and misted the surface of the Seine. High above the tracks it coursed down the high, arched windows, flooded the sills, splashing and drumming on the pavements. Inside, the station was dank and chilly.

Daven paced impatiently. He planned to open *La Revue Nègre* ten days hence, and he had no idea what to expect from the cast. As the locomotive's stack belched its last breath of steam, Daven watched the doors open at the ends of the cars and saw Caroline Dudley's performers step down, resplendent in their Harlem glad rags.

"Out spilled a little world," recalled Daven, "rocking, boisterous, multicolored, carrying bizarre musical instruments, all talking loudly, some roaring with laughter.

"Red, green, yellow shirts, strawberry denims, dresses in polka dots and checks. Incredible hats—derbies—cream col-

49

ored, orange and poppy, surmounted thirty ebony faces, wild and joyous eyes."

Suddenly a copper-colored girl in her teens, supple, electric, wearing black-and-white overalls, burst away from the other entertainers. Like a drop of quicksilver, her arms above her head, she went straight to Daven. Her dark eyes flashed and, in a birdlike trill, she cried, "So this is Paris!"

What Josephine sensed but did not know as she stood before André Daven in the soft gray light of the Gare St. Lazare was that Paris was ready for Josephine Baker. Her entrance could not have been better timed. She was walking on the stage set of "Les Années Folles," the French counterpart of America's "Roaring Twenties." Soon she would be a leading figure of the age, as much a part of her time as Proust, Nijinsky, Hemingway, Gergieff, the Dolly Sisters and Gertrude Stein.

Seven years earlier Paris, all of France, had awakened from a nightmare. World War I had left the flower of her youth strewn across the muddy fields of Verdun. Three fourths of the Frenchmen who had gone to war were dead or wounded. Two and a half million of them were men between the ages of eighteen and twenty-five. From Brittany to Savoy, in villages, cities and in Paris herself, there was scarcely a family that had not mourned a soldier. "Nothing else in the history of the Continent," wrote Malcolm Cowley, "not even the Black Death, had produced such an extravagance of corpses."

Josephine arrived in that sweet slice of time between the end of the Great War and the beginning of the Great Depression. The 1920s was a dance of survivors, wild and erotic, as well as a dance macabre. Paris was feasting, shaking off the memory of the wasted young men, the dead, the maimed, the disenchanted. Everyone wanted to forget the past, to erase the taboos of La Belle Epoque. Paris swarmed with witty, impertinent revelers in search of perpetual amusement. "When I look back over those ten years," wrote Maurice Sachs, the diabolic chronicler of the time, "it seems always to have been the Fourteenth of July. The tricolor was always flying."

Paris "après guerre" was a mecca for painters, sculptors, writers, and musicians, who were pouring in from everywhere. Russians, Turks, Swedes, Germans, English and Americans crowded the Left Bank until the cafés of Montparnasse sounded like the tower of Babel, a mad confusion of tongues.

When Scott Fitzgerald called it The Jazz Age, he was talking about a state of mind, exemplified in France not only by jazz but by "Les Six," Bolshevism, champagne baths, loop the loops in open cockpit planes, cocaine, La Garçonne, Parade, Dada, Le Fox Trot and suicide, touted by the Surrealists as a chic alternative to life after thirty.

The era was saturated with the romance of easy money. "The Jazz Age," Fitzgerald wrote, "raced along under its own power, served by great filling stations full of money. . . . Even when you were broke you didn't worry about money, because it was in such profusion around you."

Many Americans were drawn to France because that country's galloping inflation had steadily increased the value of the dollar. In 1925 the official exchange rate was at 21.25 francs to the dollar, up from 5.45 in 1919. Footloose, these rich expatriates settled in Paris and mixed with the bohemians.

Bricktop, a Montmartre saloonkeeper née Ada Beatrice Queen Victoria Virginia Louisa Smith, remembers a system of patronage at the time, reminiscent of the Renaissance. "In those years in Paris there were I can't tell you how many people who wanted to write, who wanted to paint and perform— people who had money but couldn't make it. And they used to take care of all the geniuses, the people who *could* write and paint and perform but didn't have the money. The rich ones were taking care of these. It was a beautiful, beautiful thing."

Daven was in a hurry. In order to transport the troupe of *La Revue Nègre* from the Gare St. Lazare to the Théâtre des Champs-Elysées, he had chartered a tour bus. A rehearsal was scheduled for the day the troupe arrived, and he was anxious to see them perform.

Josephine stared with delight at the comic, open-cockpit taxis that lined the curbstones in front of the station and passed in parade across the gleaming pavements. For her the bright cacophony of their horns sounded "just like Christmas music."

As the performers climbed on the bus, they jostled each other, talking, joking, sitting together. But Josephine stood on the observation platform as the bus rocked through the 8th Arrondissement, the commercial heart of Paris, peering through the scrim of rain at the fine gray buildings, the arcades and tidy shops, the smart Parisians ducking into cafés and boulangeries. Josephine was guided by a catalogue of superstitions, and she remembered it was lucky to arrive in a city for the first time in the rain. "That means happiness," she said.

The Théâtre des Champs-Elysées, made of reinforced concrete, the first such building in France, sat serenely on Avenue Montaigne, an aristocratic street lined with sedate private houses and maisons de haute couture.

On this dark morning, as a welcoming salute to the Americans, Daven lit the facade of his theatre on which the sculptor Emile-Antoine Bourdelle had chiseled the Meditation of Apollo and the Muses, using Isadora Duncan as his inspiration.

But when Josephine popped out of the bus, she ignored the architectural masterpiece as she scurried across the street with the others to a small café called Le Bar du Théâtre. On the boat train that morning, sitting for the first time at tables with whites, they'd discovered the traditional breakfast of France. They wanted more café au lait and croissants.

One of those standing in front of the theatre, waiting for the troupe to arrive, was artist Paul Colin. Talented and ambitious, trained at the Beaux Arts in Nancy, Colin had been commissioned to design the poster for *La Revue Nègre*. He was just starting out and this assignment was a plum. His poster would be pasted on kiosks from Montmartre to the Bois de Vincennes, plus walls in the suburbs of the city. Colin was determined to make it a winner.

As the performers advanced toward the theatre, dodging traffic, some of them skidding on the rainswept street, Colin could scarcely believe his eyes. "They tap danced across the Avenue Montaigne, chewing on their croissants, balancing cups of coffee in their hands."

Inside the theatre, the balcony and orchestra seats were dark. Lit by footlights, spots and floods, the stage was a white-hot desert.

Josephine stepped into the shadows behind a flat, took off her clothes and wiggled into the scoop-topped cotton bathing suit that served as her rehearsal costume. She put on white socks and patent leather shoes with straps across the insteps, looking like Mary Janes. She rolled the socks down to her ankles.

Jazz musicians, among them New Orleans prodigy Sidney Bechet, broke out their instruments—saxophones, banjos, trumpets and trombones. Bechet fingered his clarinet and blew a note or two. The drummer put his traps together and tapped out a beat. The hall was filled with Dixieland music.

A long-legged man stepped away from the wings and started to dance at center stage. Chorus girls followed, clicking a counterpoint to the drums.

As the tall man danced, he sang to the accompaniment of piano player Spencer Williams, whose hands became a frantic blur.

> *Skiddle up skat!*
> *Skiddle up skat!*
> *Oh, skiddle up skiddle up,*
> *Skat! Skat! Skat!*

The tall man finished his number and Maude de Forest, star of the show, began to sing. Maude had a weakness for gin, and whenever she took a few belts, she switched from blues to spirituals—a disconcerting performance for a revue full of jazz babies. Maude sang slowly in her deep, rich voice, "Sometimes I Feel Like a Motherless Child," as sassy chicks shimmied and buck-'n'-winged.

"*Ordre! Ordre!*" called Daven, but nobody paid attention to him.

Paul Colin sat on a folding chair, close to the footlights. As he sketched he bristled with aggravation. "I had just one day to make my *affiche* for *La Revue Nègre* so Daven could rush it to the printers and put it on the streets in time to advertise the show."

The problem, of course, was Maude de Forest. "Usually I use the star for the poster, but Maude was too fat. I wanted a poster that would '*frapper les gens*,' would evoke the soul of Harlem."

Josephine pushed into the spotlight. The hollow enormity of the theatre, far from the firetraps of the chitlin' circuit, the dingy black vaudeville theatres where she first learned her trade, might have dwarfed a lesser spirit. But Josephine was at home on a larger stage. She clowned as she danced, seeming to fill the hall to the rafters.

Colin strained forward. "Her face seemed ordinary," he said, "but her body was beautiful. And I never saw anybody move the way she did. She was part kangaroo and part prizefighter. A woman made of rubber, a female Tarzan. She had the perfect figure for a poster."

Paul Colin, a short man, projected passionate intensity. Women liked him. Now he beckoned to Josephine. She responded with a radiant smile.

She spoke no French. He spoke no English. To establish communication, Colin began to doodle. Josephine took his pencil, leaned over his pad and made a few doodles of her own. "I could see she was intelligent, perhaps too intelligent," said Colin.

Colin was not satisfied with his sketches. And he could not make careful studies in the theatre. Speaking through an interpreter, he explained to Josephine that he wanted her to come to his studio, on the Place de la République, at ten that evening.

"Place de la République. *Entendu?*"

"Yes. Yes."

"I thought to myself. She'll never come. It was her first day in Paris and my *atelier* was clear across town." But at ten that evening, twelve hours after she arrived in Paris, Josephine knocked on Paul Colin's door.

Years later Josephine romanticized her youth, her naïveté. When she talked about her first night in Paris, she presented herself as shy and innocent, afraid to go to an artist's *atelier*. She said she stood on the threshold in great confusion.

But Colin remembered another Josephine: "I indicated to her to take her clothes off so I could accurately capture the lines of her body. I have been misquoted as saying she resisted taking her underwear off. She didn't. She knew why she was there. In two minutes she was in the buff."

As she moved, striking poses, dancing a step or two, arching, bending, Colin could feel his pulse racing. He felt the essence of the woman, the tension and vigor, the hardness of a cat about to strike.

Only Josephine's feet exposed her as a city creature. Corns and bunions, aggravated by years of squeezing into ill-fitting shoes and walking on harsh urban pavements, swelled the tops of her toes.

And, if you looked at her closely, under bright lights, you saw something singular in someone so young, something seen in later photographs. Josephine, in her teens, had lines on her forehead, furrows that were battle scars of her childhood.

In the wee hours of the morning Colin walked Josephine back to her hotel on the rue Campagne-Première in Montparnasse.

The rendezvous on the Place de la République was a beginning. They were now lovers. During the following six weeks in Paris, Paul Colin took Josephine everywhere. He introduced her to the Latin Quarter, to the courtyards on the Ile de la Cité, to the forests and gardens, the vistas of the city.

The next day Paul Colin told André Daven, "It's a shame you don't star the pretty girl I had at my studio last night instead of Maude de Forest."

Daven studied Colin's drawing, done in red and black. Josephine was dancing in the center of the poster behind two Harlem dandies, one wearing a bowler cocked over his eye. Josephine wore a very short dress, her arms akimbo, her hips seeming to move rhythmically.

"Her name is Josephine Baker," Colin insisted.

"We'll see," said Daven. André Daven had other things on his mind. He wondered whether this show would open at all.

The revue was in a state of wild disorganization. Claude Hopkins's band was full of life and clarinetist Sidney Bechet was superb, but Daven could not pull things together. He was more at home with the lush cabaret of the Moulin Rouge, the feathery routines of the Folies-Bergère. Where was there a pattern in all this madness?

At the height of his frustration, at the end of an impossible rehearsal, he slammed out the stage door, took a cab to

Montmartre and walked into the office of Jacques-Charles, Paris's most talented dance hall choreographer. Daven talked to him about his dilemma. "They keep tap dancing, tap dancing, tap dancing. The show is a bore. The reviewers will pan it."

Jacques-Charles reached for his hat and went with Daven to the Avenue Montaigne. As he watched the troupe perform, he began to smile. A few years earlier, Irving Berlin had taken Jacques-Charles on a tour of Harlem's nightclubs. Remembering those torrid nights, those uninhibited displays of talent, Jacques-Charles saw possibilities here.

Through an interpreter he told the cast, "You must let me shape this show or you'll have to go back on the boat. I want total obedience. This will be your only chance."

As his first rehearsal began, Caroline Dudley's sister Katherine, who lived in Paris, bustled into the theatre with a hodgepodge of ragged, colorful costumes she had bought for Daven at the Marché aux Puces at Place Clignancourt.

Jacques-Charles pulled odds and ends out of the pile. "I mixed everything together. I put Louis XIV tricornered hats with overalls and straw hats with fur coats."

The revue was to be a fast-paced show lasting forty-five minutes. At Daven's suggestion, Jacques-Charles picked Josephine to introduce the Charleston.

After the first rehearsal Jacques-Charles knew something was lacking. The show did not build. It needed a dash of eroticism, a voluptuous note to bring it to a climax.

Looking at the gaggle of supple young dancers, Jacques-Charles saw what Paul Colin had seen. Josephine had an exquisite body. Her torso was short yet serpentine, her arms graceful, her legs long, slim and gently muscular. If she danced in the nude, she might save the show.

Jacques-Charles beckoned her. Josephine was expectant. Charles spoke in French to an interpreter. As the interpreter spoke to Josephine, she flushed. Her mouth quivered. She broke into tears.

"No . . . I'm sorry," she started to say.

Josephine, who had danced topless in vaudeville, who had stripped without hesitation for Colin, found the prospect of public nudity painful. Jacques-Charles was invading her fantasy world, dreams she had nurtured back on Bernard Street, imagining herself "in beautiful clothes, the lead in a lavish musical."

Though she wanted to star in *La Revue Nègre,* Paris to her meant silks and satins, a chance to be a celebrated performer, not a whore. Tears streaming down her cheeks, she faced Jacques-Charles. "Take me back to the boat," she said.

Jacques-Charles was unexpectedly vehement. "I'll take you back after opening night." Sensing the force of his will, Josephine went back to work.

Jacques-Charles paired Josephine with Joe Alex, a giant of a man with powerful legs and thick, muscular arms. She took off her shoes and socks. Sidney Bechet blew a wanton tune and, in a few short moments, the professional Josephine took over. She became a dancer, bringing Jacques-Charles's choreography to life.

A friend of André Daven's, sitting next to him in the front row, leaned toward Daven and said, "She's a morsel fit for a king."

After rehearsal, Paul Colin took Josephine on her first long walk in Paris.

It was warm for September. She wore no coat. If the fashion arbiters of the Faubourg St. Honoré had been called on to describe Josephine's attire, they might have called it *"Criard!"*

It was loud indeed. She wore a bright red-and-white checked skirt and blouse, green shoes and yellow socks. Dangling from shoulder straps, pressed against her hip, were a Brownie camera and a pair of field glasses.

"Her hat had a garden on top," said Colin. "It was trimmed with poppies, sunflowers and daisies."

Linking arms, Colin and Josephine strolled up Avenue Montaigne, circled the fountains of the Rond-Point and started up the Champs-Elysées. The broad, tree-lined avenue stretched ahead of them, ascending to the Arc de Triomphe. In the flower stalls flaming geraniums bloomed in brightly painted cans. *Le Figaro, Paris-Soir* and *L'Intransigeant* were piled beside poster-covered kiosks. Along the thoroughfare, open-topped motor cars and fiacres, navigated by drivers in tall silk hats, moved past in giddy profusion. Josephine lingered in front of the stylish shops, voraciously examining the sparkling jewelry and furs.

Sidewalk cafés were sprinkled with people sitting in the shade of red awnings. Bowls heaped with peaches, pears and apples ornamented the sideboards. Waiters at Fouquets, wearing crisp white aprons, served their customers carafes of wine and bottles of beer and wiped the marble-topped tables.

As Colin and Josephine threaded through the crowd, Josephine gaped at the deep cloche hats and tunic dresses, styles set in motion by Poiret and Chanel. She kept up a running commentary in a language Colin did not understand. "Her expressions were exaggerated. She laughed too loudly, and then she would suddenly go dark."

The Parisian women stared back at Josephine, at her outlandish get-up, which somewhat embarrassed Colin. "I was used to being seen with smartly dressed women, actresses and dancers from the music hall. But nothing bothered Josephine. She wanted people to look at her. She was a born exhibitionist."

Near the Arc de Triomphe they bought chestnuts in brown paper bags from a vendor. Josephine was intoxicated by Paris, thinking of the rich possibilities the city held for her. "She was ambitious," said Colin. "Make no mistake."

Five days before the opening of *La Revue Nègre,* Paul Colin's posters came from the printer. Boys armed with pastepots and rolls of posters bicycled hither and yon, plastering the red-and-black design on kiosks, fences and walls.

Advance notices of *La Revue Nègre* appeared in several papers. There was only one mention of Josephine, in the weekly arts and leisure guide, *Comoedia:* "Josephine Baker is not just a pretty Negress, she's a dancer who has a lot of spirit in her legs and a remarkable sense of caricature."

On the evening of October 2, well before the 9:30 curtain, the Théâtre des Champs-Elysées started to fill. The French fascination with American blacks, in fact with anything American, brought Parisians to the theatre in droves.

The composition of the audience reflected the bastard nature of Tout Paris in the 1920s. Old and new money, merchants and nobles, dandies and debauchees, artists manqués and flourishing geniuses mingled with each other. Surrealist painter Robert Desnos of the "oyster colored eyes" was there. Also present were Dadaist Picabia, a member of Section d'Or and creator of the sets for the Ballet Relâche; Léger, painter of giant machines; and the poet Blaise Cendrars.

While the theatre buzzed, the house lights dimmed and three raps sounded offstage. The show was about to start.

Twelve musicians wearing red coats filed into the orchestra pit and took their places. The audience turned its attention to the stage.

At first the music was soft, the rhythm carried by a snare drum. As the bass drum came into play, Spencer Williams stabbed the keyboard, picking out unexpected melodies. Clear and sweet came the notes of a trumpet following the piano's cues. Then the trumpet erupted, taking the saxophone and cornet with it.

The curtain rose majestically. The stage was bare. The backdrop was a breathtaking view of Manhattan. With a gleam in his eye, Sidney Bechet strolled out, pushing a brightly painted vegetable cart, took up his clarinet and blew a wild improvisation, bouncing gold dust off the rafters.

Another backdrop descended, a Mississippi levee. The moon glowed behind branches dripping with Spanish moss. Colored spotlights played on riverboats, bales of cotton and women in mammy caps and red bandanas.

Enter Josephine walking on all fours, bottom up, head down, dressed in rags, a tattered shirt and cutoff pants. Her black hair, slicked down with grease, shone like a bowl of caviar.

The music gathered force. The orchestra played "Yes, Sir, That's My Baby!" Josephine rose up and started to Charleston.

Gay as a child, she flung her legs out, slapping her bottom in time to the music, unleashing a galaxy of movement appealing directly to the senses. She crossed her eyes, blew out her cheeks, spun like a whirligig, twisting, bending, evoking by turns the image of a small brown monkey and a splendid tropical bird.

The women in mammy caps came to life, joining in the frenzied dance, their busts and buttocks quivering, their faces and foreheads gleaming.

Josephine, in an effort to raise the ante, leaped toward one of the artificial oaks and, clawing and slipping, tried to scramble up it.

Most in the crowd sensed a tenderness behind her grimaces and mocking style, saw her desperate clutch for fame. But some of the spectators, weaned on suave nineteenth-century music, feared a new barbarian invasion was swooping down on Paris. "Stop it! Stop it!" yelled a wild-eyed woman. "We didn't come to see this ugliness." Others whistled disapproval. But the enthusiasts far outnumbered the killjoys.

As she sang her last note, Josephine somersaulted and skipped offstage.

"She's horrible! She's wonderful!" French critic Pierre de Régnier wrote later. "Is she black? Is she white? Is that her hair I see or is her skull painted black?"

The drummer beat out a steady jungle rhythm, a tom-tom call. Josephine returned with Joe Alex to do their savage dance. She rode onstage upside-down, carried on Alex's broad shoulders. All she wore was a bright pink feather tucked between her thighs and a ring of feathers circling her ankles and neck. Alex swung her around in a slow cartwheel.

The audience gasped in awe at the magnificence of her black body. Her skin glowed as if it had a lamp beneath it. Her breasts were small and round, like two apples. Her derriere was firm and smooth, cantilevered to an exaggerated degree. "A witty rear end," Anita Loos would call it.

Josephine and Joe then engaged in a primitive mating dance, filled with ardent passion. Unlike many white women who look pale and unnatural when nude, Josephine wore her nakedness with the confidence of a panther in her pelt. She slid into and out of Alex's arms, oily as serpent's skin. Her legs moved in response to his sensuous gestures. Her fingers caressed him. Her emotions seemed beyond her control. She did not appear to be acting. Rather, she seemed like a young animal suddenly let loose.

At last Alex's hands encircled her waist. He lifted her aloft as her body quivered in a wild orgasmic spasm.

At first the audience was silent, stunned. Then they rose to their feet, shouting wildly, roaring, clapping. Some made a rush for the stage.

Josephine and Joe Alex in "The Dance of the Savages," the fiery pas de deux that catapulted her to fame. *New York Public Library*

Josephine was so frightened she ran into the wings.

As the crowd emptied the theatre, filling the sidewalks of the Avenue Montaigne, Janet Flanner, a peppery writer from Indianapolis on her first assignment for *The New Yorker,* walked out of the theatre into the night, listening to people who had seen or heard about the show. The talk was all of Josephine. "Within a half hour of the final curtain," wrote Flanner, "the news and meaning of her arrival had spread by the grapevine up to the cafés of the Champs-Elysées, where the witnesses of her triumph sat over their drinks excitedly repeating their report of what they had just seen, themselves unsatiated in the retelling, the listeners hungry for further fantastic truths.

"The two specific elements had been established and were unforgettable," Flanner continued. "Her magnificent dark body, a new model to the French, proved for the first time that black was beautiful."

She was like a revolution or a tidal wave. Not since 1909, when Diaghilev presented the Ballets Russes starring Nijinsky and Pavlova, had Paris been witness to such a sweeping conquest.

After the show tables were set up on stage and in the lobby of the Théâtre des Champs-Elysées for a supper party for the cast and invited guests.

Josephine, escorted by Paul Colin, made her second entrance of the evening, this time wearing an ice-blue dress cut on the bias, selected by Paul Colin from a Paris design house.

She sat beside Colin, staring wide-eyed at *le beau monde* of the city, hardly daring to believe that these privileged people had taken her into their hearts.

Later Josephine said something she must have begun to feel that night. "Paris is the dance," she said. "And I am the dancer."

FIVE

"Picasso I pose for many times. He did not see the outside, but saw inside. He was very intense and very strong. He pulled you to him."

—Josephine

The following morning Josephine awoke to a city bathed in sunlight. The buildings along rue Campagne-Première, her street in Montparnasse, sparkled white beneath a cloudless sky. At corner cafés, bohemians leaned back, sprawling in their wrought-iron chairs, occasionally lifting their faces to the sun.

Josephine threw open the shutters. The concierge across the street was sweeping the sidewalk, pausing to exchange greetings and bits of gossip with neighborhood merchants. "It's like a dream," Josephine remembered thinking. "Paris is so chic, so sympathetic, so gay."

Josephine dressed in a hurry, left the hotel and hopped aboard an autobus for morning rehearsal at the theatre.

Sitting on the bus in her sweater and floppy knickerbockers, once again she found she was an object of fun. Parisians thought knickerbockers belonged on English schoolboys. A passenger laughed.

Josephine invited this kind of response. "If I'm going to be a success, I must be scandalous. I must amuse people."

As rehearsal began, Man Ray, a photographer Alice B. Toklas describes as looking like ". . . an Indian potentate in miniature," arrived to take pictures of the cast. Jacques-Charles suggested they rehearse on the roof ". . . en plein air."

After photographing the group, Man Ray plucked Josephine away from the others. He positioned her against a railing at the edge of the roof, the Eiffel Tower in the background. Josephine preened, puffed out her chest, grinned, strutted and struck a pose, parodying a cakewalk. When Man Ray was finished, Josephine turned to look at the view and found she had an audience. "Since it was so warm, everybody had their windows open. The secretaries and maids and elevator operators in the adjoining buildings all applauded."

Gathering articles that week for her scrapbook, Josephine searched the papers for notices of *La Revue Nègre*. She could not read French, but she recognized the name of the show and picked out her own name from the maze of foreign words. "It was my first French lesson." Almost every paper in town, from the conservative *Intransigeant* to the radical *Paris-Soir*, reviewed the show. Josephine was widely mentioned.

André Levinson, Europe's eminent critic of classic dance, referred to Josephine in the dance of the savages as ". . . a sinuous idol that enslaves and incites mankind.

"The plastic sense of a race of sculptors came to life," he continued, "and the frenzy of the African Eros swept over the audience. It was no longer a grotesque dancing girl who stood before the audience, but the black Venus that haunted Baudelaire."

She was also reviled. Critic Robert de Flers said he experienced "shame and anger." He admitted she was supple and sensuous, but he could not understand her hideous squint. He called her performance "lamentable transatlantic exhibitionism, which brings us back to the monkey much quicker than we descended from the monkey."

Josephine welcomed notoriety. She did not mind the barbs. When an English-speaking reporter asked her what she thought of *La Revue Nègre*, she was unexpectedly articulate. "It represents slavery, discrimination and liberation. All of it is there, in the songs and dances."

She was often stopped on the street and asked for an autograph. But Bricktop remembers that at that time she could hardly write her name. "I said, 'Baby, get a stamp.' "

Jean Cocteau became one of Josephine's admirers. He saw *La*

Nineteen-year-old Josephine clowns with clarinet, surrounded by French musicians. She also played the saxophone, having learned to do so while traveling around the United States on the black vaudeville circuit. *H. Roger-Viollet*

Revue Nègre six times. But the fans who really touched Josephine's heart were the ordinary people, the crowds who worshiped her, those who saw her as a star light-years above them. Arriving at the theatre one afternoon, Josephine found a man alone in the back row, surrounded by a litter of candy wrappers. He said he did not have the money for a second admission so had camped in the theatre, waiting twenty-four hours for her next performance.

Josephine's life in Paris was unfolding with remarkable ease. Each day brought joys, discoveries. She marshaled her youth, her supernormal energies, and set out to make the city hers. She walked the length and breadth of Paris, from the Etoile to the Gare de Lyon, from the Sacré-Coeur to the Place d'Italie. She kicked through the leaves in the Luxembourg Gardens, where dahlias and asters lined the paths. She studied the pictures at the open-air galleries on the boulevard Saint-Michel, where painters hung their canvases on railings and propped them up against kiosks and lampposts.

Josephine's relationship with Paul Colin settled down and became a mutually beneficial alliance. Still new to the city, Josephine wanted an escort and a guide. She was giddy with success and admitted later, "I was in love with myself." Colin, already a dedicated bachelor, wanted *"une fille sans histoire,"* an accessible woman who was not out to ensnare him. His poster for *La Revue Nègre* was just the showcase his talent needed. It launched his career, bringing him work as an illustrator and a set designer. Copies of the poster sold as far away as New York, fetching handsome prices in Harlem. What better publicity could Colin ask for than to have his inspiration incarnate at his side, target of shamelessly greedy eyes.

Josephine met scores of people. In an era when Americans seldom mixed with the French, Josephine gained immediate entrée. Her dark skin and her eccentric habits appealed to the Gallic love of curiosities. She was taken up by people in artistic and intellectual circles as well as by *"le gratin,"* which, translated literally, means the thin, tasty crust on top of a dish, but was also a popular designation for the few French families known to be authentically noble.

Josephine attended the Salon de l'Automne art exhibition at

the Grand Palais. She went to tea dances with Paul Colin at Le Boeuf Sur Le Toit, Cocteau's restaurant on the rue Boissy d'Anglas, which featured a small jazz combo. Cocteau often took a turn on the drums. "Jazz was a better intoxicant for me than alcohol, which I cannot stand. With jazz you feel yourself pushed about by twenty arms; you are a god of noise. . . ."

Colin took Josephine to the Bal Nègre on rue Blomet in Montparnasse, started by colonial soldiers from Martinique and Guadeloupe and now frequented by Paul Morand, Kisling, André Gide, skinny solitary Jules Pascin, and Man Ray with his volcanic mistress Kiki.

Painters were mad for Josephine. "Josephine speaks to our unconscious," wrote art critic Pierre MacOrlan. "She turns upside down our way of seeing, displacing lines, calling to mind a primitive order."

French artists began to discover Negro art two decades before Josephine arrived. Painters such as Derain, Matisse and Modigliani made excursions to the Trocadero Museum, the predecessor of the Museum of Man, to contemplate collections from primitive cultures.

Picasso shocked and delighted Paris by announcing that a primitive Hottentot nude just brought from Africa was far lovelier than Venus de Milo. And now, here was Josephine, a boisterous teenager from the drab Middle West who, in one evening, had come to symbolize the violent darkness of the African woman. Picasso bowed to her triumph. "She is the Nefertiti of now."

She posed at the Beaux-Arts for Picasso, Van Dongen and Foujita. Cubist Henri Laurens pictured her doing the Charleston. In 1926 Alexander Calder caricatured her in wire, using that medium for the first time and later he did several sculptures of her. These images of Josephine are among his most remarkable works, prototypes of the mobile concept, designed to be suspended from the ceiling and to quiver in the slightest breeze, Jack Baur wrote that "a tremor of life ran through them."

The most famous rendition of Josephine was a honey-colored nude portrait painted by Domergue when she was twenty-two, for an exhibition at the Grand Palais. Josephine's

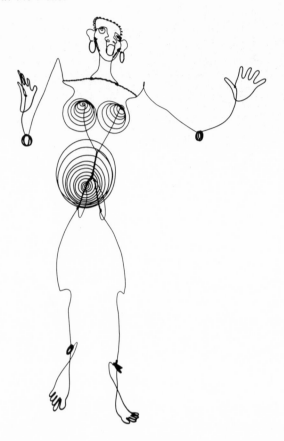

Josephine Baker, wire, by Alexander Calder. Paris
1927. *UPI*

legs are long and comely. She sits leaning forward, a white
flower in her hair, her lips moist. The painting was reproduced
on postcards and sold at bookstalls along the quay to tourists
who took them home as a memento of Parisian wickedness.

Writers saluted Josephine. Charlie Wales in F. Scott
Fitzgerald's *Babylon Revisited* watched "Josephine Baker go
through her chocolate arabesques." Colette, fifty-two when
Josephine arrived, who had shocked Paris twenty years before
by dancing seminude in a music hall, called Josephine "a most
beautiful panther." Erich Maria Remarque pronounced
Josephine *"une grande actrice."* And Paul Morand, inspired by

In her early years in Paris, Josephine spent afternoons posing for artists such as Picasso, Van Dongen, Foujita and Pascin. *H. Roger-Viollet*

her, wrote the novel *Magie Noire*. Morand saw Josephine as a *"machine à dancer,"* fueled by primordial energy. She was his idea of the indefatigable, joy-filled savage whose mind was unburdened by intricate mental processes.

To writers she was a concept rather than a person. They made her what they wanted her to be, *"une garçonne,"* the French term for a flapper. The word "garçonne" first appeared as the title of a vulgar novel written in 1923 by Victor Marguérite. In *La Garçonne* a Sorbonne student named Monique Lerbier cuts her hair, wears a man's jacket and tie, has a child out of wedlock, joins in orgies, and toys with lesbianism. Monique's mother, herself apparently something of a flapper, is described as "covering many kilometers between her first shimmy at five in the afternoon and her last tango at one in the morning." As *La Garçonne* became a runaway success, French women en masse set out to imititate Monique's style.

The popularity of *La Garçonne* helped pave the way for Josephine's conquest of Paris. In the style of Marguérite's heroine, Josephine broke all the rules. The people of Paris knew nothing about the real Josephine; they did not want to know. One reporter wrote that St. Louis was in the state of "Louisiane."

Janet Flanner, an acute observer of the Paris scene, felt no urge to probe beneath Josephine's visual impact. "The only thing about Josephine that interested me was her gift, her talent, the reception that Paris gave her and her popularity. . . . You can't expect an ignorant person to be introspective."

For French couturiers of the 1920s, engaged in liberating the female body, Josephine was a *"mannequin idéal."* Her cinnamon skin and her streamlined body reminiscent of Brancusi's "Bird in Space" was catnip to the masters of fashion.

Josephine now abandoned her overalls and red-checkered shirt, replacing them with crepe-de-chine dresses, cloche hats and lizard-skin shoes. She was welcomed into the sumptuous salon of Madame Vionnet, an artist in fabric who had introduced the bias cut. Josephine bought dresses from Elsa Schiaparelli, who promoted the vamp look. But the couturier who shaped her, who drew out Josephine's beauty, was Paul Poiret, the maniacal dictator of French couture, "the Killer of the Corset." Poiret was at once shrewd and fatuous, egotistical and imaginative, possessed of an enormous talent.

Josephine was soon hooked on Paris fashions, relishing her trips to the great design houses, an addiction that would last until her death. She loved the pomp and ceremony of haute couture: crystal chandeliers, the smell of wildly expensive perfume, saleswomen lined up like high priestesses on steps leading to the grand salon to hand out programs for the afternoon showing, the seamstresses who knelt at her feet during the fittings and who called the dresses their children, treating them with intense affection. But most of all she loved the absorption of a master designer such as Poiret when he trained his expert eyes on her. "It was for me that Poiret created the Zouave pants," she boasted. Poiret called one morning dress that he created for her *un rien,* a trifle, which cost the staggering sum of nine thousand francs.

Some couturiers sent her bills and others simply gave her the dresses, considering the peripatetic exhibitionist a walking advertisement. Bricktop arrived at Josephine's hotel room one day to find the floor covered with stacks of couturier clothes. She said, "Josey, hang these dresses up or have your maid do it."

1925. Josephine hams with bon vivant Paul Poiret, king of French fashion, who freed women from corsets and petticoats. He boasted, "I liberate the bust." *H. Roger-Viollet*

"Oh no, Brickie. They are going to take them away tomorrow and send me another pile."

As *La Revue Nègre* moved into its third week at the Théâtre des Champs-Elysées, friction developed between André Daven and his cast. Daven regarded the performers as unruly children needing surveillance. He was afraid that unless they were kept in line he might lose his investment. "Two dangers had to be watched out for in this group—the nightspots of Montmartre, where the debaucheries cost a fortune, and alcohol. America was dry and our new friends had not yet tasted champagne."

To keep his cast in line, Daven hired the doorman at the

Théâtre des Champs-Elysées to act as a security guard at the hotel. When this man appeared in a uniform with gold piping and a hat trimmed with braid, like an admiral from a Gilbert and Sullivan cast, he looked not in the least intimidating. But the cast resented what the guard stood for. To escape Daven's surveillance, to be close to the sin spots of Montmartre, most of them moved to the Hotel Fournet on the Boulevard des Batignolles, at the foot of Montmartre.

In a burst of exuberance, Josephine took a suite: two bedrooms and a living room. For the first time in her life she had a private bath. Paul Colin was disapproving. "It was a very extravagant thing to do. She didn't know how long her success would last. But Josephine didn't think that way."

With a zest that underscored all her endeavors, Josephine decorated her suite in a manner she felt befit her new life. She went to Galéries Lafayette, the Macy's of Paris, and bought a cretonne bedspread covered with bright blue flowers. She bought baby dolls in multicolored frilly dresses and set them on the pillow. But her most unusual decorating flourish was a pair of antique portable steps that she placed near the foot of her bed, "just like Napoleon probably had."

For Josephine, powerful and famous people were the kings and queens of her childhood fairy tales. They were strong. They lived in fortified castles, protected from a hostile world. They would grant her immunity from her fears.

One Sunday morning shortly after she settled in the Hotel Fournet, she went to the bird market, near Notre Dame, and bought a parakeet and a parrot. Next she purchased a goldfish, two baby rabbits and a snake. Finally she went to the Marché aux Bestiaux and picked out a fine pink baby pig.

Visiting Josephine at the Fournet, Paul Colin had trouble finding a place to sit down. The suite was a shambles. "The animals behaved as they would in a barnyard. The rabbits hopped around the room. The pig wiggled his bottom and shook his ears. He relieved himself on the floor and the carpets."

Josephine named her pig Albert for Albert Tartaglia, the maître d'hôtel of the Fournet. A hearty, hard-working Frenchman, Albert was bewitched by Josephine. Instead of being insulted at Josephine's gesture, he found Albert and the rest of the menagerie charming.

Tartaglia bought a brand-new car and took Josephine out for a driving lesson, an act of foolhardiness since Josephine had never driven and did not understand traffic regulations. She drove like mad, straight ahead, gunning the engine, never looking right or left.

SIX

"She had the genius of youth."

—Anita Loos

Of all the quarters of Paris, Josephine loved Montmartre best. Built on a steep hill, in the shadow of Sacré-Coeur's cupolas, dome and campanile, Montmartre stood at the top of the city, a sleepy red-wine village by day and a throbbing carnival of pleasure by night.

Before 1860, before Montmartre became part of Paris, it was simply a village. As late as 1925 there was still a provincial air about it. The red and yellow facades of the tumbledown houses, the mansards and chimneys jumbled together, made Montmartre seem less formal, less intimidating than other parts of the city.

"La Butte" was home turf to the expatriate black musicians who had come to Paris after the war. Its night world of dives, its cafés, bordellos and dance halls that attracted free-spending whites, reminded them of Lenox Avenue in Harlem, State Street in Chicago, Storyville in New Orleans. Yet Montmartre was better. It was part of Paris, steeped in the romance of centuries. On the Place du Tertre, lovers sat beneath café awnings, embracing unselfconsciously against a typical Utrillo tableau.

Released from the grip of racial prejudice, the black Americans relished their newfound freedom. Their music flourished in Montmartre. Sidney Bechet wrote of the place, "Any time you walked down the street you'd run into four or five people who had real talent to them. Everywhere you'd go . . . you couldn't help yourself. And everybody had a kind of excitement . . . everybody was crazy to be doing." Though Josephine is often credited with introducing "Le Jazz Hot" to the French, it had in fact been heard in Paris since World War I. In those days Lieutenant Jim Europe and his 369th U.S. Infantry "Hell Fighters" band played songs such as "On Patrol in No Man's Land" in major cities on the Continent.

After the Armistice of 1918, many black American musicians, not wanting to return to prejudice and prohibition, rode the war-battered trains to Paris. Montmartre beckoned these men to its citadels of pleasure. In Montmartre they were paid to make their music, and little by little jazz took the place of the gypsy violin. As the music heated up, so did the town. Jazz was a catchword for wild times. "Jazz could mean any damn thing," recalled Bechet. "It could mean high times, screwing, ballroom. It used to be spelled *jass,* which was screwing."

By the time Josephine arrived in Paris, jazz had a firm foothold in Montmartre. Up the narrow, twisting streets of La Trinité, on the rue Blanche, rue Pigalle and rue Fontaine, from one-story carriage sheds and cellars, the music of the Mississippi Delta drifted into the night.

Paris was free of speed limits in the 1920s. Every evening bright green and blood-red Renaults, Citroëns and Hispano-Suizas roared up the streets of Montmartre and disgorged soigné sophisticates in front of such garishly ornamented holes in the wall as Zelli's, Chez Florence and Le Perroquet.

Anita Loos succumbed to the lure of Montmartre, often making the rounds of the clubs with Cole Porter. "Paris nightlife was gay and healthy. It was just people letting off steam in the brightest kind of way. Even the people who took drugs didn't do it in a depraved sense. They just got high. And the lesbian set was so beautiful. There has never been anything like it since."

Like jazz, the Charleston was known to those frequenting Montmartre. It had come to Paris a year before, introduced by Bricktop. But when Josephine Baker took center stage at the

Théâtre des Champs-Elysées and danced the Charleston, she did it as nobody had done it before. The dance became a rage in Paris. Sales of Rodelle soaking salt soared, as foot baths were prescribed for the cure of swollen red dancers' feet. Sem, the pen-and-ink cartoonist of worldly Paris, sketched cruel satires of the rich and titled hell-raisers trying to duplicate the natural syncopation of the children of Harlem. With characteristic wry humor he called them "White Bottoms."

When Josephine met her, Bricktop was already a fixture in Montmartre. A pale, unspoiled beauty, Bricktop was small, chesty and absolutely unique. She characterized herself as "one hundred percent Negro with a trigger Irish temper." She had come to Paris in 1924 and started dancing at Le Grand Duc, a seedy dive where Langston Hughes worked as a waiter. It was owned by a gangster-nobleman, scion of a prominent French family. On warm summer nights Bricktop did cartwheels down the rue Blanche, showing off legs that one Paris reporter called "more beautiful than Mistinguett's."

Bricktop was adopted by the champagne people. Cole Porter was so smitten that he wrote "Miss Otis Regrets" for her, and a chagrined John Steinbeck begged her forgiveness with a taxi full of yellow roses after she had him bounced one night for unruly behavior. They wined her, dined her and gave her money to open a place of her own across the street from Le Grand Duc. She returned their generosity, giving free Charleston lessons to Scott and Zelda Fitzgerald, Hemingway, Cole and Linda Porter and, in a back room away from public view, the young Prince of Wales, later to become Duke of Windsor, who was too shy to practice in front of a crowd.

Josephine and Bricktop were bound together by a web of common memories and experiences. They were both black girls, raised in the Middle West, on the lam from white America. Both had been suckled on back-street jazz—Josephine on the sounds of cathouse pianos in the Valley and Bricktop on the music of State Street saloons. And both had been nurtured in black vaudeville. In her teens Bricktop toured with Jelly Roll Morton ("He was a temperamental boy. He couldn't make up his mind whether to be a pimp or a piano player, so I told him,

'Be both!' "), then became a member of the Panama Trio that included Florence Mills.

Bricktop was secure about her place in the nightclub world. She treated Josephine, twelve years her junior, like a little sister, never dreaming Josephine would overtake her. Later the two would become fierce rivals, with Bricktop jealous of Josephine's fame and Josephine envious of Bricktop's open nature and showmanship in intimate situations. But at the start of their friendship, which waxed and waned over fifty years, Bricktop was the leader and Josephine the follower.

At a time when passage to Europe was expensive, when black women were scarce in Europe, it was natural that Bricktop became Josephine's mentor and guide. "Josephine used to come into my place and ask me about everything. She'd say, 'Brickie! Brickie! Tell me what to do.' She wouldn't go around the corner without asking my advice."

The most important lesson Bricktop taught Josephine was never to mimic the rich, never to surrender her identity. Though Bricktop sometimes pocketed handouts, she did not take up the habits of the donors. "There's nothing in this world like a pork chop sandwich."

In "Brickie's parlour" Josephine met Mabel Mercer, a gentle, shy mulatto singer from Staffordshire, England. When Brickie took a break, leaving the dance floor to man the cash register or bounce a drunk, Mabel entertained. At Bricktop's banquettes lined the walls, lit from behind. Mabel sat at the tables and talked and sang to the customers in a low, rich, mezzo-soprano voice.

> *Pack up all my cares and woe,*
> *Here I go, singing low,*
> *Bye, bye, blackbird.*

When Mabel's speaking melted into singing there was often a quaver in her voice, a sound that underlined her dramatic intent. She molded the words, coloring them with subtle inflections. Josephine often heard Bricktop coaching Mabel, helping her streamline her style. "Stop waving your hands around. Cup them in your lap, like a lady." Josephine was fascinated by Mabel's delivery, her intimate way of speaking songs, and later used elements of Mabel's style.

Through Bricktop more than anyone else, Josephine became part of the crazy, free-spending world of the rich at play. At Bricktop's and Zelli's she luxuriated in what Fitzgerald called "the comforting proximity of millionaires." She shared the dance floor with Egyptian cotton kings, polo players from Buenos Aires, Indian princes and Chicago meat packers, men who came to Europe in their steam yachts and lit their cigars with twenty-dollar bills. Woolworth heir Jimmy Donahue, phoned Bricktop from a liner crossing the Atlantic. "Brickie, hold the phone in the air so I can hear the music."

Bricktop had a power base, a territory. As the owner of a *boîte* she commanded respect. This was brought home to Josephine one night when dress designer Elsa Schiaparelli, one of Bricktop's backers, entered Bricktop's with twenty-five people. When she was ready to leave, Schiap said, "Oh, Brick, you can charge this."

"I don't let anyone charge."

"But this is my place," Schiap said.

"Ohhhhhh, this is not your place. Your place is called Schiaparelli's. This is called Bricktop's. People pay at your place. You pay here. You pay or you don't come back."

Schiaparelli paid and did come back. They all came back because the greatest problem of the rich is boredom, and Bricktop knew how to rescue them from their ennui.

There was a curious law in Paris in the 1920s: Bistros had to close from midnight to 2 A.M. Musicians came to work at seven in the evening, quit for two hours, then went back to work until anytime.

Mabel Mercer remembered the night and the dawn. She left Bricktop's one morning at seven. "Louis Armstrong was entertaining. I came back about noon and Louis was still there, still entertaining. Nights were wonderful and exciting then. Dawn in Paris . . . nobody thought there was anything odd about visiting the flower market and having breakfast at dawn. Nighttime is dangerous now. It was fascinating then."

Montmartre musicians snatched a few hours sleep and reas-

Frisco and Bricktop, spirited proprietors of fashionable Parisian nightspots.

sembled for afternoon jam sessions, playing for their own amusement, giving their best at these private get-togethers. Sidney Bechet found it a challenge to play for other blacks. "You got to *go* some to play for Negroes."

Musicians often gathered at the Hotel Fournet. At one of these sessions Josephine met Jocelyn Augustus Bingham, who called himself Frisco. As Bricktop was a sister to Josephine, Frisco became a father, giving her the reassurance she craved. Their relationship lasted fifty years.

Born in Jamaica, Frisco had been a San Francisco longshoreman, had worked his way around the world cooking on freighters. He had been a doughboy during World War I and, after the war, decided to make a life in Europe instead of the United States. "I was born for nourishment, not for punishment."

Tall, black and handsome, with straight white teeth and a ramrod posture, Frisco was a vivid personality, a man of many talents. He could speak nine languages, including Portuguese,

Arabic and Magyar. He played the piano and danced at various Montmartre clubs, including Chez Florence and Le Perroquet, before opening his own place, Frisco's, at 12 rue des Martyrs. There, when Josephine met him, he was making a fortune playing for high society. "The Ritz sent me five tables every night."

Afternoons, before he drove off in his Rolls Royce to pay house calls on the rich, to give them Charleston lessons, Frisco left his apartment on the rue de Rome and stepped around the corner to join the fun at the Hotel Fournet. "The Fournet wasn't a great hotel, but it was good enough for parties. They were just a bunch of kids in there, yappin', talkin' and singin'."

Sometimes Josephine left the sessions, suddenly craving solitude. She would shut herself away in her suite, sitting on her cretonne bedspread, surrounded by her pets and frilly dolls, stunned by her success, trying to take it all in.

Often Frisco followed her there. They would sit together on her bed. "I'd talk to her quietly. 'Jo,' I'd say, 'you're in the right country now. You just behave yourself and you'll go far. Very far.' "

Frisco remembers that in the soft fall light of a Paris afternoon, she looked much younger than her nineteen years. "She was such a baby then. She had the sweetest eyes."

As October gave way to November, the mulberry trees in the Jardìns des Tuileries surrendered their leaves, carpeting the geometric lawns with pointillistic patterns of umber, yellow and vermilion.

Traversing the garden, en route to the theatre, Josephine passed the bocci players in the statue-studded park and watched the black balls roll along the dusty ground. She felt the bite of autumn in the air, a chill wind signaling the coming of winter, a season she despised. Josephine had another reason to feel apprehensive: She would soon be leaving Paris. On November 19 *La Revue Nègre* was scheduled to close and go to Berlin for a six-week run, and then on to Moscow for the final leg of the tour.

Josephine loved Paris as she had loved no other city. Berlin and Moscow were remote, unknown. And returning to New York, to anonymity, was unthinkable. Even if she triumphed in

Gotham, played the lead in a Broadway show, she could not stay at the Plaza or the St. Regis. Here in Paris, when someone stood up as she entered a restaurant it was to applaud her, praise her, not to show her the door.

Josephine now saw that she was more than the dancing sensation of Paris. She was becoming a symbol. To the French she epitomized the New Woman. Today it is unlikely that a nude dancer would be a feminist idol, but in Paris in the 1920s her name meant freedom. French women were in revolt. During the war many of them had taken men's jobs in industry or had managed offices and farms. They had grown accustomed to a measure of freedom and wanted to keep it. Yet, because they were still denied the right to vote, the right to enter the professions and politics, to open a bank account or to buy contraceptives, real freedom was still out of reach. So, pitched against staggering odds, la femme française fell back on her sexuality, using it as her prime weapon in her battle for liberté and égalité, to say nothing of fraternité.

Women demanded the right to romance, licit or illicit. The cocottes of La Belle Epoque were being driven out of business by upwardly nubile young women defecting from petite bourgeois households, who smudged their eyes with charcoal and painted on blood-red lipstick with such trade names as "Eternal Wound." They tattooed their derrieres with roses and wore flimsy underwear with crossword puzzles printed on them. They flaunted ankle bracelets, drank cocktails, smoked cigarettes and—*quelle horreur!*—cut their hair.

With her small breasts, boyish hips, clipped black hair slicked down with goo, Josephine embodied many of the tendencies, tastes and aspirations of the epoch.

As popular idols often do, Josephine listened to her public. In an article prophesying that Josephine might usher in a new era of romanticism, Paul Brach suggested she drop her cross-eyed clown routine: "Josephine Baker, will you be serious for one night? Wear a becoming hairdo with giant plumes, like the white stars in our shows. Have a long train carried by twelve black pages. Make a majestic entrance and sing a soft sentimental song of your country."

This was perhaps the worst advice she ever received. She

would never again recapture her almost Chaplinesque genius for comedy, which she demonstrated in those early days in Paris.

As her fame became real to her, so did the prerogatives of celebrity. People were willing to pay for her company. Power was new to Josephine and she used it without discrimination. Mostly she went out with the people who would pay, but even at other times she exacted her tribute. One of Josephine's admirers, a young architectural student living on an allowance from his father, adored Josephine and sent flowers to the Hotel Fournet every day. Josephine liked him. He was teaching her French and they laughed together at her accent. But soon Josephine changed the relationship. She was sitting with the student at the Restaurant Calvini on the rue Pigalle. They had finished supper and the student pulled out his billfold to pay the check. As he opened the billfold, Josephine spotted a thousand-franc note. She reached for the note and put it in her purse.

"That's my allowance for the month," the student said. "If you take it I won't have any money to live on."

"If you go out with artists you must pay," Josephine replied.

The student forgave her, insisted on seeing her as often as he could, but soon saw that he was playing a losing game. Standing in the lobby of the Théâtre des Champs-Elysées waiting for Josephine one evening, he told Caroline Dudley, "I've given Josephine all my money and she's given me nothing in return. Nothing."

As *La Revue Nègre* was about to close in Paris, Paul Derval, director of the Folies-Bergère, came to see the show. "I was immediately fascinated by a marvelous girl, built like a Tangara figurine, whose explosive personality seemed to set the very stage afire." Derval returned the next evening and, after the show, introduced himself to Josephine. "Would you like to star in my next Folies review?" he asked.

The Folies-Bergère was the biggest, splashiest and best-known music hall in the world, a showplace for Loie Fuller, Maurice Chevalier and the fabulous Mistinguett, whose photograph, larger than life, decorated the facade.

Derval produced a contract and Josephine signed it, knowing that in order to go into rehearsal for her Folies show she would have to abandon Caroline Dudley and *La Revue Nègre.* She knew her departure would deal a death blow to the show; it was not strong enough to continue without her and would close prematurely.

Josephine put Derval's contract in her purse, deciding to go with *La Revue Nègre* to Berlin and face the problem later. In fact, she was not sure what to do. Maybe she would stay with *La Revue Nègre* and maybe she would not. Of course, she would not tell Derval she was leaving Paris. He expected her to start rehearsals soon.

As Josephine boarded the train for Berlin, she was saying good-bye to the happiest ten weeks of her life, to a time when her talent was fresh and raw. She was saying good-bye to the first flush of romance with a city that had given her love and respect.

French writer Fernand Devoire summed up the feelings of pleasure-sated Parisians when he said: "Josephine Baker, our lives on the banks of the Seine were weary and depressing before you came along. In the eyes of Paris, you are the virgin forest. You bring to us a savage rejuvenation."

Devoire's words were translated for Josephine, who smiled and turned them inside out, expressing how she saw the City of Light, the center of all her dreams, the paradise so far removed from the slums of St. Louis. "To me," she replied, "Paris is the virgin forest."

SEVEN

"Berlin needs its sensations as a fish needs water."

—Joseph Goebbels

As the Paris–Berlin express crossed the border and cut through the rich German heartland, the thick forests and cold December streams of a land that had tasted the bitter defeat of war, Josephine, sitting with her snake Kiki dozing in a hatbox on her lap, surrounded by the rambunctious troupe of *La Revue Nègre*, stared out at the countryside and wondered what lay ahead.

She was curious to see Berlin, a city renowned for its glamor and its queer, fascinating excitement; eager to know if Berliners would take her to their hearts the way Parisians had done. But by not being honest with either Carolyn Dudley or Paul Derval, Josephine was sabotaging both their plans. Caroline Dudley was relying on Josephine to stay with the company not only through the Berlin run but also for the six weeks the show was booked to play in Moscow. At the same time, completely unaware that his wily headliner had left town, Paul Derval set in motion the vast creative and technical machinery of the Folies-Bergère in preparation for his spectacular 1926 revue.

When Josephine and the other performers disembarked at Potsdammer Station, a policeman, posted at the exit of the terminal, smiled and handed them metal tickets with the numbers of taxicabs on them. His courtesy characterized the daily routines of the city, a civil orderliness that contrasted vividly with the moral anarchy of the doomed metropolis.

As the cabbie piloted through the shrill traffic from Potsdammer Station to the Hotel Bristol, located on the festive Unter den Linden, the Piccadilly of Berlin, Josephine stared with delight at the white sea of electric bulbs flooding the bawdy Friedrichstrasse, the Jäger and Behrenstrasse, the throbbing arteries of Berlin's night world, where every building boasted a cabaret, a bordello, a dance hall, or some other lively form of *Amusmang*. To Josephine the Berlin dives looked like giant ocean liners, giddy incandescent ships propelled by their orchestras, sailing under dark night skies.

Though she stayed in Berlin less than two months, in that brief time she would become one of the magic names in the haunted city—along with Greta Garbo, Lotte Lenya and Marlene Dietrich—during what Germans called *Die goldenen zwanzigen Jahre,* the Golden Twenties.

Postwar Berliners saw a far different person from the "La Bakaire" of later years—the *soignée vedette* who spoke in modulated cadences (the result of speech lessons from an actor at the Comédie Française), the humanitarian earth mother and accomplished performer who tailored every one of her responses in a press conference to fit the Baker image.

In Berlin Josephine displayed a joyous pagan appetite for life, a hunger to grab at new experiences with both hands. Her way of dancing, a "frenzied fertility rite set to the syncopated rhythm of jazz," reflected much of her inner state, a craving for action without reflection, a deep need to sate her physical senses in a desperate effort to keep at bay the hobgoblins lurking in the dark corners of her psyche, the fears and loneliness that had stalked her since childhood.

She thought she was Cinderella. She was convinced that if she failed to keep running from her cruel beginnings, stopped for a moment to look at her garden of horrors, she would find herself back in St. Louis again, trapped and doomed to oblivion. One lover avowed that she even preferred coitus standing up because it gave her instant release and she could do it while dancing.

People used the word "oversexed" when speaking of

Josephine in Berlin. *George Hoyningen-Huené*

Josephine. But it is hard to say how many of the stories were true and how many were wild fabrications, so easy to pin on a performer whose stage dancing captured exactly the sexual tempo of her time.

"She was a beast for sex," says a composer who knew her in Berlin. "She was looking for the perfect penis, and she looked hard," recalls an Austrian vaudeville actor who worked in Berlin's music halls and swears that he remembers a queue of men waiting outside her hotel room at the Bristol to see if they measured up. Rumor, never substantiated, had it that she worked in a high-class brothel in her after-hours.

"Sex was like champagne to her," says an old friend. "She didn't need conversation. It would last twenty minutes, perhaps one hour, but it was body to body the whole time. She was a free spirit 'way back. Just because a man spent an hour with Josephine, he could never feel that he owned her." But was that how she really felt? Frisco, who was playing in a club in Berlin at the time, remembers, "She was so happy if a man told her that he loved her."

At daybreak of her first Berlin morning, Josephine, an insomniac, wandered the streets, getting a feel of the city.

Her two favorite places in Berlin would reflect the extremes in her personality: the Berlin Zoo, filled with animals great and small with which she felt a communion stronger than she felt with people, and the colossal "Vaterland," a section of Berlin in which there were restaurants and specialty shops selling merchandise from countries all over the world. In the "Vaterland" Josephine bought boxes of tourist items, indulging in her voracious need to acquire material objects.

Postwar Berlin was a jungle city full of contrast, barbaric and beautiful, grim and gay. Along the wide thoroughfares, lined with massive gray buildings, unheated trams clanged and swayed past shoddy shops and peeling billboards. On busy street corners one-legged war veterans stood in the foul slushy cold, selling bootlaces and cocaine. Below ground level, cellars were stuffed with criminal gangs posing as wrestling clubs. On bleak side streets, where hunger reigned, children huddled on doorsteps of grimy stucco buildings or scavenged in garbage cans.

Despite its rickety scenario, *La Revue Nègre,* which played at the Nelson Theatre, was almost as popular in Berlin as it had been in Paris. After the finale, the audience became so excited by Josephine that they carried her offstage. With her clipped, shiny hair and taut athletic body, Josephine appealed to both sexes, an asset in a city where, at that time, androgyny was held in high esteem.

Dancing every night to sellout crowds, Josephine mesmerized the hard-boiled cosmopolites who were fascinated by her rare mix of innocence and sensuality. According to one spectator, "The women of Berlin were never the same again." *Berliner Illustrierte,* the world's first picture magazine, called her "a figure of contemporary German Expressionism."

German Expressionism, the style of radical figurative art in northern Europe at the beginning of the twentieth century, was really less a style than a cluster of attitudes: harsh dissonant shapes, broken-bottle cubism, an appetite for the primitive with extreme jumps of tone between limelight and gloom.

Expressionists bubbled with fantasies about noble savages, the racial purity of undeveloped societies pantheistically idolizing the jungle as the Eden of happy animals. No wonder then that they saw Josephine as a primordial force responding to the ultramechanized age that Europe was entering at the time.

This mechanized society had appeared at its epitome in Fritz Lang's masterpiece of the silent cinema, *Metropolis,* and at its smoothest in the school of design at Weimar, known as Bauhaus.

When Josephine was told that she symbolized German primitivism, she visualized prehistoric cavemen. "What are you trying to say?" she retorted. "I was born in 1906 in the twentieth century."

Unwittingly, Josephine became a standard-bearer for another popular German movement, *Freikorperkultur,* nudism. This was a lively political issue and an open sore to right-wing Germans, hell-bent on purging the citizenry of any ideas that remotely smelled of decadence. Berlin nudists did not bow gracefully to conservative forces. Both factory workers and hoary-haired university professors espoused nudism to free themselves from the neuroses of modern society.

Right-wing Germans, whose ranks were increasing daily, regarded Josephine as a threat to the Aryan ideal. The Brownshirts passed out pamphlets condemning her, labeling her *untermenschen*, subhuman. Josephine simply dismissed them as a nuisance, about all they seemed at the time. "I'm not immoral," she said. "I'm only natural."

The chaotic nature of German politics was in large part the result of the special madness brought on by the inflation that followed World War I. The Germans had been forced to withstand the humiliation of a lost war, the exactions and arrogance of the victors, and the annexation of the Ruhr and Rhineland. But worst of all, far more demoralizing than the defeat of their armies and the political upheavals that followed the Armistice, was contending with the worst inflation in history. People trundled wheelbarrows of marks through the streets in an effort to buy a loaf of bread.

By the time Josephine arrived, the worst of the inflation had passed, only to be followed by a new era of false prosperity. Profiteers who had made fortunes selling Germany short during the inflation invested their winnings in real estate, new construction, new enterprises and stock market speculation. Nowhere were the spending sprees of the fat-bellied "Schiebers" more obvious than in Berlin's nightclubs, the kinkiest and most garish dives in Europe.

Berlin's nightclub world welcomed Josephine as a long lost daughter. "In the dance halls," said Josephine, "when I walked in, the musicians stopped playing. They stood up and saluted me."

Berliners were just beginning to discover jazz—they pronounced it *yats* and considered it "knorke," which loosely translated means "nifty." Duke Ellington had come to Germany in the summer of 1925 with his all-black revue *Chocolate Kiddies*, thus setting the stage for Josephine. Bessie Smith records blared over Berlin radio, and in smoky overcrowded bars a wanton clarinet and the chuckle of saxophones made merry until the night was worn away.

Because she was a celebrity as well as a notorious character,

Josephine was invited everywhere. She was seen at all the smart places: at the shabbily splendid Romanische Café across from the Kaiser Wilhelm Memorial Church, a café that could seat one thousand customers; at Uncle Tom's Cabin, a restaurant and beer garden where the literary clique gathered; at the Kuka, which opened at three in the morning and catered to artists, bar girls, journalists and writers; and at the Residenz Casino, or "Resi" as it was affectionately known to Berliners, not merely the gayest of the city's dance haunts but the gayest in the world. Among its primary attractions were its telephones, one on every table so that a customer could call any other customer and become familiar and its post office through which one could send such items as perfume, cigars and cigarettes, liquor or cocaine.

Josephine also attended the popular pervert balls, about which writer Otto Friedrich wrote: "Even the Rome of Suetonius had never known such orgies." As the honored guest at one, Josephine remembered a haze of smoke, balloons and paper snowballs. "It was a veritable can of herrings . . . men and women flattened against each other."

Claude Hopkins, the band leader of *La Revue Nègre,* had a brief fling with Josephine at this time. He found her wonderfully warm and charming, "a sweetheart," and he delighted in seeing a little brown-skinned girl dazzle the worldly Europeans. "High society really went for her," says Hopkins. "The Krupp family, they came to the show almost every night to see her."

One night, after a performance of *La Revue Nègre,* Josephine was swabbing off her stage makeup with cotton dipped in alcohol when a knock came at her dressing room door.

"Come in," she called.

The man who entered was short and stocky and somewhat handsome, with wavy hair and extraordinary cobalt-blue eyes. Josephine felt as if she were being pulled into a magnetic field. "My name is Max Reinhardt," he said. "I saw you in New York in *Shuffle Along.* I have an acting school here in Berlin, and I would like you to become one of my students."

Making inquiries about Reinhardt later, Josephine would learn that he was the most famous director in Germany, a fact that did not particularly impress her. "I was used to such descriptions by now. Everyone I met seemed to be 'the greatest,' 'the most eminent,' 'the finest.' Perhaps this was sometimes the case, but in my ignorance how was I to know?"

Viennese by origin and trained as an actor, Reinhardt was one of the most influential and original theatre producers in the world when Josephine met him. He had arrived in Berlin in 1894, when he was twenty-one, playing in Otto Brahm's repertory company at the Deutsches Theatre. Eleven years later, when he became head of the company, he set out to revolutionize the fundamental techniques of the stage. To him, the theatre was a place for display, for spectacle and magic. Using the plays of Shakespeare, stretching all the possibilities of light and stage, he was a master of gigantic productions and a genius of the mob scene.

Reinhardt was particularly interested in pantomime, use of the body to portray story and emotion, and consequently founded the International Pantomime Society, which he inaugurated at the Salzburg Festival.

When on his first trip to New York he saw *Shuffle Along*, Reinhardt was awed by the blacks' great talent for mimicry, largely developed in black vaudeville. "I have never seen such wonderful possibilities," said Reinhardt. "I should like to do something with it."

When Josephine premiered in Berlin, Reinhardt decided to make her one of his protégées. He saw Josephine as a great raw talent who could be molded into a truly remarkable comedienne. He knew she needed years of training and he wanted her to sign a three-year contract to study at his acting school— one of the best in the world—where he was certain he could draw from her all there was to evoke.

Pudgy Marlene Dietrich was a special student there. Earlier that year she had played a minor role in George Wilhelm Pabst's classic *The Joyless Street,* with an aloof young actress who was also plump then named Greta Garbo.

Josephine recognized that Reinhardt was offering her an exceptional opportunity. And years later, whenever she told the story of her life—which she did in five coauthored autobiographies and numerous articles—she always mentioned his offer. At the time Reinhardt spoke to her, however, she could not decide whether to accept his invitation or follow through on her contract with the Folies-Bergère.

Thinking that Josephine was just teasing him, Reinhardt pursued her with added zeal. He squired her around Berlin, introducing her to the great personalities of the day.

In its culture as well as its decadence, Berlin was one of the most exciting cities of the world in the 1920s. Its bacchanalian esprit acted as a natural magnet for the creative and intellectually gifted. Refugees from the Russian Revolution, the avant-garde from Austria and Hungary, and American writers fleeing the intellectual barrenness of their homeland converged in a whirlpool of talent.

The "dramatis personae" illuminating Berlin in the 1920s was phenomenal: Vladimir Horowitz, Yehudi Menuhin, Lotte Lenya, Pola Negri, Le Corbusier, Kurt Weill, Kandinsky, Dorothy Thompson, Albert Einstein, Bertolt Brecht, Mies van der Rohe, Sol Hurok, Werner von Braun, Joseph Goebbels, Paul Klee, Rudolph Serkin, Herman Hesse, Vladimir Nabokov, Walter Gropius, and a frustrated architect and paperhanger, Adolf Hitler.

One evening Josephine and Reinhardt were guests at a stag party at Karl Vollmoeller's apartment, located on the Pariser Platz. Vollmoeller was an amusing and quirky playboy with a rapacious appetite for decadence. He combed the city to find eccentric personalities to invite to his much-talked-about parties as he reveled in mixing all types, from the "Strichjungen"—boy prostitutes found in the "daisy bars"—to shy odd ducks from the corners of recherché cafés. His late-evening "at homes" usually included ballet masters, dancers, publishers, writers and actresses who had been "just discovered."

Count Henry Kessler, a playwright and bon vivant sometimes known as the "Red Count" because of his liberal politics, kept a diary that is an excellent record of life in Berlin between the wars. A regular at Vollmoeller's soirees, Kessler wrote vividly of the night Josephine lit up the party. Four or five men in dinner jackets, among them Reinhardt, amused themselves with half a dozen naked girls who alternated between squirming on the floor like a pack of lizards and dancing feverishly to American jazz blaring from a Gramophone.

Josephine danced apart from the group, alone, engrossed in her thoughts. She wore only a pink muslin apron. Kessler was bewitched by her purity of style. To him she was an ancient Egyptian performing an intricate series of movements without ever losing the basic pattern, like a dancer in the court of Solomon or Tutankhamen.

A woman named Landshoff, a niece of Germany's foremost publisher, Samuel Fisher, danced over to Josephine. She wore only a dinner jacket. With their matching cropped haircuts, they looked like two young boys. Kessler watched as they slid to the floor and lay in each other's arms, "like a rosy pair of lovers," oblivious to the men who stood over them.

To Kessler, Josephine seemed curiously unerotic. "Watching her inspires as little sexual excitement as does the sight of a beautiful beast of prey."

Kessler decided to write a pantomime, starring Josephine, which he hoped Reinhardt would produce. The show would be half jazz and half Oriental, the music to be composed perhaps by Richard Strauss.

To promote his idea, Kessler invited Reinhardt and Josephine to a large dinner party on February 26, during which he would discuss the plot of the pantomime among a group of his friends. On the evening of the dinner, Kessler cleared his library to give Josephine ample room to dance. But when his honored guest arrived, it was clearly apparent that she was in no mood to shine.

As much as Josephine craved attention, she liked it on her terms, which were often hard to decipher. If she suspected that she was being put on display as a vulgar item for the titillation of the curious, she withdrew into herself. When two patrician-looking German women walked in on Kessler's gathering, she retreated to a corner and sulked.

When Josephine felt insecure she turned inward, seemingly oblivious to the fact that people were focusing on her. She could be in a room with twenty people and still be by herself. At such times, her power to mesmerize appeared to vanish as she almost seemed to become physically smaller.

As Kessler started describing the ballet he had in mind for Josephine, she quickly snapped out of her solitary mood and hung on his every word. Said Kessler: "My plot is how Solomon, handsome, young and royal (I have Serge Lifar in mind), buys a dancer (the Shulamite, Miss Baker), has her brought before him, naked, and showers his robes, his jewels, his entire riches upon her. But the more gifts he lavishes, the more she eludes him. From day to day he grows more naked and the dancer less perceptible to him. Finally, when it is the King who is altogether bare, the dancer utterly vanishes from his sight in a tulip-shaped cloud. . . ."

Josephine loved the idea of playing the vanquishing woman. How soon, she asked, would the part be ready for her? She spotted a Maillol statue of a nude woman and began to compose grotesque movements in front of it, copying the pose of the sculpture, resting against it in bizarre postures, talking to it. "Then she danced around it with extravagantly grandiose gestures," wrote Kessler, "the picture of a priestess frolicking like a child and making fun of herself and her goddess. Maillol's creation was obviously much more interesting and real to her than we humans standing about her. Genius (for she is a genius in the matter of grotesque movement) was addressing genius."

Josephine never performed Kessler's pantomime, nor did anyone else, and she did not attend Max Reinhardt's acting school. A surprise visit from Monsieur Lorett, Paul Derval's agent, persuaded Josephine that she had to decide whether to remain in Berlin and work under Reinhardt, go to Moscow with *La Revue Nègre,* or return to Paris and the Folies-Bergère.

Derval first learned that Josephine was in Berlin when a friend of his returned from Germany and told him that Josephine was appearing there. Frantically he got in touch with Monsieur Lorett, who took the first train to Berlin, to wait in the biting cold for two hours outside the stage door of the theatre where Josephine was performing. At last he was admitted, only to learn that Josephine had little intention of honoring her Paris contract—though she might think it over on consideration of an extra 400 francs per performance. This would make her salary 27,000 francs, about $5,400 a month, making her one of the highest paid performers in Paris.

"What could I do?" said Derval. "The show was too far advanced for us to cancel it, and there would have been no point in taking her to court. I surrendered."

Josephine could not bring herself to tell Caroline Dudley that she was leaving *La Revue Nègre,* so she asked Sidney Bechet to deliver the news.

The cast was angry at the thought of the show closing, but instead of venting their anger on Josephine, whose temper they feared, certain performers made Caroline Dudley the scapegoat. "I'm going to have two men guard you," Bechet told Dudley, "because somebody might cut your throat."

Dudley paid the boat fare back to New York for anybody who wanted to go. This, combined with her loss from the show's early demise, put her $10,000 in debt. To recoup some of this, she tried to sue Josephine for the $10,000 loss. Despite the lawsuit, she never blamed Josephine for her defection. "How could I blame her? She was a bastard off the floor. She was kicked around all her life."

Returning to Paris in March, Josephine rented a two-room apartment on the rue Beaujon near the Etoile. Montmartre would be where she worked and relaxed, but for day-to-day living she wanted a good address.

Rue Beaujon was a quiet street, a short walk from the scrupulously manicured Parc Monceau where, in free moments, Josephine would sometimes wander. But most of her time was spent at the Folies.

In six weeks of rehearsal prior to the opening of *La Folie Du Jour,* Josephine had her first taste of what it is like to be at the hot center of an extravaganza costing over half a million dollars and utilizing the talents of more than five hundred people.

The Folies-Bergère, which opened in 1869, was the first music hall in Paris. Through the years it had achieved a worldwide reputation as the Arabian Nights of the common man, a citadel of pleasure where foreign visitors often went on their first night in town.

The cheapest tickets entitled the holder to stand in the "promenoir." This peculiarly Gallic element of interior architecture is a walking area off the lobby of the theatre where spectators could stand at the famous Folies bar, immortalized by Manet, and sip an apéritif or stroll into the darkened theatre and watch the show. The immense lounge was a popular hunting preserve for *demimondaines,* hustlers who preferred the cozy "promenoir" to the harsh realities of the street.

Josephine could not have chosen a better era to be a Folies star. Music hall entertainment reached its apogee in Paris between 1919 and 1935. In the Twenties the Folies was a temple of mirth, an amorous and eccentric institution that has never been equaled since. The postwar boom afforded lavish spending on public entertainment. This was the reign of nudes and sumptuous decors, the ascendancy of electricians, of engineers and intricate stage machinery, of the maître du ballet and of equating stars with royalty. "I loved and adored them," Tallulah Bankhead said of the Folies' shows, "those big, idiotic showgirls . . . those big idiotic spectacles. They were really wonderful."

The three-story Folies-Bergère building was a factory very much like the MGM lots in the 1930s and 1940s, the difference being that at the Folies they were producing only one show at a time. In little rabbit warrens in the basement, one hundred workers of every profession utilized their talents to prepare for the show: wardrobe designers, makeup artists, machinists, electricians and accessory specialists all bent their skills to the task. There was a forge, a carpentry shop, an embroidery workshop, a room with several miles of sequins ready to be attached to dresses and another filled with the plumes of tropical birds. The fabrics required for a revue might measure 500 kilometers—the distance from Paris to Lyons; 17 kilometers of ribbon were used to execute a special curtain.

In *La Folie Du Jour* Derval skillfully combined the vast trappings of the Folies-Bergère—a full orchestra playing Irving Berlin tunes, collapsible stairs, three-dimensional sets and elaborate fireworks—with Josephine's hoochy-koochy dancing. Only blonde and red-haired nudes were cast, to heighten the vivid contrast with Josephine's dark skin. She, meantime, regarded every chorus girl and chorus boy, the choreographer, stage manager and even Paul Derval himself, as little goblins expending their energy to make her shine as the star.

To an extent, it was her egocentrism that made her see things this way, but it was also her sharp sense of professionalism and of self-protection that made her want everything to be the best. Minute details of lighting, every trick in the makeup man's repertoire, the ordered workings of the intricate stage machinery, all demanded her attention. Josephine radiated so much enthusiasm that her energy had a catalytic effect on performers and crew, causing them to push their talents and skills to the limit. This trait would stay with her.

But her severe mood swings confused and irritated many of the workers. She could be sobbing uncontrollably one moment, then ten minutes later be bubbling with joy. The seamstresses at the Folies, accustomed to the professionalism of Maurice Chevalier and Mistinguett, did not know what to make of Josephine. She was often late, and once arrived wearing a nightgown under her fur coat. Like many who would wait on her, they were enthralled by her charm yet afraid of her moods. She could change very quickly from softness to anger. Sometimes, in the middle of a fitting, she walked away, leaving the seamstresses posed on their knees ready to pin a hem. She said of herself, "I don't have the calling to be a pincushion."

A week before the show opened, the 1926 Folies program came from the printer. Josephine dominated it, not just because she was the star, or because of her dark skin, but because her hard athletic body, radiating kinetic energy, captured the eye by its sheer blazoning vitality. She was a new kind of sexual woman.

As in the 1890s with such American stars as Lillian Russell, Nora Bayes and Maude Adams, plump pulchritude was still the physical ideal in the 1920s. Chorus girls averaged ten more pounds than they do today. The Folies program contained lumps of fleshy beauties, marshmallow tributes to Peter Paul Rubens, draped around Ionic columns, sprouting from potted palms or resting supine on chaise longues.

At the entrance to the Folies on rue Richer, Paul Derval had erected towering color photographs of Josephine. Above the marquee an immense bank of electric lights spelled out her name. For the first time ever her name was up in lights.

Over the years the Folies had featured Yvette Guilbert, Loie

Fuller, La Belle Otéro, Liane de Pougny, Colette, Charles Chaplin and Mistinguett, as well as female impersonator Barbette, known as "the jazz-age Botticelli"; the Dolly Sisters, the spoiled stepdaughters of Paris; Fernandel; and a chorus boy who would later be one of France's greatest actors, Jean Gabin. Josephine was taking her place among some of the world's brightest stars.

Josephine wrote home to her mother and, in her broken English riddled with misspellings, described the preparations for the show in fairytale language. Surprisingly, she also wrote to her husband Willie Baker, inviting him to join her in Paris. Was this a generous gesture made out of guilt for deserting Willie, or did she really miss him?

Willie was working as a Pullman porter in Chicago. He still loved Josephine but knew she was moving in a world where he would be relegated to the role of hanger-on, and he was too proud for that. "I told her I wouldn't go unless I had a job over there," said Willie. "I don't ride on the coattails of no woman."

EIGHT

"As irresistible as the Queen of Sheba, Josephine Baker is the current rage of the Parisian stage. Indeed, she is all but the dictator of Paris."

—*Vanity Fair*

The opening of *La Folie Du Jour* was an occasion. The highlight of the show occurred when a vast iron cage, egg shaped and painted gold, gradually descended from the lofty ceiling of the house to the level of the orchestra. As its gate opened horizontally, Josephine was revealed standing on a giant mirror. She wore only three gold bracelets on her upper arm and a girdle of rhinestone-studded bananas around her hips. Looking like a Delaunay painting come to life, a visual blur of legs and arms, Josephine danced the Charleston. The bananas trembled like Jell-O on a fork. Then the cage closed over her and she was pulled slowly up again into the distant dome of the theatre.

She reminded e. e. cummings, who was in the audience, of "a creature neither infrahuman nor superhuman, but somehow both; a mysteriously unkillable Something, equally nonprimitive and uncivilized, or beyond time in the sense that emotion is beyond arithmetic."

A film clip made of Josephine's banana dance ran as a "short subject" in movie houses throughout the United States. One spectator in Columbia, South Carolina, became so excited he sprang to his feet and yelled louder and louder, "Do Jesus! Do Jesus! I have never seen a woman dance so good before in my life."

Josephine in her celebrated banana costume. Banana-clad Josephine
dolls sold by the thousands to children in the streets and in the Bois de
Boulogne. *Granger Collection*

Josephine as the "Dark Star" of the Folies-Bergère. Newspapers called her "the most photographed girl in the world." *Photographie Girauden*

Soon it seemed that everybody in Paris was boasting that they had been introduced to Josephine. *Vanity Fair* said: "Since the war the two Americans best known in Europe—known for different reasons, of course—have been Woodrow Wilson and Josephine Baker."

Josephine, swinging from a trapeze at the Folies, tossing violets to her audience, seemed to embody the spirit of the Twenties, the pain and poignancy, the unrestrained joy of the Jazz Age. She was the Ebony Venus, the Black Pearl, the Creole Goddess. Newspapers called her "the most photographed girl in the world." Bananas, nature's witty phallic symbol, became her professional trademark. Like Chaplin's baggy trousers, her bananas for a time were the most talked about, the most cartooned costume in Europe. Banana-clad Josephine dolls sold by the thousands to children in the streets and in the Bois de Boulogne. Cocktails, bathing suits and hair goo were named for her. She was said to paint her fingernails with fourteen-carat gold, for which Countess Anna de Noailles, France's beautiful lyric poet, tagged her "the panther with the golden claws." The countess was so taken by Josephine that she wrote a poem about her, which Josephine admitted she could not understand in English or in French.

Josephine carried the bananas with her for years, dancing in them in cabarets and theatres across Europe and throughout South America. Even when her body reached the point where it looked better clothed, she held on to the bananas. At the Josephine Baker Museum in Dordogne, filled with waxen figures depicting scenes from her life, they were exhibited with panoply worthy of Nefertiti's right elbow.

Josephine's skin became a fashion focus. On the Place de l'Opéra there was a giant moving doll of Josephine in a shop window next to a display for Valaze Water Lily beauty cream. The sign for the exhibit said: "You can have a body like Josephine Baker if you use Valaze cream."

At the time Josephine did not understand that the color of her skin was a major component of her success. She spent an hour each day in her dressing room at the Folies trying to bleach herself white by rubbing herself all over with lemons.

Years later she would come full circle, exaggerating the importance of her blackness, claiming credit for the suntanning fad that swept Europe in the 1920s, filling the beaches of the Côte d'Azur, Biarritz, Deauville and the Venice Lido. "Whites tried to do all they could to be like me. They put oil on their whole bodies and went to sea. Baked the whole day. Some of them got sick. They said to me, 'Isn't it beautiful to be kissed by the sun in that way.' "

Though Josephine's makeup did not set a trend, she looked better in the current style than most people. She went to Hélène Rubinstein for advice and Rubinstein, who believed that a face can cost as much in upkeep as a Rolls Royce, gave her the full treatment. She blacked Josephine's eyes with kohl, taught her to apply a sticky foundation called Crème Gypsy (which dried to a light ochre), accented her full lips with a dark lipstick to make a vivid contrast with her strong white teeth, and Brilliantined hair.

Her first season at the Folies, Josephine was the consummate "enfant gâté." She seemed to delight in getting away with as much as possible. She liked the power of having everything depend on her arrival.

Waiting for Josephine became an infuriating ritual. Minutes before showtime, the stage director was out on the street corner looking for her car. The orchestra conductor stood, baton poised, waiting for her entrance. On stage the girls glanced anxiously toward the wings. Some nights the orchestra played extra interludes; sometimes management altered the order of the acts. Just when all hope was gone, Derval recalled, "suddenly the stage door banged open, a hat went flying, a fur coat was thrown to the floor. Leaving a trail of clothes, shoes and underwear, Josephine Baker tore past me en route to her dressing room." One evening when the stage manager found her dressing room door locked, he kicked open the door to find Josephine sitting on the floor naked, eating a lobster with her fingers. Josephine promptly put on her scanty costume and walked on stage, still chewing.

Josephine could not stand being alone. She was always ready to talk to anyone, and she could not resist inviting people to have a drink in her dressing room between acts. Derval was lenient about Josephine's friends to an extent. "But Josephine considered every animal in creation her friend," said Derval. "She had rabbits nesting in the wardrobes, white mice in the drawers, and cats, dogs and birds more or less everywhere. A baby tiger and a boa constrictor were among the more exotic of her acquaintances. One day I put my foot down when Josephine befriended a young goat. There was a scene, of course, but by that time I was used to her scenes."

When the rabbit dung reached barnyard redolence, Derval took Josephine to court. After some haggling she reluctantly agreed to leave her menagerie at home. Josephine felt that when human beings let her down her pets would be there. "I tell them everything, my joys, my hurts."

As Josephine's fame grew, so did demands on her. It was June, and Paris was at the height of the "grande saison."

Josephine lived *la vie Parisienne,* flitting like an exotic butterfly from one event to the next. There were at least three fetes every evening. After performing at the Folies, she would always appear somewhere, often contributing her services as a guest performer.

Ernest Hemingway told A. E. Hotchner about his first meeting with Josephine, at Le Jockey in Montparnasse, a lively *boîte* with a great orchestra and generous drinks, decorated to resemble an American saloon:

> Was in there one night with Don Ogden Stewart and Waldo Peirce, when the place was set on fire by the most sensational woman anybody ever saw. Or ever will. Tall, coffee skin, ebony eyes, legs of paradise, a smile to end all smiles. Very hot night but she was wearing a coat of black fur, her breasts handling the fur like it was silk. She turned her eyes on me—she was dancing with the big British gunner subaltern who had brought her—but I responded to the eyes like a hypnotic and cut in on them. The subaltern tried to shoulder me out but the girl slid off him and onto me. Everything under that fur instantly communicated with me. I introduced myself and asked her name. "Josephine Baker," she said. We danced nonstop for the rest of the night. She never took off her fur coat. Wasn't until the joint closed she told me she had nothing on underneath.

Josephine was constantly in motion, as if to protect herself against being rejected. On one level she realized she was an outlet for the sexual repression of the Western world. And having grown up in the sultry streets of the Chestnut Valley tenderloin district, where sexuality was accepted as a part of life, she regarded the whites who swarmed around her with a certain amount of disdain. At the same time, unlike Bricktop who felt secure enough to be herself, Josephine yearned to be part of the white fashionable "monde," to which she was now exposed by virtue of her talent and her notoriety.

In order to secure her place in this milieu, Josephine went out of her way to be amusing. She could always be counted on to make people laugh. Life looked different with her. It became comic, funny, less drab than usual. She brought one out of the commonplace.

Lucius Beebe, one of the classic American snobs of this century, recalled what Josephine meant to the postgraduate Yale men having their sojourn in Europe, the obligatory "rite of passage" before going to work somewhere. "The vistas of the world were wide and inviting," wrote Beebe, "filled with horse cabs, onion soup for breakfast, ties from Charvet, drinks with Berry Wall at Ciro's, and the hideous binges staged by those American students who were theoretically practicing architecture at Versailles. And Josephine Baker—Mlle. Bakaire, as the French called her—was the undisputed queen of Montmartre.

"You started the evening in the right quarter at Maxim's or penetrated the transmaritime Rive Gauche to get a pressed duck at Frédérick's. Later you went to the Bal Tabarin to be pawed by the feather-boaed huzzies at the illimitable bar and see the can-can ... eventually you ended the night wherever Mlle. Bakaire was holding forth, or you were nobody. It was as much a ritual as Sunday night dinner at the Ritz or banking with Ha-Ha Harjes."

The cruel condescension at the core of much of the flattery she received pained Josephine. The trend-setters who vied for her company were, at the same time, laughing their cynical laugh at what Paul Morand called "her stone-age gambolings" and her fractured grammar in two languages. Said Bricktop, "She couldn't speak American, let alone French."

The social cartoonist Sem (Georges Goursat), who like Toulouse-Lautrec drew the circus of his time, the circus of society, with a wicked pencil, caught these feelings of condescension toward Josephine in a profile he sketched of her dancing. The top half of her torso is elegant and theatrical, bedecked with jewels, but a monkey tail swings from her derriere with a fly buzzing around the tip.

Josephine concealed her fears and ignorance with bravado. The first time she ate crayfish, for example, she chewed it with the shell because she did not know better. Rather than admit her faux pas, she continued eating it that way in order to be shocking.

Though constantly surrounded by people, Josephine was lonely. She was trying to make her way in a world that was educationally and experientially beyond her ken. She lacked the intellectual baggage to exchange bons mots with the cognoscenti; she had been given no chance, as yet, to acquire the elegancies and artifices of French society. She was not yet the graceful, sophisticated hostess of later years. It was only natural for her to feel unsure, frightened and, at times, lost in her new surroundings.

Once asked what she thought of cubism, she replied, "I think a work of art should look like what it is supposed to look like. Nowadays, when an artist paints a bouquet of flowers, he just puts paint around the way we did when we were children. I think that's awful. A little while ago a lady showed me a tiny little picture which had been very expensive. Didn't I think it was absolutely lovely? It was made by Penazso. What was his name? I posed for him. Ah yes, Picasso. It was just a couple of stupid streaks. Awful!"

Josephine was a mythomane. She edited her life, camouflaging the ugly parts with cosmetic adjectives, sanitizing salacious encounters and interlarding nasty episodes with self-justifying anecdotes. If one of her statements was called into question, she was outraged. "I don't lie. I improve on life."

She wanted her public to think that men showered presents on her simply because they admired her "art." In many of her accounts about her suitors, the men emerged as victims. They were silly old goats made pathetically vulnerable by their sexual appetites; for example, a minor dancer at the Folies, whom Josephine had persuaded to act as her secretary during working hours, came to her to say that a rich industrialist was offering a hefty sum for the privilege of Josephine's company. No shrinking violet, Josephine demanded the money in advance and suggested that a nice diamond would cap the deal. The day of the rendezvous, the doorman at the Folies handed Josephine a box with a stone "as big as a frog's egg," plus the stipulated fee.

They dined at El Garron, a tiny restaurant on rue Florentine, with overcrowded rooms and an Argentine atmosphere. The pianist was blind. "I ate like an ogre," said Josephine. "I drank champagne and I danced like a fool. I laughed. I amused myself! But afterwards it was a different story. He wanted to take me to his place and he gave his address to the taxi driver."

Josephine raised such a fuss that the old man lost his temper, whereupon she threw herself at the mercy of the cabdriver, explaining that she was Josephine Baker of the Folies-Bergère. Was there any chivalry left in Paris? Yes! *Mais oui!* The cabbie forced the man from his hack and drove Josephine to her door.

By making fun of her suitors, Josephine was blocking the chaos in her life. The changing stream of lovers passing through her apartment did not make her happy. Her terror of being alone propelled her into physical intimacy with strangers, which, with her great pride, left her with a feeling of self-loathing afterward.

Josephine was perplexed by the rules of the game in Paris. She did not realize how fixed, how traditional French society was. She thought her success at the Folies was a *passe partout.* She could not have been more wrong. To be sure, her stardom provided entrée into a fascinating way of life, but one that had nothing to do with the respectability for which Josephine hungered. The Folies, the Opéra and the Comédie Française were the time-honored suppliers of mistresses for French aristocrats, government officials, successful bookmakers and Argentine millionaires, as well as visiting dukes and princes.

The backstage door of the Folies faced onto the rue Saulnier, a dimly lighted street where a silent parade of Rolls Royces stood in a neat line. The owners sat in the back of their cars waiting for the dancers. Sometimes one of them sent in a bouquet of flowers with an expensive bracelet or anklet tucked between the petals.

It was not only a question of sex; Paris had the best bordellos in the world. But to sleep with a dancer from the Folies-Bergère was to realize a dream, to possess the glamorous. "It hurts me to confess it," said Albert Camus many years later, "but I would gladly trade ten conversations with Einstein for one first encounter with a pretty chorus girl."

During La Belle Epoque, at the turn of the century, the headliners at the Folies were considered *poules de luxe,* who earned enormous amounts of money and spent it prodigally on jewels of all sorts and sizes.

They were part of a dazzling hierarchy known as the *dégrafées,* the unbuttoned, or as the boulevard wits called them, *les grandes horizontales.* These women ruled as queens of their separate world. Endless newspaper columns were devoted to their lovers, their furs, their rampant aigrettes and cascading birds-of-paradise. Like Josephine, they arrived out of the blue and were not about to go back to oblivion. Daughters of shopkeepers, cabdrivers, county clerks and God-knows-what, they had started out honestly enough as nursemaids, artist's models, milliner's assistants. But their beauty and love of a good time had led them to the more enjoyable and profitable scarlet path. The music hall was a perfect display case for their assets. It was, as Colette said, "the one profession for which you don't need any training."

During La Belle Epoque, when kings and princes traveled to Paris for some official "unofficial" reason such as a diplomatic reception or a military review, the Quai d'Orsay kept a red list of pretty women meritorious enough to receive royal homage. The three women whose names appeared at the top of the list were known as *les trois grandes*—Caroline Otéro, Liane de Pouney and Emilienne d'Alençon. Each performed, at various times, at the Folies-Bergère; each was blessed with beauty, wit, charm and intelligence.

These women were not great respecters of men, however exalted. Emilienne d'Alençon, a sugary blonde with rosy dimples, instructed her maid one Sunday morning to tell King Leopold of Belgium, who was at the door, that she received no one before eleven o'clock. Leopold had the good humor to say: "Let her sleep. I'll come back after Mass and take her out to lunch."

The most vivid of the three was Caroline Otéro, a voluptuous Spanish gypsy dancer. Her magnificent breasts inspired the architect of the Carlton Hotel in Cannes; its twin cupolas are still known as *les boîtes à lait de la Belle Otéro.*

She considered her sexual power the equal of any royal

power. After being ordered to give up her box at the Comédie Française to Czar Nicholas, who arrived unexpectedly with his retinue, Otéro swept past His Imperial Majesty shouting in her voice of Andalusian brass, "All right, I'll leave! But from this day on, I'll never again eat caviar!"

With the waning of La Belle Epoque and the growing sexual freedom that followed World War I, *les grandes horizontales* became extinct, fading the way of all flesh, but the grand tradition of diamond-digging dance hall girls lived on with Gaby Deslys, the Dolly Sisters and Mistinguett. Gaby Deslys, whose extravagance helped King Manuel of Portugal lose his throne, augmented her stage earnings with several "love affairs." Sporting rose tattoos on her breasts, she entertained suitors at the Hôtel de Paris for a minimum fee of $500 a night.

With certain notable exceptions, these women seldom married into the milieu of lords and ladies or the wealthy men of business with whom they consorted, for this would probably have ended the careers they adored. They knew also that they could never really be accepted. Josephine, in her early years in Paris, did not know this.

Josephine was not only trying to break out of a cast taboo imposed on her as a Folies dancer, she was also overlooking the fact that she was not to the tricolor born. "Frenchmen will make love to, or enjoy a temporary affair with any female," wrote long-time Paris resident Elliot Paul, "from a hopping Hottentot to a pale six-foot Finn, but they seldom marry foreigners."

The obstacles in Josephine's way became more apparent when she entered into a liaison with the owner of a large automobile company, a man she referred to only as Marcel, never going into detail about him or the short, bitter chapter he represented in her life. Marcel set her up in a lavish apartment on the Champs-Elysées. He showered her with baubles and added to her menagerie, bringing home mice, parrots and a miniature monkey. He even built her a marble swimming pool within the apartment. Josephine mistook all this as the prelude to a permanent commitment. The subject of marriage began to weigh on her mind. She could not be carefree. Each day her worries intensified. What would become of her? Her entire capital was her youth, her body and her dancing. Without telling Marcel that she was already married, she broached the subject of their future, adding, "I'd like to have a baby."

Marcel made it clear that not only was she totally out of his social sphere, she was black as well. There was no hope for a marriage between them.

Rejected, Josephine moved back to the rue Beaujon. A fierce dignity supported her through this period. No matter how hurt she was, she would never let people see her cry. But vulnerability was written across her face.

During these unhappy months, the fall of 1926, Josephine caught bronchial pneumonia, a potentially lethal illness in the days before sulfa drugs. She was confined to bed for three weeks. The sickness drained her energy and reinforced her feeling of isolation, even though her apartment was constantly full of people. "I shook like a coconut tree . . . I was alone."

Paul Colin, Josephine's early protector and guide, saw less and less of her now. He was disillusioned by the commercialism of her new success. "As soon as she started sticking feathers in her ass and trying to imitate Mistinguett," he said, "I lost interest in her."

Timing played a key role in Colin's success, as it did in Josephine's. Paris was in the midst of a wholesale crush on everything Negro. Babangi masks, heads wrapped in turbans, bracelets extending up the arm were the rage.

Sarah and Gerald Murphy, the essence of Twenties' expatriates, who lived near Josephine at 2 rue Greuze, entertained visitors by singing pre-Civil War folk songs and spirituals in two-part harmony. *Vogue* proclaimed: "The Negro is at last coming into his own. The most distinguished art critics say his sculpture is better than that of Phidias; the musicians say he composes better than Beethoven; the dance-enthusiasts add that he dances better than Nijinsky; and the cabaret and music hall proprietors admit that he pays better than anyone."

This period in Paris was dubbed *Le Tumulte Noir*—the black tumult—and Colin decided to publish an album of his lithographs using that name, to be issued by *Editions Success.*

Josephine agreed to help boost Colin's book by writing a few prefatory remarks. With only a fifth-grade education and elementary French, she obviously needed help. Colin asked Marcel Sauvage, a journalist for *L'Intransigeant* and a burgeoning poet, to assist her with the introduction.

Sauvage, who spoke no English, arrived at Josephine's apartment with an interpreter. She greeted them wearing a rose-colored bathrobe, open at the front.

The apartment was a mishmash, cluttered with discarded clothes, records and an odd assortment of paraphernalia: a bust of Louis XIV, a bowl of hundred-franc notes, an Empire cabinet, a noisy parrot, a Gramophone and a seven-pound dictionary Josephine said she never opened.

Josephine padded around the apartment, her Turkish slippers clip-clopping as she walked. Music blared from the Gramophone. The telephone, tethered by an extra long cord, rang incessantly, vexing Josephine who could not understand what most of her callers were saying. She pointed to a copy of *Contes de Fées*, a collection of fairy tales, explaining to Sauvage that she was trying to learn French from the stories.

Josephine finally sank into a leather chair, tossed one slipper in the air and answered Sauvage's queries through the interpreter. She talked fast, waving her hands, punctuating her flapper Harlem accent with breathy expletives. *"Formidable! Merveilleux!"*

Together they composed the preface for *Un Tumulte Noir,* which the publisher reproduced in Josephine's inimitable scrawl. Her handwriting was characteristic and revealing: large, handsome, sweeping and childlike. As with many performers whose handwriting grows larger as their egos expand, Josephine's had already reached the point where two, three or four words swept entirely across a page. Her flamboyance was as decorative as her costumes, onstage or off.

Referring to the Negro invasion of La Ville Lumière, she wrote, "I'll say it's getting darker and darker in Paris. In a little while it shall be so dark until one shall light a match, then light another to see if the first is lit or not."

Sauvage was fascinated by Josephine. He decided to collaborate on her memoirs. "My colleagues thought I was crazy, but I recognized that Josephine was not just a dancer, she was a phenomenon."

Josephine responded with unalloyed glee. "Write my memoirs. Oh là là!" She burst out laughing.

Busy with his job at *L'Intransigeant* during the day, Sauvage worked with Josephine at night after she had finished at the Folies and had made her customary tour of the gutbuckets of Pigalle. Sauvage often brought his wife Paulette along, and together they listened to Josephine tell the story of her first nineteen years, romanticized, often fictionalized, conveyed in pidgin French.

In addition to writing her memoirs, Sauvage was pressed into service as a secretary. The papers reported that Josephine received forty thousand love letters, and while even she admitted the figure was slightly exaggerated, she was indeed receiving a lot of mail, which lay about her apartment in clumsy stacks. So many of the letters contained marriage proposals that Sauvage devised a form letter for Josephine by which she kindly refused the offers. There were lots of requests for money. An African, living in Bordeaux, asked her to set him up as a game hunter. Mash notes invited her for "rendez-vous." "Meet me at Métro Le Peltrier at 6:30 this Sunday." One man included a baby picture of himself as an inducement to Josephine to sleep with him.

Passing many nocturnal hours in Josephine's apartment, Sauvage had an opportunity, as few others did, to see her life from the inside, to analyze the real world behind the press clippings, which Josephine, with her obsession for appearances, did not want people to know about. "Josephine was *une fille de joie* in those days," said Sauvage. "She had many affairs at the same time. She could make love to one man on one night and to another man on another night and it didn't bother her. She lived to make love. But she was terribly proud. She never wanted people to think that she was just a call girl."

During her interview sessions with Marcel Sauvage, Josephine ticked off an inventory of her bounty with an élan that would bring a blush to the cheeks of Lorelei Lee, the gold-digging heroine of Anita Loos's *Gentlemen Prefer Blondes*. "I got sparkling rings as big as eggs, 150-year-old earrings that once belonged to a duchess, pearls like buck teeth, flower baskets from Italy, six lacquered Chinese chairs, toys that run on electricity, Russian ivory elephants cut by the poor people of Siberia, a bear, a duck, lots of stuffed animals, peaches . . . great big strawberries, perfume in a glass horse, four fur coats, and bracelets with red stones for my arms and legs." On her twentieth birthday one lothario gave her a brown Voisin car upholstered in brown snakeskin.

"She was a woman who was constantly pursued by men," says Sauvage. "But not by affection, but sexual curiosity. It was not tenderness. And she was looking for tenderness."

One night Josephine announced to Sauvage that she had hired a daytime secretary to file her press clippings and to help answer the backlog of correspondence. The secretary was a journalist named George Sims, just then beginning a most successful career as an author of mystery stories, many published under the pseudonym of Simenon. Over the years, using seventeen pen names, the prolific Simenon would publish more than five hundred books, translated into dozens of languages.

He was twenty-three years old at the time and had come to Paris from Liège, a small town in Belgium. Like Josephine, Simenon was pushed out into the world early and carried with him the unhealed wounds of a miserable childhood.

Josephine first met Simenon shortly after her arrival in Paris. He had been one of the stage-door Johnnies who clustered around her at the Théâtre des Champs-Elysées. Josephine once gave him seventy-five dollars and asked him to mail a money order to Carrie in St. Louis because she did not know how to fill out the forms.

Simenon was very much the provincial, hungry for life and eager to gain experience, all of which would become fodder for his novels. Sexually, he was supercharged. He wrote that at twenty he clenched his fists at the thought there were women in the world he would never possess, and he set out quickly to redress this parsimony of fate.

His wife was a painter. Under the guise of securing models for her, he canvassed Montmartre, searching for prostitutes. "During my first days in Paris," Simenon wrote, "I would leave the arms of one woman at eleven o'clock in the morning and go back to another only a few moments later, and be obliged to accost a professional or go to a house of assignation to begin all over again twice the same afternoon." In the evenings, wearing elephant-leg pants in a "bois de rose" color, he idled in dance halls and cabarets looking for what he called "the common denominator." He felt he could know people better seeing them tiddly and raising Cain rather than working at their everyday occupations. In Montmartre he reconnected with Josephine and willingly accepted the invitation to work for her.

Sauvage had already met Simenon. Now that they were both employed by the same boss and their jobs overlapped, their acquaintance grew to a friendship. "We both found it *très gênant*," says Sauvage, "trying to answer letters while Josephine walked around her apartment completely nude."

It soon became apparent to Sauvage that Josephine was smitten with Simenon. "He was her physical ideal, tall and handsome, with broad shoulders and clear skin."

Josephine and Simenon were explosive together. She was quite possibly the most uninhibited woman he had ever met. She, too, liked lovemaking on the spur of the moment, standing up, alfresco, under water, *"n'importe comment."* But, alas, Simenon was not in love with Josephine. She was an adventure to him, a chapter or a footnote in a long book of conquests.

After a few months Simenon quit his job. Though he and Josephine remained friendly, she did not take his rejection with equanimity. Her sense of loneliness increased. She was subject to severe depressions, balanced by periods of unbelievable vigor. She could not trust men; to trust was to be hurt.

Josephine now plunged into her reckless social life. Paulette Sauvage remembered many nights when Josephine returned to her apartment alone, overstimulated from marathon dancing. She washed the grease out of her hair, went to bed and called in her little bird voice, "Madame Sauvage. Venez! Venez!"

Sitting next to her bed, Paulette Sauvage held Josephine's hand and told her fairy tales, repeating the same stories again and again, fantasies about birds and animals and kings and queens. "She looked like a little pickaninny lying there listening to me. Her eyes were like saucers."

Josephine was the highest paid entertainer in all of Europe. Her fame—and her income—increased as tourists returned home from their visits to the Continent and raved about the black girl who brought Paris to its feet. Journalist Robert Ruark recalled, "When the American thought of France, he thought of the Folies-Bergère, Le Louvre and Jo Baker, just about in that order."

Her luxury, her aura, masked her pain. Poet and essayist Langston Hughes, one of the most gifted writers spawned by the Harlem Renaissance, who had admired Josephine in *Shuffle Along,* passed through Paris and dropped her a note saying he wanted to meet her. It was 1926 and Hughes had just published his first book of poems, *The Weary Blues,* which expressed the exoticism of the era.

As Hughes stood in front of the Folies' stage entrance waiting for Josephine, she pulled up in the Voisin. Her chauffeur, resplendent in his beige uniform with gold buttons, opened the door for her. With Hughes following, Josephine swept into the backstage corridor. Just inside the entrance, a maid received her cloak. As she walked down the hall, another maid took her gloves and purse. Inside the dressing room, a maid put the makeup towel around her neck. Another removed the shoes from the star who as a child had been so poor she was forced to wear a discarded pair of high heels to grade school; now Josephine owned over 150 pairs of shoes.

Hughes was dazzled by the scene. "Here indeed was a star," he wrote years later, "treated as no star I have ever seen, white, black, green, grizzly or grey, treated in America." And yet, as Josephine talked to Hughes, reminiscing about Harlem, the Cotton Club, Small's Paradise, Connie's Inn and the many friends they had in common, he realized how truly lonely she was, how nakedly vulnerable. "She wanted to come home. She wanted to come home."

NINE

"Paris is the American dream."

—Alice B. Toklas

One night Josephine walked into Zelli's, a popular dive high up on rue Florentine, catty-corner to Bricktop's. Zelli's was a big, raffish, cavernous room lined with tables decorated with B-girls whose business it was to "mount the check." The place resembled nothing so much as a dime-a-dance hall on the old Barbary Coast. "The broads who worked Zelli's were high-class broads, depending on the time of night," says jazz musician Jack O'Brien, who played there. Zelli's was also populated by sleek-haired, wasp-waisted men who guided women of "a certain age" up and down the dance floor.

An American hangout, attracting a wide range of regional and social types, Zelli's catered to aging satyrs, Texas ranch-hands and peppery Rotarians anxious to embrace the vices they denounced at home.

Zelli was king of the district. An American of Italian extraction, he achieved the status of sainthood in the quarter because of his generous treatment of down-and-out expatriates. "He had two or three trunks of jewelry," says Bricktop. "And he took care of everybody. He'd slip a fellow a diamond to get him off the hook with his rent." Any Zelli regular who died broke in Paris received a funeral on the house.

Josephine came into Zelli's often to see a friend named Zito, an Italian immigrant who worked there as a caricaturist, drawing sketches of American tourists. Often Josephine arrived just as Zito was quitting for the night, and together they would tour Montmartre.

But on this particular evening Zito had a cold and wanted to go straight home. Before leaving Zelli's, he introduced Josephine to a cousin recently arrived from Rome. His name was Guisseppi Abatino, but he called himself Count Pepito de Abatino. Zito suggested that Pepito escort Josephine for the evening.

Pepito was a lean, handsome man in his late thirties. He had dark, intense eyes, olive skin and a spacious forehead framed by thick dark hair slicked back at the sides; he resembled Adolphe Menjou. His air of self-possession immediately intrigued Josephine.

Pepito had just begun working at Zelli's as a gigolo, prefer-

Josephine and Pepito de Abatino, her "no-account" count who pretended to marry her. *UPI*

ring, like most of his colleagues, to call himself a professional dance instructor. As with chorus girls, many gigolos regarded their jobs as simply way stations. Rudolph Valentino and George Raft were but two "professional dance instructors" who went on to bigger things.

Usually young, elegant men of South American type—even if they had been born in a London suburb—gigolos in the Twenties often had more work than they could handle. It was a dancing era and everybody wanted to learn the new steps. Of course a gigolo's duties were not confined to teaching "La Foxtrot" or "La Charleston." Many middle-aged American women, willingly paid for masculine companionship. "Husbands and wives took separate vacations in those days," says Bricktop. "Some rich women reserved the same gigolo year after year."

Although a little old for the job, Pepito had the requisite appearance and temperament to be a gigolo. Not only was he handsome and suave, but he was a master of the art of flattery, knowing just the right words and accent to make a little brown wren feel like a bird of paradise.

Before Pepito assumed the title of Count de Abatino, when he was simply and inelegantly Guisseppi Abatino, he worked as a stonemason in Palermo, Sicily. His metamorphosis from laborer to ersatz noble was a tribute to his imagination and audacity. (In the 1920s, many Italian males away from home had a title of some sort; the "nobility" was dubious, if not devious, and often resulted in profitable marriages and even more profitable divorces.)

Like many ambitious people, he was restless and frustrated by the perimeters of a lazy provincial town. He set out for Rome in the only suit he owned and with but a few lira in his pocket. He loitered in dance halls along the Via Veneto, principally the Imperial, where he met Josephine's friend, Frisco. In that razzle-dazzle world with its great emphasis on appearances, Pepito's matinee-idol face and sleek manner made him a natural companion for those desiring an escort. He cadged meals from his benefactors, looked at the ceiling whenever it was his turn to buy a drink, and perfected his skill on the dance floor. Soon Guisseppi was able to buy another suit. Then he bought a monocle, a walking stick, a few more suits. He took to wearing white and yellow spats.

When Zito wrote to Guisseppi, describing his spendthrift customers in Montmartre, Guisseppi sensed that Paris held more fertile pastures for his charms. He decided to pay Zito an extended visit. On his trip over the Alps he acquired the title Count Pepito de Abatino.

Even though the Montmartre establishment knew that Pepito was Zito's cousin and an ex-bricklayer, the knowledge did not stop Pepito from creating a history commensurate with his phony title. Like any international city, Paris is hospitable to impostors, and Pepito's story was as good as anyone's: "I was a lieutenant in the Arditi, one of Italy's crack regiments. I was an excellent horseman who won recognition in Rome and in other Italian cities for my equestrian prowess. After attending a school for diplomats in Rome, I worked for the Italian government in its department of foreign affairs. Bored with paperwork and the endless round of cocktail parties which diplomacy entails, I took a leave of absence to come to Paris, hoping to find a more interesting position, a job which would enable me to exercise my imagination."

Knowing that Zito had never made any claims to aristocracy, Josephine must have realized that Pepito created himself. Still, she was charmed by him.

Josephine and Pepito spent the night in Montmartre, traipsing from one nightclub to another, dancing and talking. Pepito played the avid swain. He told her that he had watched her at the Folies and that her performance was unlike anything he had ever seen. He vowed to get to know her. As he talked he flicked the ashes from his cigarette, deftly held in the air with a holder he waved like a baton. Other times he adjusted his monocle, inspecting her more closely as if she were an objet d'art.

At dawn they walked into Bricktop's just as the musicians were getting ready to go home. Bricktop, with her saloon-keeper's shrewd eye, immediately sized up Pepito. "Josephine," she said, taking her aside, "what are you doing with this bum? He can't even buy a glass of beer."

Josephine shrugged her shoulders. "Zito has a cold."

"That count business was the biggest fraud," Bricktop later said. "He was no more a count than I was a duchess—and I could have called myself a duchess but I was too smart. I knew better."

Undaunted by Bricktop's rebuff, Pepito launched a campaign to win Josephine, pursuing her with a flourish that only the Italians can muster. A Frenchman can utter a fair amount of nonsense, but his native sense of restraint and inborn logic stop just where the Italian begins. Pepito wrote her love notes. He waited for her every evening after her performance and accompanied her on her nightly swing of the clubs, holding her hand as she stepped from her car, holding the door for her, holding her coat for her, holding her chair for her, pouring her champagne, keeping track of her pets. He understood Josephine's craving for esteem and affection, and he gave it to her in spades. He was as well oiled as an Italian salad.

Josephine fell in love with being loved. For her, Pepito was like the magic mirror in *Snow White;* he assured her that she was the most stunning belle in Paris—which at that moment she was. But she reveled in his doting.

There is an old French proverb, "To be loved is a strength; to love, a weakness." Josephine, as the recipient of love, was in control, but she did not know then how much her dependency on Pepito would grow. At times, the balance of power would shift to him.

Pepito quickly became a fixture in Josephine's apartment, frightening away all competitors. Her affair with him, which lasted nine years, had a somewhat steadying influence on Josephine. She did not become monogamous, but the compulsion for wild promiscuity was gone.

Despite his dapper clothes and pretense of gentility, it was obvious that Pepito was not in a league with Josephine. True, both were dark complexioned with straight white teeth and compelling eyes, but Josephine had the patina of success *and* its reality. Said Marcel Sauvage, "Picture a stonemason with a star."

Pepito saw a role for himself in Josephine's life; in fact, that was part of his attraction to her. He wanted to be her manager.

He appealed to Josephine's persistent fear that she would drop into oblivion. Pepito promised to turn her into a polished performer. More important, he spoke the magic words to her: "I'll make you a lady."

She would have singing lessons, dancing lessons and French lessons, and she would learn how to use a knife and fork and how to carry on small talk. She could sing opera and act in plays and perform in movies. He would be her impresario.

Pepito's first move was to line up endorsements. An Argentinian chemist had patented a hair-straightening pomade and planned to use the Corsican singer Tino Rossi to advertise it; after listening to Pepito's pitch, he decided to use Josephine. The grease, christened "Bakerfix," was an enormous success. It became the French equivalent of Dixie Peach Pomade, used at that time by blacks in America.

Josephine enlisted Pepito's help in launching a project that had been gestating in her mind since she first arrived in Paris. She wanted a nightclub of her own, in Montmartre. Paul Derval did not consider Josephine's voice strong enough for the Folies, and Josephine reasoned that if she had her own nightclub she would be able to develop her singing voice.

Backers were easy to find in the inflationary period of the late 1920s. Since no one could be sure what money would be worth from one day to the next, the wisest thing seemed to be to spend it immediately on something offering a quick return. A nightclub was ideal. Pierre Loy, a doctor who had been one of Josephine's "protectors," agreed to finance the club.

Pepito, normally as temperamental as a cheese soufflé, with a fierce Sicilian jealous streak that bordered on the violent, became extraordinarily passive and conciliatory when one of Josephine's admirers was about to part with money. He stayed in the background until Josephine and Dr. Loy signed the lease for the cabaret.

Like many Sicilians, Pepito had a genius for organization and a shrewd sense of business, two qualities Josephine notoriously lacked. They decided he would act as manager, hiring the help, overseeing the dining room and balancing the books.

Chez Joséphine opened on rue Fontaine on December 14, 1926, the same month and year as La Coupole, Hemingway's legendary hangout in Montparnasse. The club was an immediate success, pulling in so much money the first few weeks that Josephine bought Pepito a diamond-and-platinum watch exactly like the one just given by Bricktop to her man of the moment.

Josephine had hired an ebullient black American woman named Freddie to do the cooking at her nightclub. But since she loved to cook, too, she prepared many of the specialties herself. The cuisine was an intriguing mix of soul food and "Cordon Bleu." Chitlins (the small intestines of pigs, usually served fried and greasy), rooster combs, greens, and black-eyed peas were given equal billing with "canard à l'orange" and "shrimp pâté." For herself, Josephine liked spaghetti and red pepper, "cannibal sandwiches"—beef tartar—and plover eggs.

Josephine's pets were allowed to wander through the club. Holding a champagne glass in one hand and talking to the customers, Josephine would feed her nanny goat "Toutoute" with the other hand. Her pig "Albert," whom Josephine doused with Worth perfume, fattened himself in the kitchen to such an extent that he had trouble squatting under the boiler where he slept. The situation became critical when his ever-widening girth broke some of the boiler pipes. "We had to break down part of the kitchen door to get him out," said Josephine. "Poor pig!"

Chez Joséphine became one of the regular stops for the international crowd as well as for middle-class American tourists, who were flocking to Paris in growing numbers. Describing the curious mixture of humanity in Paris at the time, Janet Flanner wrote: "Europe's prewar royalty was by now mostly in exile, on tour, in trouble, without power, or in a nightclub. . . . The highlights were French countesses, still penniless since the French Revolution; Georgian princes left over from the Russian International; Italian male nobility set rolling northward by the march on Rome; Austrian barons with a tireless smile—these and similar and sundry innocents and sophisticates helped animate the Right Bank by day and Montmartre by night."

Pepito, who always had one eye on the cash register and knew that Milwaukee beer barons often spent more than Castilian countesses, lavished attention on the tourists flocking to Chez

Josephine kicks high for customers at Chez Joséphine, her *boîte* in Montmartre. *Keystone*

Joséphine. He played up to the schoolmarms and sales gal-vanizers, giving them the opportunity to meet a "real" count. He introduced such "divertissements" into the nocturnal fiesta as playing tennis with paper racquets and balls, and he sold quantities of foot-long Josephine dolls.

The high point of the evening came when Josephine made her entrance. John McMillan, a writer assigned by *Vogue* to do an article on "La Bakaire," was sitting at a table waiting for her one night. "Josephine Baker is the Lulu Belle of Paris," McMil-lan would write. "I could think of nothing else as I saw her for the first time passing through the room. . . . She had just ar-rived from the Folies-Bergère, accompanied by her maid, her chauffeur and a white Eskimo dog. She came in without a wrap, and the length of her graceful body, which is light sealskin brown, was swathed in a blue tulle frock with a bodice of blue snakeskin, worn with slippers to match.

"The frock was cut excessively low in back, with a huge diamond ornament at the waist. On her left hand she wore an enormous diamond ring and on the wrist of the same hand a very impressive bracelet. Her hair, which grows in tight curls, was plastered close to her head with white of egg and looked as though it were painted on her head with black shellac. The woman is like a living drawing by Aubrey Beardsley or Picasso."

After changing into an ostrich feather or two, Josephine gave her clients their money's worth. "I never amused myself more," she later said. "I made jokes, I caressed the skin on the heads of bald-headed messieurs: they never laughed harder before. Everybody did the Charleston, the boys, the maîtres d'hôtel, the cook, the cashier, the errand boys, the goat and the pig. . . . And me, I dance, I dance. I laugh, I burst out laughing, I pull the nose the closest to me, the ears, the hair, the beard, and all in the midst of streamers, balls and all night the lights keep changing."

Josephine was beginning to gain confidence. She was now twenty years old, basking in the comforting glow of money, rapturous attention, fame and young success. And she loved her cabaret. Only her singing did not receive the reception she had hoped.

When she sang the blues the tourists applauded. But the

Colette in the late Twenties. The most famous French woman writer of her time, Collette adored Josephine, calling her "the most beautiful panther" and "little brown daughter."

jazzmen who played on "La Butte de Montmartre," who knew Bessie Smith, Ethel Waters and Adelaide Hall, did not take Josephine seriously. "Being musicians, we knew she stank," says Jack O'Brien. "She was a chorus babe, a big-shot dame, but a lot of it was due to luck."

Of all the people who came to her nightclub, the person who gave her the biggest thrill was Colette. Here was the most famous French woman writer of that time, and she was seeking out Josephine.

Following Colette's divorce from her first husband, the tyrannical Willy who locked her in her room every day and forced her to write, Colette desperately needed money. In order to support herself, she decided to become a music hall performer.

Colette, like Josephine, delighted in shocking the bourgeois. She appeared topless and in lesbian scenes and was a great success. Maurice Chevalier wrote that in her youth Colette had "the most exciting, appetizing bosom in the world."

Now in her fifties, her hair short and frizzy, she had a thin, hard, painted mouth. She was no longer slender—her face and figure had broadened, accentuating her shortness. She looked much like a withered, badly made up Mickey Rooney.

She followed the revues at the music halls with active interest and she adored Josephine, calling her "the most beautiful panther" and "little brown daughter." Colette came into Chez Joséphine and presented its owner with a copy of *L'Envers du Music-Hall*, a novel based on the author's experiences as a dancer at the Folies-Bergère; she had written it in 1912, when she was thirty-nine. After that, Colette wrote Josephine loving notes from time to time on doily paper.

Josephine was not intellectual enough to admire Colette's writing; it is indeed probable that at the time of their meeting Josephine had read nothing more than the titles of Colette's books. But she knew Colette had a golden name and, years later, whenever she spoke of her, people listened. When Josephine was middle-aged, making her exhaustingly numerous "comeback" and "farewell" tours, pulling in the crowds as a nostalgic piece of a bygone age, she would say: "In Paris, in the Twenties, we were young and gay. Hemingway, Picasso, Colette and me. We ran up and down the Champs-Elysées. And the older people thought we were crazy."

Les Mémoires de Joséphine Baker, Recuillis et Adaptés par Marcel Sauvage appeared in 1927, produced in paperback by Kra, a well-known publisher located on the Left Bank. The cover has a caricature of Josephine by Paul Colin, a profile of her head shaped like an elongated egg, dominated by a black skull and two renegade spit curls. One black eyelash juts out from the oval, like a diving board awaiting a diver.

Of the four autobiographies Josephine coauthored in her lifetime, the first is by far the best. Highly whimsical, with only a tenuous connection to fact, it nonetheless captures her febrile essence, uncontrived and unadorned, before she began to think of herself as a legend. In a chatty style she shows an independence of spirit, an unsentimental directness and a breezy curiosity about life. She shares her recipes for corn beef hash and hot cakes, includes some Negro spirituals, a sampling of her love letters and snatches of poetry dedicated to her.

She writes as if she were telling a fairy tale. "My father and my mother met at school. Their parents didn't want them to marry. So they got married anyway and they were very poor because they had no one to help them. They were abandoned."

The memories of her dark childhood—brief as it was—are woven with a mixture of philosophy and poetry. The hurts and deprivations and hours of hunger and loneliness are all seen "through a glass darkly," but seen, as it were, with an amalgam of pain and pleasure.

She talks extensively about her body, a harbinger of the narcissism that dominated her later years, and she throws in some offbeat beauty tips, probably none of which she practiced: "The best toilet water is rainwater, it keeps indefinitely. . . . Bathe in the milk of violet petals. Moisturizers made from bananas fight wrinkles. Rub strawberries on your cheeks to give them color. Swim as often as you can. Animals which live on land are never as elegant as fish."

Josephine thought of her body as her primary asset, a blessing from God that helped compensate for her many handicaps. She felt threatened by physically unattractive people; in her memoirs, referring to the men injured in World War I, she said: "Regarding warfare, I don't understand it, but it disgusts me. I have a strange fear of men lacking an arm, leg or eye. I am sorry for them, but I have a physical revulsion for anything crippled."

As soon as her autobiography was published, the French Association of Mutilated War Veterans threatened to sue. Josephine issued a denial, blaming Marcel Sauvage for fabricating the statement. Sauvage produced the manuscript in galley form, on the borders of which were notes by Josephine, proving that she had gone over the manuscript prior to publication.

Pepito stepped in immediately when he realized that a lawsuit—*any* lawsuit—could prove costly; after all, considering the methods by which he functioned, what was his was his, and part of what was Josephine's was his, too. He knew which side of the bed his bread was buttered on. Accordingly, he quickly advised Josephine to place all her money and assets in his name so that she would be immune from legal sanctions. Josephine said later that her money was in both their names, hers and Pepito's; brother Richard and Bricktop disagree, however, saying that it was all in Pepito's name. Whichever, one fact was palpably clear (though it was perhaps not so to Josephine at the time): Pepito now had a legal hold on her that would determine the course of their relationship.

One of the most interesting aspects of Josephine's first autobiography was what she saw ahead for herself at the age of twenty-one:

THE FUTURE

Yes, I will dance all my life, I was born to dance, only for that. To live is to dance. I would love to die breathless, exhausted, at the end of a dance—but not in a music hall.

I am tired of this artificial life, weary of being spurred on by the footlights. The work of a star disgusts me now. Everything she must do, everything she must put up with at every moment, that star, disgusts me. Bad choices, sad choices.

I want to work three or four more years and then I'll quit the stage. I'm going to make a home for myself in Italy or in the Midi of France. I am going to buy land on the Riviera.

I will marry an average man. I will have children, plenty of pets. This is what I love. I want to live in peace surrounded by children and pets. But if one day one of my children wants to go into the music hall, I will strangle him with my own two hands, that I swear to you.

At twenty-one she was talking about a conflict that persisted throughout her life. Josephine had a deep need for family and a need for a home, a place to sink roots. Yet try as she often did, she could not wrench herself away from the spotlight; she could not stop working. She was so restless, in fact, that she now took an afternoon job dancing at the Acacias, an elegant "thé-dansant" off the Etoile.

The Acacias was originally owned and managed by Maurice Chevalier and a comedian from the Casino de Paris named Saint-Grenier. By the time Josephine worked there, the establishment had fallen into the hands of a small, stout social climber from San Francisco named Elsa Maxwell.

While they were redecorating the Acacias, in preparation for its reopening, Josephine went over several times to watch. "I love colors for themselves, blood-red and yellow, the yellow of the egg," she said. "Colors have an astonishing physical effect on me. They make me drunk, they exalt me. . . . I took the gold powder in my hands and I shook it on my arms. I smeared it on my body. I had a shower. A shower of gold powder."

Between the Folies-Bergère, Chez Joséphine and the Acacias, Josephine was dancing at least ten hours a day. Part of her drive sprang from a need to prove that she was as good as anybody else. Despite her remarkable success, she was still an outsider, a black American amidst the alien corn. Pepito was also in exile and he, too, had known the taste of prejudice. Sicily and the Italian mainland are two different cultures. Sicilians are darker; the illiteracy rate is high and their slums are notorious. Romans talk about "Sicilians and their knives" the way some Americans talk about blacks. Josephine and Pepito's mutual feeling of isolation strengthened the bond between them.

Josephine even encountered some prejudice in France. When the American tourists invaded Paris in the 1920s, they imported much of their way of life, and some of their discriminatory attitudes were adopted by the French. Traditionally, French prejudice toward blacks was oblique. In French papers published for children—*Cri-Cri, Pierrot* and *Le Petit Illustré,* for example—blacks were often portrayed as drunkards and buffoons, beings created by God for the entertainment of white men. But the idea of excluding a black person from a public gathering place would have been unthinkable in France before the late 1920s. As the value of the American dollar rose and the French franc declined, and transatlantic travel became more convenient, French business people, eager for maximum profits, sometimes succumbed to American-style prejudice.

This was dramatically brought home to Josephine when she and Pepito tried to rent a suite in a hotel on the Right Bank. They were refused because the management feared that a "colored guest" would reduce American trade.

One of the most humiliating racial rebuffs Josephine experienced occurred on an historic night that started out so happily for her.

On May 20, 1927, Charles Lindbergh, a shy young man of twenty-five, climbed into the cockpit of his gray-white monoplane, *The Spirit of St. Louis,* and took off from Roosevelt Airfield, Long Island. Thirty-three and one half hours later he arrived in Paris. "This boy of ours came unheralded out of the air," wrote American Ambassador Myron Herrick, "and circling the Eiffel Tower, settled to rest as gently as a bird on the field of Le Bourget."

About twenty-five thousand people were waiting for him. Lines of soldiers, ranks of policemen and stout steel fences went down as the crowd ran to greet the conqueror of the Atlantic. Many of the French, who had never heard of the Missouri metropolis, assumed that Lindy's plane was named after Louis IX, who was Saint Louis, as a compliment to them.

Paris feted him. In the Place de l'Opéra electric signs flashed the news. On the streets, in the Métro, in cars, motion picture houses and theatres, wherever people gathered, it was "Lindbergh! Lindbergh! Lindbergh!" Even the tramcars flew the Stars and Stripes.

At the Folies-Bergère, Josephine stopped the show. *"Bonnes Nouvelles!* Ladies and Gentlemen. Charles Lindbergh has arrived!" She was thrilled to make the announcement. "My heart almost burst with pride and joy. Americans and French alike were delirious with happiness."

After the show Josephine was invited by friends to a chic restaurant, l'Abbaye de Thélème, to toast Lucky Lindy. The room was filled with revelers. All of a sudden a clear, strident voice silenced the party. An American, sitting with his wife at the table next to Josephine, called the waiter over and said, "At home a nigger woman belongs in the kitchen."

While everyone in the room waited to see what would happen next, the manager rushed over to the table. After the couple repeated their complaint, he said, "You are in France, and here we treat all the races the same."

For Josephine it was a brutally cold reminder that she would never completely escape from bigotry. "I thought if the floor could open up and swallow me, it would be a blessing," she said.

Josephine's mind was soon occupied by professional problems. Her second season at the Folies proved almost, but not quite, a flop. Louis Lemarchand, author of the revue, christened it "Un Vent de Folie," A Gust of Madness. Derval billed it as a hyper-revue, hoping to put the show over with a flashy adjective.

The problem was Josephine, and she knew it. Fashions pass—more quickly in Paris than elsewhere. Josephine Baker, dancing in bananas, was already a tired gimmick. Writing in *The Dancing Times*, Arnold L. Haskell said that Josephine "always seems to be playing up to what the public wants the Negro to be." Another reviewer said it would take more than a gust, it would take a cyclone to get Josephine to stop wiggling in the same old way.

Her charm over the French seemed to be broken. The critics ground her down to a caricature. "The breath from the jungle," as Erich Maria Remarque had called her, was starting to go stale.

During this uncertain period, when Josephine did not know what would become of her career, she and Pepito discussed getting married.

Josephine yearned for respectability. She still felt the sting of being tagged a *fille de joie*. Alfred Ogden, a New York lawyer, recalls that as a young man in Paris, "If you got into a taxi and asked for Chez Joséphine, the driver asked if you wanted her apartment or her nightclub."

"How strange it was," Josephine would later write, "up until now I had been the one who pleaded with my lovers to marry me. This time it was just the opposite; I was the one who hung back. I didn't try to analyze my reasons. I loved Pepito. I depended on him. He dealt with all my problems. He handled all my baffling tedious paper work. He had abandoned everything for me. I was his entire life. His jealousy was enough to prove he loved me. Yet deep down inside me there was something that refused to say 'I do.' "

Josephine never mentions that she was still the wife of William Howard Baker, Pullman porter, jockey and doer of odd jobs. By instituting a divorce suit, Josephine would call atten-

tion to the fact that she was a married woman, a vital statistic
she had successfully concealed from her European audiences.
Josephine wanted to be a bride, to bask in the publicity heaped
on a celebrity who marries, but she also wanted to stay clear of
legal tangles.

She resolved her conflict with an ingenuity that was totally
Josephine. In mid-June 1927 she simply announced that she
and Pepito had been quietly married at the American Embassy
on the third of the month, her twenty-first birthday. Unfortunately she hadn't mastered the first rule of prevarication: Never
change your story. "One day she claimed they were married at
the Embassy," says Marcel Sauvage, "and the next day it was
supposed to have happened in Italy. I didn't know what to
believe." Paul Derval lost no time quibbling over details. Seeing
the publicity value in the match, he had a sticker printed and
slapped over every picture of Josephine, topless in bananas,
scattered around Paris to advertise "Un Vent de Folie." It read:
COUNTESS PEPITO DE ABATINO.

On June 20 Josephine held a press conference for American
reporters to discuss her "marriage." She was the quintessential
newlywed, radiant and bubbly. "I'm just as happy as I can be,"
said Josephine. "I didn't have any idea that getting married was
so exciting. I feel like I'm sitting on pins and needles. I am so
thrilled."

Josephine's high loud voice monopolized the gathering, leaving Pepito, barely conversant in English, little chance to speak.
She held up her diamond wedding ring, weighing sixteen
carats, and explained that she would not be wearing it because
it was too heavy. "That ain't all he gave me either. I got all the
jewels and heirlooms that have been in the Abatino family for
generations."

Journalists had heard Pepito referred to in Bricktop's and
Zelli's as "the no-count Count." Moreover, the Abatino family
tree could not be found in any European stud book or any
Italian genealogy. When a reporter asked about Pepito's
lineage, Josephine fielded the inquiry with aplomb. "Sure he's a
count. There ain't no fake about that title. I had it looked up
and verified by a private detective in Rome before I signed on
the dotted line. He's got a great big family there and lots of

coats of arms and everything. I understand they live in a big swell château, and as soon as my contract with the Folies-Bergère is finished, I am going down to visit them.

"You know, Pepito had a good job before he met me, with the Italian government. But he couldn't work and make love to me at the same time, so he had to give it up."

Pepito readjusted his monocle, giving Josephine a puzzled look. If the gentlemen of the press did not believe everything she said, they proved they were gentlemen by letting the remark pass.

A correspondent for *The New York World* asked if Pepito would be joining Josephine at the Folies. Josephine shook her head. "I ain't going to let my honey go on the stage, but we are going to make a movie together. It's a comedy against a background of nobility—and if he shows any sheik stuff, I will take him to Hollywood to be trained."

The press conference did the trick. Scores of papers in the United States carried news of the first American colored girl to marry into European nobility. No one seemed to care if it were true; it was a good story.

Americans in 1927 were much more devoted to their newspapers than they are today. Rudolph Valentino dictating his memoirs from the spirit world; "Shipwreck" Kelly sitting on a flagpole for seven days; Alice Reighly stomping the hustings, campaigning for the Anti-flirt Movement; Albert Einstein trying to cope with his absentmindedness; a convict in Sing Sing taking a "hot squat" on the electric chair, blasted into eternity with the headline "ROASTED ALIVE." Anyone whose name was in the newspapers was automatically a celebrity—scientist, senator or murderer.

Much of the news in the Negro community in 1927 was too sad to be churned out as amusing copy. Sixteen black men were lynched that year. The Mississippi River, where Josephine was baptized into the True Life Baptist Church, overflowed from Arkansas to the Gulf of Mexico, leaving thousands of whites and blacks homeless and destitute. The whites received decent housing, but the blacks, most of them poor tenant farmers, were forced to live under appalling conditions.

Josephine's "marriage" was a happy news item. The black

press took it seriously, brushing aside any reference to Pepito's phony credentials as a racist tactic on the part of whites to sabotage Josephine's triumph. On Wednesday, July 6, 1927, *The New York Amsterdam News*, the leading black paper in the country, ran an editorial titled "The New Countess," which began:

> Indications are that Josephine Baker, now Countess Pepito di Albertine [sic], has made a more auspicious venture on the sea of matrimony than any number of American white women within memory. Of course, Josephine, unlike so many American white women, didn't go to Europe in quest of a titled husband, and the fact that she now has one certainly must be as great a surprise to her as to everyone else. This is a little contrary to the "he that seeketh, findeth" theory that so many white women dote on, backed up by their accomplishments or wealth or both, who annually seek titled husbands abroad. Some of them find both title and husband and are happy ever after; while others awake one fine morning to the fact that they have a scheming white elephant on their hands, with or without a real title.

The Pittsburgh Courier, a black paper circulated primarily in the Middle West, ran a picture of the couple sitting in the back of Josephine's touring car: Pepito's head held erect in patrician arrogance, his eyes full of mocking condescension; Josephine, leaning close to him, a fur coat slung over her shoulders, a crocheted scarf wound tight around her forehead, smiling out at the world with the serene felicity of an aristocrat.

But the person who was most surprised by the announcement of Josephine's marriage was Willie Baker, who read about it in *The Chicago Defender.*

In black towns across America, Josephine's marriage to a Roman count was greeted with wonder. Her odyssey became a folktale told again and again. By bamboozling the press, Josephine inadvertently helped create a whole new level of aspiration for young, ambitious blacks fighting for the chance to work as postal clerks, schoolteachers, milkmen and salesgirls. Think big. The sky's the limit.

Scores of ebony girls hightailed it over to Paris in the 1930s, hoping to duplicate Josephine's success. Bobby Short, the black supper-club singer, remembers when he was working as a child entertainer in his hometown of Danville, Illinois, playing the piano at neighborhood parlor socials and ladies' teas, and listening to the women talk about Josephine.

They chewed over the stories—the bushel baskets full of diamond bracelets and anklets; how New York mayor "Gentleman" Jimmy Walker would not leave Paris without seeing her; how the Prince of Dahomey courted her and the King of Zambezi offered to relinquish his throne for her.

"She was an image to them," says Short. "She was that kind of intangible thing they loved because they had conceptualized her into some sort of dream. 'Josephine Baker. My God!' they said to each other. 'She's conquered France and now she's married this count.' " It was true Cinderella.

TEN

"To be a curiosity is a painful profession."

—Josephine

Now that Josephine and Pepito were officially a couple, so to speak, their lives acquired a common goal: to make Josephine as famous as possible. But they realized that in order for her to continue to bewitch her public she would have to become a skilled performer.

Josephine's style of dancing, her dizzy variations on the Charleston, was on its way out—outlived by its "ankular" cousin, the wittier and far more subtle tap steps. What's more, Josephine had trained as a chorus girl, scarcely the most trying apprenticeship. "Today's chorine," wrote critic Gilbert W. Gabrill in 1927, "instead of spending eight years acquiring an art, spends just about two shakes of a lamb's tail learning a strut."

Josephine knew that she needed time and tutoring to extend her dancing repertoire beyond the instinctive level of exotic movements. She realized, too, that she had to develop a singing voice.

Her upper range was full of bubbling birdlike tones, and she knew how to yodel, stretching out the voo-de-o-doos. She sang the blues with such exquisite poignancy that it often brought a lump to the listener's throat. But Josephine did not know how to project her voice, "throwing the velvet" as they used to say in Harlem, and that handicap was especially troublesome to her as a music hall performer working large auditoriums.

Jimmy Daniels, a black singer and dancer who performed in both New York and Paris and watched Josephine on stage at various times over a period of forty-five years, summed up her real dilemma: "She was the most glamorous human being I have ever seen. She was one of the great poseurs. But I must admit quite frankly that I could not pin down any great talent, except flair. She was the quintessence of a star, yet she wasn't a great dancer and she wasn't a great singer until late in life. In the end, she turned out to be one of the best French singers of all time."

Josephine was deluged with offers to perform in cities around the world, from Athens to São Paulo, from Helsinski to Marrakesh. She even received nibbles from New York, and she longed to go back. She vacillated on the issue. She was afraid that in New York her choreography might be viewed as little more than gymnastics, a recapitulation of her *Shuffle Along* routine.

Florence Mills, with whom Josephine had appeared in *Shuffle Along*, had died suddenly in the summer of 1927, still young and at the peak of her fame. She left a place in the world of black entertainment for a pixyish dancer with a high, delicate voice. Josephine wondered if she was seasoned enough to go back to New York and make it big on home ground, perhaps even take Florence's place.

But Florence Mills had been an enormous talent, a singing and dancing star not only in New York but in London and Paris as well. She began performing as "Baby Florence Mills"; she was a cakewalk champion at six. When she was eight, in 1900, she sang "Hannah from Savannah" in Williams and Walker's *Sons of Ham*. Later, in her teens, she became a member of the Panama Trio with Bricktop and also appeared with the Plantation Ten in vaudeville. After a hit engagement with Lew Leslie's Blackbirds in London, she returned to New York, where she died after a routine appendectomy.

Her death and her heartwarming funeral were the subject of much discussion among the black community in Paris. Josephine heard about the thousands of people who had lined Seventh Avenue in Harlem to watch the cortege pass. As the chorus girls from Lew Leslie's Blackbirds, dressed in gray, marched behind the coffin, an airplane released flocks of blackbirds overhead. The funeral was one of the greatest tributes Harlem had ever given a performer.

Painfully aware of the role timing had played in her Paris success, Josephine feared that instead of filling Florence Mills's shoes, she might be unkindly compared and criticized. Feelers from Hollywood, which Josephine ballooned into solid offers when talking to the press, frightened her more than they enticed her. If she was typecast as an exotic dancer in Europe, what would they do with her in Hollywood, where black women were cast as pickaninnies, whores, slaves or domestics?

Pepito, attracted by the American dollar, urged Josephine to let him investigate the inquiries from Hollywood producers. But whenever he pressed her about it, she backed off. "They'll make me sing Mammy songs."

In the meantime, film opportunities developed in Europe. Paul Derval arranged for Josephine to star in a short movie, *An Excursion to Paris,* which was nothing more than a series of scenes of her dancing the Charleston on a mirror in front of a Cubist painting of American skyscrapers. It was modest, to be sure, but sufficiently large to whet Josephine's appetite for the cinema. The experience convinced her that she could be a success in the movies. She was unabashedly thrilled when she saw herself projected on the screen. "Pepito! Look at me! Look at me! Aren't I wonderful?"

A few months after the release of *An Excursion to Paris,* a stranger approached Josephine backstage at the Folies-Bergère with an offer to appear in a full-length feature film. Josephine recounted the incident in a highly poetic fashion:

A man came, from where? How? And who was he? I know absolutely nothing. A man. You know, that mysterious person who is everywhere, behind all the doors, listening and not speaking, who skates like a shadow in the wings, in the artists' dressing rooms, that you run into as if by chance, at all the intersections, behind a taxi, in the restaurants, the grocery stores, the cinemas, at the hairdresser's, at the candy merchant's, behind a bed of begonias . . . the Intermediary. Mr. Intermediary. A man full of schemes and smiles.

Mr. Intermediary was a representative of Maurice Dekobra, a well-known French writer and author of a best-selling postwar potboiler, *La Madone des Sleepings,* the story of a woman driven mad by passion.

Aware of Josephine's box-office appeal, Dekobra wrote a silent movie scenario specifically calculated to cash in on her "native charm." Titled *La Sirène des Tropiques,* the film was a silly bit of frippery about a dim-witted girl from the Antilles named Papitou, who abandons her equatorial island to try her luck in France.

The gross amateurism of *La Sirène des Tropiques* was typical of many French movies produced during the 1920s. French cinema lagged far behind its American counterpart. After the war Paris boasted few theatres for silent movies. Those that dotted the fashionable arrondissements had the air of legitimate theatres rather than the aura of neighborhood movie houses. The still new medium was considered greatly inferior to the music hall.

When Paris became aware of the growing success of the American cinema, theatres of the same type were installed the length of the "grands boulevards," where for generations the French bourgeois had gone to watch melodramas and bedroom farces. Now hall after hall closed down, to remodel and reopen with a silver screen and projector. Everyone was pleased with the increasing number of imported American films; the French flocked to see Mary Pickford, Rudolph Valentino, Chaplin, the Gish sisters and Gloria Swanson. By the time shooting began on *La Sirène des Tropiques,* there were nearly two hundred movie theatres in Paris.

Imported with American films were the prejudices that account, at least partially, for Josephine being cast as a bright-toothed darkie struggling to dance her way off a tropical island. Hollywood's stereotyping—not just of blacks but of other races and ethnic groups as well: loud Irish drunks, stoic Englishmen and demure English ladies, Italian gangsters, lazy

Mexicans—was so effective that it influenced filmmaking in
Europe. In German films blacks were usually scene setters, such
as jazz musicians in a nightclub; Italian cinema presented blacks
as Roman-Nigerian slaves; at least one film depicted a black
French soldier as a happy-go-lucky, carefree tap dancer.

Josephine reported to work daily at Studio Eclair in Epinay, a
suburb north of Paris, for the shooting of *La Sirène des Tropiques*.
The opening scene featured a native village consisting of a nest
of grass huts made of new yellow straw.

On the adjacent set a crew was filming the execution scene
from *Madame Récamier,* based on the memoirs of Jeanne-
Françoise Récamier, a woman of great beauty and charm who
inspired passions during the French Revolution. The scene
called for a huge guillotine flanked by tumbrels, while the
juxtaposition of the two sets produced a few scenes of its
own.

Blacks costumed as natives watched the procession of
princesses and marquises, dressed in ornate costumes and
hooped petticoats, rich brocades and satins, topped with fantastic coiffures, as they queued up for the blade. The "natives"
danced the Charleston on one set while decapitated heads fell
into a wicker basket on the other. During breaks, the blacks and
the "sans-culottes" drank together like brothers. "You can see,"
said the studio head, "that the Niger's not very far from the
Seine."

Because Josephine had no cinematic education, she did not
understand camera angles, lighting techniques or positions.
She found it as difficult to work within a chalk-lined area as she
found it hard to change from the grandiose, overplayed gestures of the music hall to the narrow, close nuances of the film.
She saw herself as a prisoner in a magic circle, standing in a ring
of harsh lights. The spotlights made her bug-eyed, and she had
a problem getting to sleep for several weeks after the film was
completed. Even worse, her ego and personal pride were
scathed. She felt she had been used. "They didn't understand
my nature at all," she said later. "They didn't bother to study
my nature, to use my nature." She was right.

Alain Romains, a French musician who had been tutored in
jazz by blacks, composed the score for *La Sirène des Tropiques.*

During the filming he and Josephine, being of opposite temperaments, "merged" like oil and water.

Romains was a friend of Bricktop's, so when they came to a nightclub scene in the film, he suggested to the director that they have Bricktop play the owner of the bistro. Knowing Josephine's sensitivity about her singing voice, he added, "Bricktop sings Cole Porter songs like a dream."

Josephine's temper exploded and she stormed off the set. The idea of having another black female entertainer in *her* movie!

Recalling Josephine's jealousy and uncertainty, Romains said, "In France we have an expression, *tirer la couverture à soi,* which means that when there are two people in a bed, the one who keeps pulling the bedcovers over for himself is a pig. Josephine was a blanket hog."

Romains contends that Josephine functioned well only when she was the center of attention. She was not suited to be an actress in the true sense because she could not lose herself in a character. "Her magnetism was the collective energy of all the people surrounding her and working for her," he says. "Hypothetically, it's as if you are out in the snow and everybody huddles close to you to keep warm. But if they go away, you will freeze. Josephine was that way. Unless she had an entourage, she couldn't shine."

With *La Sirène des Tropiques* completed, Josephine prepared to set off on her first extended world tour. The itinerary, planned by Pepito, was lengthy: twenty-five countries.

In several cities on the tour, Pepito had arranged for tie-ins with local nightclubs. After performing at the theatre, Josephine would dance at a cabaret, each temporarily named Chez Joséphine. By doubling her appearances, their income would double.

Before departing, they closed Chez Joséphine in Montmartre. She had mixed feelings about leaving Montmartre, a world of pimps and johns, jazz and the blues, Bricktop and Frisco, and her old friend from *La Revue Nègre,* Sidney Bechet. It was a world in which she felt at home because it was so much like Chestnut Valley in St. Louis. It was like leaving home a second time.

But Montmartre had lost much of its charm for Josephine. Fights broke out constantly, as if they were an integral part of the area's scenario. Down the street from Chez Joséphine, Bricktop's piano player, Crutcher, was shot dead by a jealous woman. Sidney Bechet, embroiled in a drunken gun battle in a café, accidentally hit a bystander in the leg. Bechet was jailed, then deported.

The caliber of tourist was changing. American affluence made it possible for a wide spectrum of the population to travel. In 1927 the dollar was worth about fifteen francs, and thus for Americans life was extremely cheap; a pound of butter cost one franc, "déjeuner" at a neighborhood bistro was three or four francs. Continentals scoffed at the marauding bands of American tourists who had pocketbooks for hearts.

F. Scott Fitzgerald wrote of his transplanted countrymen: "With each new shipment of Americans spewed up by the boom, the quality fell off, until toward the end there was something sinister about the crazy boatloads. They were no longer the simple Pa and Ma and son and daughter, infinitely superior in their qualities of kindness and curiosity to the corresponding class in Europe, but fantastic Neanderthals who . . . in the distortion of their new condition, had the human values of pekinese, bivalves, crétins, goats."

Each week the newspaper columns signaled a new disappearance of order. In mental hospital wards, in drying-out clinics, in rest retreats, people were trying to put their minds back in order, to regather their forces, to make the trip back to reality from their artificial paradise.

Josephine felt a revulsion toward this sort of excess. All her instincts, based as they were on firsthand knowledge, mitigated against dissipation.

She had seen too many burnt-out cases in the Chestnut Valley. She rarely drank to excess. She tried cocaine, but it held no allure for her because she feared and resented anything that would enslave her or break down her will.

Josephine left Paris reluctantly, afraid she would be forgotten. But she need not have worried, for reports of her escapades throughout Europe and Latin America were followed with interested delight by the scandal-loving Gauls. One person who remembered her fondly was Gaston Doumergue, President of the Republic. He attended the French salon of 1928 at the Grand Palais, the most important art event of the year. Passing by a long line of portraits of cardinals, generals and kings, he spotted a nude full-length painting of Josephine by Marlette Leslie Cotton of New York. The image provoked a wide smile from Doumergue.

And, while she was gone, Josephine achieved gastronomic immortality, or a semblance thereof. Parisian chefs, always responsive to the fluctuating populace of La Ville Lumière, took to naming "specialities" after notable Americans. At the famous Tour d'Argent, which lays claim to being one of Paris's oldest and finest eating houses, diners had a choice of "canapé Clarence Mackey," "filet de sole Edison" or "poire Wanamaker." Anyone nostalgic for "La Bakaire" could dine on "poulet Josephine Baker."

Josephine's first world tour covered two years, 1928 and 1929, and represented a distinct turning point in her life. Ever since her teenage days on the black vaudeville circuit, she had loved to travel; she savored the excitement of departure, the mystery and discovery of a new place. Now, for the first time, she would travel by aeroplane, hopscotching across Europe and South America. Despite a surfeit of landscapes and people, she was like a child. She never became blasé. She spent most of her time either living in fantasy or in the timeless present.

In Barcelona the famous gypsy dancer Macarona taught her the flamenco, which Josephine would later use in her nightclub act. In Budapest she took a steamer down the Danube, finding, as many visitors to the romantic city do, that the Danube is not blue; nor, at least in the environs of Budapest, is it particularly beautiful. But Josephine saw it as wide and powerful, and was reminded of the Mississippi. In Bucharest Josephine encountered fleas in her hotel bed and cows in the lobby. She adapted to the rustic metropolis by walking the streets barefoot, causing some residents to mistake her for a gypsy.

Through direct exposure to so many diverse countries and cultures, Josephine began to develop her ideas about the brotherhood of man, her deep feeling that all people are part of one family and that skin color does not matter.

Though she would later contradict her credo many times, Josephine felt that every human being has a soul, an ability to understand and to foster friendship, and the capacity to create beauty. To the many homes she would create throughout her career, there came brown men and yellow women, blacks and whites; Josephine's heart had no boundaries nor her love any color lines.

When Josephine made her first world tour, however, many countries in Europe and South America were in political turmoil. Because of the unstable social and political climate following World War I, the Western world was experiencing a massive pull to the right. Stories, always elaborate and risqué, preceded her. To conservatives in the countries she visited, she represented unbridled liberty and licentiousness: the living, if not practicing, embodiment of the "free love" philosophy that was supposedly rampant among artists, performers and intellectuals who did not live by the rules of society. She was simply one more example of "the world gone to hell," the depraved and immoral habitat of Isadora Duncan, Gordon Craig, Man Ray, Eleanora Duse, Gabriel d'Annunzio, Salvador Dali and, of course, Hollywood. As performers and innovators they were to be seen and, perhaps, acknowledged, but they were not to be emulated or admired.

Though Josephine often spoke of the pain of being treated as a curiosity, she loved being embroiled in dramas, especially those in which she was the star.

In predominately Catholic countries, Josephine was like a red flag before the bull of the clergy-dominated political parties. "The Catholics pursued me with Christian hate," she said, "from railway station to railway station, from city to city, from one province to another."

Nowhere was Josephine the subject of more controversy than in Vienna, where the first rumblings of Nazism could be heard. In 1928 Vienna was still wedding-cake decorative, but the cake was gray and crumbling from the inside. For centuries the city had been the gay, glittering capital of the Austrian Empire. Under the greedy and autocratic Hapsburgs, the city had been the center of an immense ramshackle state.

Outside Vienna, the Austrian nobles, many of whom owned great estates that they ruled like independent potentates, led frolicsome and often debauched lives. But on the collapse of the Hapsburg Empire, socialism became the dominant form of government. The Socialists were determined to make it possible for the common worker to enjoy life just as well and fully as the rich and titled.

When Josephine arrived, Austria was cut off from its former territories by political boundaries and tariff bills. Vienna was at the center of what little was left of Austria, a small country that could not possibly support the capital's two million inhabitants, or even itself. Vienna had become a purulent focus of discontent, a hotbed of political ferment. Yet one theme common to most groups was that of racial superiority.

Austria's population was almost purely Germanic, and among many the feeling was very strong that the Nordics were the true elect—the real "chosen people."

Elitist thinking in the main was directed against the Jewish businessmen and the intelligentsia; it was a combination of fear and hatred because the Jewish people owned most of the biggest businesses and held many high academic positions. Josephine's appearance in the city now brought to the surface latent anti-Negro sentiments. Nordic racists contended that black skin was a sign of innate inferiority; Negroes, therefore, were less fit people who would simply have to go the way of the dinosaurs, into extinction. Evolution had spoken, and oblivion was the destination of the "unfit."

As always, Josephine's fame as a risqué dancer preceded her, so the stage was set for widespread opposition. Provocative posters, showing her clad only in pearls and an ostrich feather, were spread throughout the predominately Catholic city to announce her forthcoming appearance at the Ronacher Theatre. Newspapers carried exaggerated accounts of her life in Paris, depicting her as a diabolical harlot from Harlem who enslaved men with her carnal charms.

The students, members of uniformed youth movements, the foot soldiers in various right-wing political parties that would supply the moral force for Nazism, declared their intention of preventing Josephine from performing. Extreme Nationalist

Josephine with Pepito, greeted by men about town in Vienna. Her appearance caused riots in the streets. Church bells chimed to warn citizens that "the demon of immorality" had arrived. *Keystone*

party radicals even went so far as to speak of *Negerschmach,* the insult it would mean to the white population of the city if Josephine appeared on stage. Protest rallies were organized for her arrival.

Opposition to performers such as Josephine was part of a gradually developing Nazi master plan to label all exotic, advanced art—Stravinsky, Picasso, Schoenberg, Alban Berg, Kandinsky, Marian Anderson—"Negroid" and to discredit it as unworthy of the Aryan.

As Josephine and Pepito rode in a horse-drawn carriage

down the Ringstrasse, one of the finest boulevards in Europe, on the way to the Grand Hotel, church bells pealed from every quarter of the snow-laden capital. The Catholic clergy, who vehemently opposed Josephine's appearance, had arranged to have the churches ring their chimes as a warning to the citizens of Vienna that "the devil incarnate, the demon of immorality" had arrived. A pamphlet was thrust into Josephine's hand bearing the headline "Can She Be Punished As She Deserves?"

Two days later the City Council issued a decree forbidding the Ronacher Theatre from featuring Josephine. They used the technicality that the new theatre manager had not received the necessary stage concession.

Pepito immediately began negotiations with another theatre, the Johann Strauss, and a date for Josephine's appearance was set for a month hence. But this gave the right-wing forces time to mobilize their strength. A deputation of Nationalist party members now called on Minister of Interior Hartleb and handed him a petition stating that the party was receiving thousands of letters daily protesting Josephine's "brazen-faced heathen dances." They warned that her appearance would produce riots and possibly bloodshed. In short order the controversy over Josephine became so heated that the Austrian parliament decided to hold a debate to decide, once and for all, whether she represented a threat to public morals.

While Josephine waited for the showdown to begin, she enjoyed Vienna's many diversions. Despite the stark realities of postwar life, the city was full of gaiety summed up in the word *Gemütlichkeit,* for which there is no equivalent in any other language. It means many things—the coziness of laughing with good friends, easygoingness, light-headedness and fun. "To be in Vienna was like being in a musical comedy," says Anita Loos. "The very beggars in the street had style, a sense of humor and impeccable manners."

Josephine joined in the happy-go-lucky life of the Vienna coffeehouses, sitting at the heavy tables and hoisting her stein of beer in the company of dark-haired paunchy men and golden whores. In this bohemian atmosphere, Josephine encountered a man who would become her champion.

His name was Adalbert Sternberg, better known as Monschi.

He was a member of the Austrian House of Lords, the parliamentary body that was to decide Josephine's fate. He was also a hard-drinking middle-aged charmer who, with natural geniality and warmth, made friends wherever he went. He enjoyed taking up the cause of the downtrodden.

A relaxed Catholic who practiced his faith with the ease of breathing, Sternberg's religion was in his blood as well as his soul. His family had been one of the oldest and wealthiest in the Austro-Hungarian empire. His coat of arms was the star of Bethlehem: Legend said his ancestor Gaspard had been one of the three kings who came to worship the Christ child. The Knights of Sternberg were first mentioned in Czech history in the year 1100. Sternbergs had prospered and survived in the kingdom of Bohemia for nearly 1000 years.

Monschi enjoyed entertaining his colleagues in the Austrian parliament with his wit and Rabelaisian humor. Josephine's case provided a perfect occasion for him to amuse his cohorts and make a few points.

As the government officials gathered in the parliament building, a classical Greek structure rather foreign to the Viennese temperament, newspaper reporters held vigil in the antechambers.

Even Josephine, with her shrewd eye for publicity, could not have devised a more intriguing way of capturing the attention of the press. This incident became one of a long string of happenings on her first world tour that substantially contributed to her mystery.

To open the debate, Dr. Jerzabezh, a leading member of the Clerical party and a practicing physician in Vienna for twenty-five years, gave an impassioned speech in which he called Josephine "a savage" who would corrupt the character of the Viennese if allowed to appear in public "dressed only in a postage stamp." Following Jerzabezh's oration, other deputies rose to talk of Josephine's "perverse" acting and to comment unfavorably on her figure.

Finally Sternberg took the floor. He began by calling Josephine one of the representative people of the epoch. She was a force of nature who exposed the juiceless quality of a civilization cut off from its primordial source. "Whites don't know how to dance," he said. "Only blacks conserve in dancing its human and sacred quality."

Sternberg then attacked Jerzabezh head-on: "The highest ideal of human art is always the female nude, and that part of the unclothed female which strikes fear in the heart of Deputy Jerzabezh is always represented without dread in real art. Besides, he who combats nudism blasphemes God who created the human nude."

Sternberg then instructed his colleagues to go to St. Peter's in Rome to look at the pictures in the dome. "The most daring nudes that one can see in the world are there in the house of the Pope. Therefore, what is the meaning of this campaign of poorly educated priests against Josephine?"

Count Sternberg won the day. Josephine was permitted to perform. But there was still a great deal of opposition from the clergy.

On the morning of Josephine's Vienna debut, the Reverend Father Fey, a Jesuit priest at St. Paul's Church, offered a special mass for her prodigal soul. The church was packed. In his sermon Father Fey, like Count Sternberg, cited Josephine as a symbol of a decade. However he saw her not as a living objet d'art but as the embodiment of decadence. Father Fey's sermon was so compelling that many of his parishioners donned their best clothes and rushed to the Johann Strauss Theatre that evening to see this merry Magdalene.

Josephine surprised her audience by appearing in a beautiful, long, cream-colored gown. Before the hushed and amazed Viennese, she sang "Pretty Little Baby," a Negro spiritual from slave days when black men were beaten down with fatigue and despair by their Christian masters. She received a standing ovation. Throughout her three-week engagement in Vienna the Johann Strauss was packed every night.

Ten years later the Aryan student soldiers who protested in the streets against Josephine finally had their day. In 1938 Adolf Hitler took over the city of Vienna. He commandeered the elegant Weinzinger Hotel and chose the suite of the hotel owner for himself. As he was turning in that night, Hitler looked above the bed to see a photograph of Josephine staring down at him.

Josephine's fans were as zealous as her enemies. In Prague a stampede of people rushed Josephine when she alighted from the train, threatening to tear off her clothes. A riot quickly developed in which several windows in the train station were smashed and several people went off to the hospital with injuries.

Josephine scrambled to safety atop a limousine. Only when a phalanx of policemen surrounded the car was it able to move slowly ahead. The boisterous crowd pursued and would not allow her to go to her hotel until she had been driven around the city. Perched on the car roof, Josephine waved to the crowds in the manner of visiting royalty.

After Czechoslovakia Josephine went to Budapest, where the lusty Hungarians proved just as fascinated by her as everyone else. Yet mixed with the bouquets and bravos, she once again came face-to-face with the searing ugliness of Aryan racism.

On a holiday break during her first world tour, Josephine skis with Pepito at St. Moritz. *Lynx*

One night while Josephine was performing at the Royal Orpheum Theatre on the Boulevard Elizabeth in Budapest, student agitators hurled ammonia bombs at her, shouting, "Go back to Africa." Josephine continued to dance, but later admitted that she was badly shaken by the event.

Instead of trying to shield Josephine from the unpredictable mobs, Pepito was determined to bleed as much publicity from her notoriety as possible. Every day he had a new scheme. He even arranged for Josephine to ride through downtown Budapest in a little buggy pulled by an ostrich. But his most inspired stunt was to challenge one of Josephine's admirers to a duel.

A handsome Hungarian cavalry officer, André Czlovoydi, came to the cabaret where Josephine worked every evening after she finished performing at the Orpheum. He began writing love poems to her in his schoolboy French. It was a harmless crush that would have had no significance if Pepito had not decided to make an issue of it.

Pepito was capable of transforming his jealousy, though real enough, into a role advantageous to their traveling carnival show. And so when André handed Josephine a poem in which he called her "the black sun of the city of light," Pepito proceeded to slap André on the cheek and challenge him to a duel.

Seconds arranged for the meeting at dawn at St. Stephen's cemetery.

In the meantime Pepito got the message across to André that this was not to be a serious affair. André, realizing what a hero it would make him to his comrades to fight a duel over Josephine Baker, agreed to the ruse.

On the morning of the event Pepito, who had mobilized a full corps of reporters (a notable feat considering the early hour), wielded the foil with a flair worthy of Scaramouche. Josephine, screaming at the top of her lungs, gave a performance so riveting and unnerving that it was difficult for anyone to tell whose side she was on.

Pepito was finally scratched on the shoulder, which brought an abrupt end to the combat, since it was a duel of the "first blood" rather than a duel to the death. On examining the wound, the seconds decided that the bloodshed was sufficient to satisfy the honor of the contestants. Everybody left the field contented.

One month later *The New York Times* printed an Associated Press item from Zagreb, Yugoslavia, about Alexius Groth, a twenty-one-year-old Budapest draftsman who had become infatuated with Josephine and had followed her from Budapest to Zagreb, besieging her with flowers and love letters. He stabbed himself and fell at her feet as she was leaving a nightclub. "He wounded himself severely but may recover," the item concluded.

Josephine would eventually set the story of Alexius's stabbing in Budapest rather than Zagreb, and she did not mention his name. Did she forget the name of the man who stabbed himself for want of her love? Indeed, did she ever know it?

When Josephine returned to the United States in 1935, a reporter found the stabbing incident intriguing enough to try to pin her down about it. Josephine smiled and replied, "That's what I love about Europe. Something different happens every day."

ELEVEN

"It's important to achieve something in life."

—Josephine

By the time Josephine reached Copenhagen on her first world tour, she had received enough praise and vilification to turn even the most well-adjusted person into a full-blown schizophrenic. How could she be the "Angel of the Black Race" and the "Devil Incarnate" at the same time?

Fortunately, after the Inquisition spirit of the Catholic countries, Josephine was treated by the Scandinavians more as a work of art than a trained circus animal. In front of the Palace Hotel, gentle, well-mannered Danes stood with their noses pressed against the window of the lobby, trying to catch a glimpse of her—not simply because she was Josephine Baker, the dancer, but because she was black. In Denmark, where most of the population is fair and blond, blacks were considered fascinating novelties.

Josephine was buoyed by her reception.

At her press conference, held upon arrival, Josephine beguiled the corps of reporters by reciting one of her favorite fairy tales, Hans Christian Andersen's *The Emperor's New Clothes*. She told the story in French, with broadly acted gestures, as if the reporters were children.

Whenever she could avoid it, Josephine did not speak in English, for the mistakes she made betrayed her lack of educa-

153

tion. But because she was not French, her errors in that language were not held against her. On the contrary, they were considered endearing. One reporter remarked, "I didn't think the cool French language could be so delightful. It is quite an event to hear Josephine Baker talk with such a lovely voice."

Robert Mountsier, an American journalist based in Copenhagen, spent a few hours with Josephine in her suite at the Palace. During the interview Josephine alternated between playing with the three dogs she had acquired in her travels— Baby Girl, a Pekinese; Alphi, a Brussels Griffon; and Fifi, a Brabançon—and writing a long letter to her mother in St. Louis.

Afterward, Mountsier cabled *The New York Sun:* "Last year the best known American in the Scandinavian section of the world was the blond Lindbergh; this summer the winner by any contest for the most popular American would be Josephine Baker."

After Copenhagen Josephine visited Stockholm, where the royal family turned out to see her. It was then that Josephine met Gustav, Crown Prince of Sweden.

In *Remembering Josephine,* published in 1976 and written by Stephen Papich, Josephine's manager during her comeback tour of the United States in 1960, the author describes a torrid romance that allegedly took place in the late 1920s between Josephine and Gustav.

Papich includes in his book a picture of the prince when he was about twenty-four or twenty-five, a strikingly handsome young man with Nordic features, clear blue eyes and sandy blond hair. Papich tells his readers that the picture shows Gustav as he looked at the time Josephine met him. In fact, in 1928 Gustav was well into his forties and, although he kept in shape playing tennis, he looked distinctly middle-aged, a situation not helped by the fact that he wore pince-nez.

Josephine, Papich claims, gave him a kiss-by-kiss account of her affair with the Prince, although, Papich adds, that Josephine's talent for embellishment made it impossible to separate fact from fiction. Nor does the author attempt to do so, as he describes in Josephine's words an enchanted evening she spent with the Prince, sharing the bedroom in the royal car of a train speeding through the heart of Sweden. A few fragments of the tale go as follows: "I'll never forget that bed. It was like something out of a Hollywood movie. It was like a dream. It was a bed shaped like a swan. . . . I just dropped my dress. I didn't have anything on. I was ready for anything. . . . I looked like a little boy with my slicked down hair and my hard little dancer's body. I wondered if he'd like me when he really saw me. I even wondered if he knew that I was a colored girl."

Regardless of how much of the account is true, the experience of meeting, talking with and perhaps even going to bed with royalty instilled in Josephine the belief that she had a direct line to world leaders. This special relationship with the powerful, she felt, gave her the right to try to influence their thinking. Over the years Josephine wrote long advice-filled letters to a variety of statesmen, including Juan Perón, Khrushchev, Robert Kennedy and de Gaulle. Her letters often went unanswered, but Josephine never relinquished her belief that she could influence world affairs.

In the summer of 1929, Josephine traveled throughout South America on the last leg of her tour. The long stretches of time spent getting from one place to another—sitting on boats, in trains and on planes—provided an experience alien to her nature: She was forced to sit relatively still. During these long journeys Josephine confided in Pepito, revealing to him incidents from her childhood. She told him about the terrifying experience of being forced to leave home to work as a maid when she was only eight years old. She told of how the husbands of women she worked for would grab her bottom as she washed dishes or scrubbed the floor. She told about yearning to escape, of her fantasy, kindled by fairy tales, of moving to a land where there would be kings and queens. As a result of these long soul-searching talks, Josephine and Pepito decided to write a novel based on her youth. It was published in Paris the next year, 1930, under the title *Mon Sang Dans Tes Veines,* "My Blood in Your Veins."

Set in Massachusetts, the story tells of a young black servant named Joan who works for the Barkleys, a family of wealth and prominence. They live on a large tract of land called The Oaks, which—strange for New England—resembles a plantation.

Joan falls in love with Mrs. Barkley's son, Fred, who is forced to renounce her because of her black skin. Then, to please his mother, Fred becomes engaged to a New Orleans belle. Before the wedding Fred is injured in a riding accident and requires a blood transfusion. Joan donates several pints of her blood and, subsequently, dies of weakness.

Reviewers called *Mon Sang Dans Tes Veines* corny, amateurish and melodramatic, which it was. Despite Josephine's celebrity, the book sold poorly. Yet the novel affords a rare glimpse of Josephine's psychological machinery. She saw Joan's magnanimous gesture as a ritual sacrifice in the manner of Christ surrendering His life on the cross to atone for the sins of men.

Lest any reader miss the point, the title page of *Mon Sang Dans Tes Veines* is an illustration of the lower half of Jesus' body nailed to the cross. The legs are slim, androgynous and, at first glance, could easily be mistaken for Josephine's. Three black men are kneeling at the foot of the cross, raising their hands in supplication to the crucified figure.

"Josephine thought of herself as a member of the Holy Family," says a friend, "but it was not always clear which role she thought she was playing. Sometimes she pictured herself as the black Madonna, other times as the child of God, and the Virgin Mary. But that picture gets to the core of Josephine. She felt that all her life whites had tried to crucify her, to kill her spirit."

As Josephine boarded the *Lutetia* departing from Rio for Europe, she began to worry about Paris. She was ready to take on the great city again, but would the Parisians welcome her back as a polished performer? After all her recent triumphs abroad, she now knew that she wanted to have her biggest success in Paris, to settle there and buy a home. Could she do it?

On the *Lutetia* Josephine sang and danced for the passengers in the ship's salon. Le Corbusier, the "monstre sacré" of modern architecture, was in the front row and was enthralled by the black American show tunes she sang. "They were fantastically beautiful, touching, rich, inventive, generous and decent," he would report. When Josephine sang "Baby" he was moved to tears.

Le Corbusier was returning from one of his jaunts through

South America, where he had been lecturing on his then remarkable architectural theories. He had declared war on cities, denouncing them as "stone deserts," unhealthy and chock-full of useless, finicky objects, a jumble inherited from a past age. His own architecture reflected the man: massive, virile, elemental. He loved rough materials, unpolished but not denatured.

Le Corbusier was a student of jazz, which he considered "the expression of the new epoch." After the show he invited Josephine to his cabin. She took with her a little guitar and delighted him by singing some more blues, including the number Florence Mills had made famous, "I'm a Little Black Bird Looking for a Blue Bird."

> *Never had no happiness,*
> *Never felt no one's caress.*
> *I'm just a lonesome bit of humanity*
> *Born on a Friday, I guess . . .*

Le Corbusier devoted part of each day to painting and sketching. As the *Lutetia* plied the Atlantic, he made several drawings of Josephine in the nude in his cabin. "Josephine Baker, known around the world, is a small child, pure, simple and limpid," Le Corbusier wrote in his journal. "She glides over the roughness of life. She has a good little heart. She is an admirable artist when she sings, and out of this world when she dances."

"Corbu" and Josephine were kindred souls, so it was only natural that a shipboard romance should develop between them. Although faithful and considerate when he was home in Paris to his wife Yvonne, a gypsy Monegasque, Le Corbusier enjoyed his liberties when traveling. Women generated an intense excitement in him, which he considered moral by its very force.

He was a brilliant companion, precise and functional in everything except his speech. He rambled backward and forward while talking, and even slipped sideways, until he found a colorful expression—badinage was not his forte—and then would stop short in self-admiration.

For the ship's costume ball Le Corbusier blackened his face, an amusing combination with his thick owl-shaped glasses, but eschewed Josephine's banana costume, in favor of striped convict's trousers and an Indian army guard's vermilion coat. "Not being a handsome fellow," he explained, "I keep my anatomy out of sight." Josephine dressed as a white-faced clown, her eyes encircled in black. The effect on the ship's company was no less than the two of them had sought.

Although Pepito could be the firm and cunning businessman, when it came to exploiting Josephine for money he had a soft interior, and her infidelities hurt him deeply. Josephine was his purpose in life, his entire existence. He fought to foster and maintain his control over her, fluctuating between keeping her on a long tether, letting her have her head and—when fiercely jealous—enforcing severe regulations upon her. But how could Pepito, stonemason turned impresario, intelligent but not brilliant, compete with Le Corbusier? Pepito was a moon to Josephine's sun, and he realized that there were times when he had to withdraw. She simply would not tolerate his jealousy.

Pepito was slowly and irretrievably slipping into the rank of an employee. Josephine no longer bothered introducing him as her husband. And he countered with the one surefire weapon he possessed: financial control. With his shrewdness he had their finances so enmeshed that Josephine would have to pay a very high price to break free.

But Josephine was not in any way ready to rupture their relationship. Pepito was the greatest personal inspirer she had ever known. He was an astute observer of the niceties of protocol and the superficialities of class, and he was doing everything in his power to keep his pledge to turn Josephine into a lady. He engaged tutors to teach her French, Spanish and German; he shared with Josephine a sense of fashion, helping to change her garish flamboyance into a style uniquely her own. And he polished her rough edges: "Hold your fork this way, Chérie. Chew with your mouth closed, Chérie. Don't speak in such a loud tone of voice, Chérie." Like Pygmalion's Galatea, Pepito's Josephine proved receptive and responsive.

When they returned to Paris, Josephine was the consummate cosmopolitan: urbane, softer, more subdued. All the outward appearances of breeding were there, as were many of its inner feelings. Josephine had acquired a greater confidence, and though she would always be plagued by insecurities, she would never be a maundering pinchbeck.

Pepito now signed a contract for Josephine to star in the 1930 revue at the Casino de Paris. Though not as famous as the Folies-Bergère, the Casino de Paris was considered by many to be a higher class of entertainment, with more imagination and taste than its rival.

When Josephine went into rehearsal, the Casino was the subject of intense curiosity. Henri Varna, a dapper vaudevillian and opera star, and a former music hall comic with a Roman physique named Oscar Dufrenne, had just purchased the theatre for nine million francs. Varna had risen from playing small roles at the Théâtre de Belleville to become director of the Palace, Concert Mayol and the Empire. Since childhood, theatre had been his passion.

Varna was a veteran producer, a man of confidence and firmness with remarkable flair. He was guided by his dreams, and the sureness of his vision gave him a creative courage unbridled by any traditional ideas of what a music hall should be. Varna incorporated his Jesuit education into the music hall by setting many of the scenes in churches and convents. This idea was later "borrowed" by Derval at the Folies-Bergère, where one season he had Josephine sing Schubert's "Ave Maria" between nudie skits.

Varna, who could see that Josephine had made quantum leaps in her career, believed she was now ready to be presented to the Parisian public as an accomplished performer.

Despite Varna's support, Josephine felt wary of the other members of the cast. The chorus boys and girls for *Paris Qui Remue*, "Paris Which Stirs," did not believe she was of the caliber to be a Casino headliner. Their opposition to her was spearheaded by Earl Leslie, the American choreographer of the show and Mistinguett's lover at the time.

"La Miss" was no spring chicken. Past fifty, but with no intention of relinquishing her title as queen of the French music halls, Mistinguett had launched a campaign to undercut Josephine through Earl Leslie.

Darling of the French music halls, Mistinguett, at about the time Josephine met her. Said Maurice Chevalier: "Mistinguett was Paris —the symbol of gaiety and good humor and courage and heart."
Culver Pictures

The history of the Casino de Paris was that of Mistinguett. If Gaby Deslys gave it the kickoff, Mistinguett assured its triumph. Sometimes comic, sometimes sad, she could be a caricature or a beauty. In middle age she could still play the little sixteen-year-old florist or the pathetic waif, without appearing ridiculous. She was also the great lady, walking down the celestial stairs, exposing her impeccable legs with plumes on her head and a satin train trailing behind. Maurice Chevalier summed her up: "Mistinguett was Paris—the symbol of gaiety and good humor and courage and heart."

Mistinguett could also be a first-rate bitch, and the more she aged the more impossible she became. Upon arriving at the Gare du Nord a few days before one of her opening nights at the Folies-Bergère, she overheard a railway porter remark that she was getting to look like a she-baboon. According to Paul Derval, "the resultant explosion was a foretaste of the atomic age."

After *La Folie Du Jour,* when Paris was abuzz with Josephine, Mistinguett did everything she could to belittle her. Michael Gyarmarthy, who was to become the creative director of the Folies-Bergère, remembers Mistinguett turning to him at a dinner party and asking, "What's the name of that 'petite Nègre' who dances in bananas?"

One evening Mistinguett pushed her scorn of Josephine too far. With Pepito, Josephine went to a movie premiere at Cinema Apollo. They were standing in the lobby when Mistinguett swept in with a brace of *jeunesse dorée,* foppish young men known as the Gilded Youth.

As giddy tourists rushed to her pleading for autographs, Mistinguett called out to Josephine in her resonant voice, "Well, Pickaninny, why don't you come up and salute me."

In an instant Josephine forgot everything Pepito had taught her. She cut through the swarm of tourists. Digging her nails into Mistinguett's arm, she spat in her face.

La Miss, like a true child of Mènilmontant, the red-light district in the shadow of the cemetery Père-Lachaise, spat back.

In the music hall milieu, the grand staircase of the Casino de Paris was the show business equivalent of walking on the altar of God. In this context Earl Leslie tried to write Josephine off as an unworthy earthling.

"You are not going to have her walk down the same stairway as 'Miss'?" Leslie asked Varna.

"Pourquoi pas?" said Varna, dismissing him.

Varna knew Josephine had everything needed to become a great star. He supplanted Pepito as Josephine's Svengali. He made her practice coming down the stairs with a book on her head. Then he had her master the descent with two books, and finally with six—over and over again. And he taught her to bow graciously, "like a grande dame before the rabble."

Josephine listened respectfully to his advice. She understood that he was the instrument of her success, and she accepted his ideas with enthusiasm.

"Is that right, Monsieur Varna? *C'est magnifique,* Monsieur Varna. You think I could do that?"

"Mais oui, voyons!"

Oscar Dufrenne, Varna's partner, had certain reservations about Josephine. He did not believe that her voice was strong enough or interesting enough for a Casino show. Therefore he thought it would be best if she did not sing at all.

While Dufrenne and Varna were arguing this issue one evening, Vincent Scotto, the songwriter for the show, dropped by. Scotto, an extremely popular composer, in the course of his career wrote four thousand songs and a dozen operettas. He helped give the period its flavor, and he had a knack for finding *the* song to launch a young artist. Scotto had just started working on *Paris Qui Remue.*

"Do you have a song for Josephine?" Varna asked as Scotto walked in.

"Oui! Oui!" said Scotto. "I was walking down the rue Chaussée d'Antin, on my way over here, and all of a sudden it hit me. I stood in a doorway under the portal of a house and wrote it. Listen:

> *J'ai deux amours,*
> *mon pays et Paris.*
> *Par eux toujours,*
> *mon coeur est ravi.*

"Do you like it?" he asked.

Varna loved it, as all of Paris would come to love it. "J'ai Deux Amours" became Josephine's theme song, which she sang at every performance she gave for the rest of her life.

To publicize *Paris Qui Remue,* Varna bought a baby leopard from Hagenbeck in Hamburg and gave it to Josephine. She named the leopard Chiquita and paraded around with this eye-catching accessory, eye-catching not only for his magnificent spotted coat but for the diamond choker around his neck. Years later Josephine would pawn the choker for $20,000.

It was tres à la mode during the Twenties and Thirties for actresses to have exotic pets. Here Chiquita strolls with his mistress. *UPI*

Josephine and Chiquita were a match for each other. It was almost as if she found her opposite number in the animal kingdom. But Pepito's relationship with Chiquita was strained. Although tolerant of Josephine's animals, he did not like sharing the bed with the leopard. Chiquita, on his part, reacted negatively to Pepito's nervousness. He did not enjoy motoring with Pepito, who drove too fast, in jerky spurts, hitting the brakes at red lights and hurling Chiquita against the dashboard.

To get people talking about her and the show, Josephine took Chiquita to a production of *La Bohème* at l'Opéra. During Mimi's tragic death scene, Josephine let Chiquita's leash go and he hopped into the orchestra pit. The next day one of the newspapers announced that Josephine was trying to devour all of Paris.

Josephine took to strutting down the Champs-Elysées with Chiquita-*cum*-choker. "You couldn't get within blocks of her," Bricktop recalls. "Everything stopped cold. The Frenchmen and the women too would come running up to her. 'Josephine!' 'Belle Joséphine!' 'Bravo Joséphine!' "

Josephine also took Chiquita to a New Year's ball given by Count and Countess Etienne de Beaumont—Proustian characters who were great connoisseurs and patrons of the avantgarde. The Beaumonts' balls were usually charity affairs for war widows or Russian refugees. This one, held in 1929, was a farewell to the 1920s.

Les Années Folles were drawing to a close, and the curtain was lifting on *Les Années Difficiles*. Across the Atlantic, storm clouds gathered with the first rumblings of the Depression. The Wall Street crash of Black Tuesday, October 24, 1929, signaled the beginning of the Great Depression. Soon the famous skyscraper suicides would begin. "You had to stand in line," cracked Will Rogers, "to get a window to jump out of."

The evening *Paris Qui Remue* opened, the auditorium of the Casino de Paris—a splendid citadel of pleasure, decorated with Chinese lacquer—was full of critics ready to write Josephine off. They considered it amusing that the "half-breed" was being presented by Varna as a polished performer.

The stage manager gave the signal. Josephine entered, her head supporting a plume so high it almost hit the ceiling, so wide it touched both right and left sides of the stage. As eleven projectors danced over her like an astral body, the orchestra boomed.

Josephine walked down the golden staircase. The chorus boys followed her, offering her to the public. Her walk was magnificent; for the rest of her career it would be a trademark of Josephine's presence. It was her great panther strut. At the bottom of the steps, like a rascal, she winked at the public.

Janet Flanner, having covered Josephine's first performance in Paris for *The New Yorker,* was in the audience. Her review was both laudatory and nostalgic for the Josephine who used to be:

> If you can get away for a day or so, it might be a good plan to fly to Paris and spend the evening at Josephine Baker's new Casino show. . . . It is . . . one of the best in years, is as full of staircases as a Freudian dream, has excellent imported British dancing choruses of both sexes, a complete Russian ballet, trained pigeons, a live cheetah, roller skaters . . . the

four best can-can dancers in captivity, a thriller in which Miss Baker is rescued from a typhoon by a gorilla, and an aerial ballet of heavy Italian ladies caroming about on wires.

Perhaps, however, enough is seen of Miss Baker in the present instance, for she has, alas, almost become a little lady. Her caramel-colored body, which overnight became a legend in Europe, is still magnificent, but it has become thinned, trained, almost civilized. Her voice, especially in the voo-deo-doo's, is still a magic flute that hasn't yet heard of Mozart—though even that, one fears, will come with time. There is a rumor that she wants to sing refined ballads; one is surprised that she doesn't want to play Othello. On that lovely animal visage lies now a sad look, not of captivity, but of dawning intelligence.

Alexander Calder also returned to see Josephine, having "done" her in 1926 and 1927. This time he captured a very different Josephine. In 1926, when he created his first wire mobile caricature of her, he gave Josephine an Al Jolson pose, her hands thrown in the air as if she were singing Mammy songs. In his 1927 sculpture Josephine is softer, more confident, less frenzied. Calder emphasized her womanliness by giving her full breasts and a large belly, a shimmering spiral which, when the mobile is suspended from the ceiling, quivers with the slightest breeze.

Calder's 1930 caricature would be a total departure from the first two for at that time he perceived the Josephine who had undergone a major overhaul in her stage presence, who had been tamed through singing lessons and acting lessons, who was now the handiwork of a shrewd manager and the smooth machinery of a top music hall. He streamlined her features—the hands hang lifelessly at her sides—giving her none of the intense vitality radiating from the first two models. Strangely, in this mobile he gives Josephine a masculine persona. The jaw is hard, the mouth strong, the shoulders wide and square. There is even a small phallic appendage between her two wire legs. For now, as an established star, Josephine was permanently cast in the traditional masculine role of breadwinner. Her paycheck supported Pepito, maids, gardeners, hairdressers, couturiers,

Josephine in 1930, at the height of her fame as a music hall performer. *Keystone*

veterinarians, pedicurists, voice teachers and makeup artists.

But, for the moment, Josephine was oblivious to the pitfalls of stardom. Pepito culled her best reviews of performances over the last five years and had them printed in a limited edition, illustrated with caricatures of Josephine.

In *Paris Qui Remue* Josephine was seen by the royal family of Denmark, the ex-king of Spain, the king of Sweden, and the king of Siam, who graciously offered her an elephant, probably the only animal she ever refused.

News of her latest triumph at the Casino reached many

people who knew her in the United States, including Mother Jones of the Jones Family band, that ragtag group Josephine had sung with on the streets of St. Louis and with whom she had stayed briefly in New Orleans, all living and eating in one roach-infested room.

Mother Jones wrote Josephine a brief note to say, "I think of you. Your success has given me pleasure." She included a photo of herself playing the trumpet and also a rusty old nail with a lock of her hair wrapped around it, a shaman her husband, a student of voodoo, considered a good luck charm.

Josephine presented the nail to Henri Varna. "I am this nail and you have hammered me into shape."

TWELVE

"I dreamed I was floating nude down a stream on a
lily pad and the stream was lined with thousands of
cheering fans. That might be heaven."

—Josephine

In 1929 Josephine and Pepito bought a house in Le Vésinet, a
villa suburb resting serenely on the western banks of the Seine,
forty-five minutes by car from the heart of Paris. The thirty-
room turn-of-the-century mansion, at 26 Avenue Clemenceau,
is still standing today, basically unaltered from when Josephine
bought it.

Inside the high iron gates, past the gatekeeper's cottage, a
long white gravel driveway lined with ancient oak trees leads up
to the house; the trees grow in such abundance that the property is named Le Beau-Chêne, the beautiful oak.

The villa, built of red and gray brick, has as many pointed
turrets and dormers as anything King François I ever knew.
The front facade is embellished with medieval shields, oeil-de-
boeuf windows and an *auvent*, or canopy, shaped like a fan,
over the front door.

For Josephine, it was a dream come true. She had not had a
permanent address since she lived at 1632 Bernard Street in St.
Louis. Now she had a suitable outlet for her long pent-up nesting instincts. She stayed at Le Beau-Chêne from 1929 to 1947,
eighteen years, a span that despite volcanic ups and downs, she
considered the happiest in her life.

The village of Le Vésinet was not simply a bedroom commu-

Le Beau-Chêne, the beautiful oak, Josephine's thirty-room turn-of-the-century mansion in Le Vésinet. *Hrand*

nity for the great city in Josephine's time, any more than it is today. Le Vésinet has a sense of place and atmosphere all its own. The land upon which it is built was originally a park, an extension of the forest of St. Germain-en-Laye and, like the forest, part of the rich hunting preserve of the French kings in the seventeenth and eighteenth centuries. In the nineteenth century, when Napoleon III ruled France, a group of bankers approached him and secured his permission to build a university there and make Le Vésinet a magnet for scholars.

Although the university never became a reality, the bankers did succeed in creating a planned community, developed under rigid zoning laws specifically designed to keep gluttonous developers at bay. The industrial section of the town was restricted to one part of the village. The residential area was landscaped to provide large patches of greenery, dotted with neatly trimmed gardens, spacious lawns and artificial lakes.

At the center of Le Vésinet, called Le Pecq, was a flourishing open market where farmers sold their fruits and vegetables. The market was not unlike Soulard, St. Louis's wholesale pro-

Josephine and Pepito in the East Indian room of Le Beau-Chêne. They are going over the script of *ZOUZOU*, her most successful movie, in which she played opposite Jean Gabin. *Seeberger*

duce center, where, as a five-year-old, Josephine had scavenged to help feed herself and her family.

The beauty of the village made it a natural attraction for artists and intellectuals, as well as wealthy businessmen who valued the tasteful architecture and good town planning. Painter Maurice Utrillo, the sculptor Bordelle, actor Jean-Louis Barrault, philosopher Émile Cartier and dress designer Jeanne Lanvin all owned mansions in Le Vésinet. Free spirits also found the town to their liking. One Englishwoman had a stairway installed leading directly from the back door of her villa to her bedroom so that her lovers, who usually worked at menial jobs, could bound up the stairs to her boudoir without using the front door which, considering their station in life, would have been inappropriate.

Josephine called Le Beau-Chêne her "shanty." At the same time she poured her vast energy into converting it from a somber, inadequately lit rich-man's dwelling into a cheerful country retreat which, in every way, reflected the unique character of its owner.

There was no overall decorating plan, but the mixture was undeniably charming. A Louis XIV room, swimming in gilt; an East Indian room, complete with temple bells; little salons, big salons, a billiard room, a studio for Josephine to practice her singing and dancing. All these came together to make a home that was both luxurious and warm. Dozens of life-size portraits of Josephine dominated the walls of the first and second floors, her compelling eyes blazing out from every turn and landing.

The enclosed sunporch, one of the most handsome rooms in the house, painted robin's-egg blue, served as Pepito's office, where he spent long days poring over the business aspects of Josephine's career and filing her clippings.

She devoted special care to her own bathroom, a place in which she was free to bask in the splendor of her own body. The walls were a solid bank of mirrors. The bathtub, coated in silver reflecting metal, enabled her to see herself from every angle while she bathed. Josephine was a body narcissist rather than a face narcissist. She never considered herself a beautiful woman, but she knew her body was one in a million. This was "dirty Josephine," who the girls at Lincoln School in St. Louis had teased because she always looked so grimy. Now she spent hours on end performing her ablutions, pampering the instrument of her success.

Josephine shopped for antiques on the rue Royale and in the Gobelin district. She bought an enormous bed from the Directoire period, which Pepito tried to convince the press had once belonged to Marie Antoinette, and a suit of fifteenth-century armor for the foyer.

Josephine made provisions for the animals she had already had and those she planned to acquire. She oversaw construction of henhouses and rabbit hutches alongside the greenhouse; a metal filigree aviary was built into one of the ridges of the villa and filled with exotic birds—parrots, macaws, cockatiels, and cockatoos. Monkey cages, stacked one atop another, cluttered the room next to the master bedroom. Soon the estate came alive with ducks, chickens, geese, pheasants and turkeys. Sometimes they joined in an earsplitting zoological chorus. Josephine joked to friends, "I so love the quiet of the country."

Chiquita, who enjoyed his position as most favored animal at Le Beau-Chêne, passed his time eating the ducks that scuttled about the artificial ponds on the property. For treats, Josephine fed him live pigeons she brought home from the Casino show.

Under Josephine's supervision, her three gardeners arranged red and yellow coleus plants across the front lawn to form JOSEPHINE BAKER in giant letters.

In the greenhouse Josephine raised orchids, while behind her villa she realized a long-cherished dream: to have a vegetable garden, which she tended daily, bringing fresh onions, potatoes, cabbage and black-eyed peas to the table. Her garden was as healthy as any kitchen patch down in Dixie.

Josephine loved gardening so much that even though she was proud of her satin-textured hands and delighted in filing and buffing her nails before painting them gold or scarlet red, she would then go out in her garden and knead the rich dark earth, letting the soil cake under her fingernails.

At the far end of the front lawn, more than a quarter mile from the house, partially obscured by the bushes and oak trees, Josephine created her Temple of Love, a semicircle of marble Corinthian columns decorated with statues of Diana, Venus and Circe, women whose bodies Josephine felt complemented her own. The columns surrounded a large pool filled with goldfish and water lilies. The bath was made of marble, like the fountain, and here Josephine would relax on warm afternoons.

The blackberry bushes beside the Temple of Love did not completely obstruct the view from people passing along the street; neighbors occasionally paused to glimpse the bucolic scene. René Sandaran, a resident of Le Vésinet, who dropped by one day to request a contribution from Josephine for a charity event given by the local sporting club, found it somewhat disconcerting to carry on a conversation with the famous

Josephine at Les Halles. *AGIP*

Josephine Baker as she paddled nude amidst her water lilies. He later recalled, "She was adorable."

Josephine was often talked about in the village, but never as an object of ridicule or moral reproach. On the contrary, she was considered a charming addition to the town, and was particularly beloved by the small shopkeepers. Like a good French housewife, she walked to market every day, usually with one of her Russian wolfhounds on a leash.

She enjoyed gossiping with the store owners, asking them about their families and chatting about personalities in the town. In true French fashion, she haggled over prices. One of these merchants, Madame Henriette Levoisier, owned a small company that supplied coal to the village. Whenever Josephine went into the store, remembering the bitter winters when she was forced to steal coal from the freight cars as a child, she asked Madame Levoisier for the names of those families in the village who could not pay their fuel bills. Josephine would then settle the overdue accounts. And at Christmastime she always made sure that the poor families received double their usual supply to tide them through the winter. Now in her nineties and living in a nursing home, Madame Levoisier still vividly remembers Josephine's continuing concern for the unfortunate. "She was generosity itself."

In the marketplace, not far from Madame Levoisier's store, was the lighting fixture establishment of George Guignery, with whom Josephine became friends when she commissioned him to rewire Le Beau-Chêne. She had hired the department store Galeries Lafayette to do the lighting in the house, but she did not find their ideas theatrical enough. So she asked Guignery to remove their lighting and start from scratch.

Guignery, enchanted with Josephine, drew upon all his technical skills in order to fulfill her fantasies. He installed giant spotlights to accent the Grecian statues surrounding her Temple of Love. He built a grid of white bulbs across the front lawn to illuminate the horticultural sign of Josephine Baker, and strung small lights around the cylindrical aviary on the north side of the villa.

At night, Le Beau-Chêne glowed like a little patch of the Tivoli Gardens while the birds in the aviary made a charming cacophony. "I think she imitated her birds when she sang," says Guignery's wife Hélène, "because she sounded just like one of them." Perhaps the parrot that sang "J'ai Deux Amours."

Josephine distributed cards with a map of Le Vésinet printed on them and an arrow pointing to Le Beau-Chêne, inviting friends and strangers to drop by her villa. The house was nearly always filled with interior designers, writers, couturiers, choreographers, directors, secretaries, musicians and chorus girls from the Casino de Paris, as well as a host of luminaries including Jean Cocteau; Cécile Sorel, the doyenne, or oldest leading lady at the Comédie Française; and dress designer Elsa Schiaparelli. Even Bricktop and Frisco dropped by occasionally.

"Josephine had to have been here before as a queen or something," says Bricktop. "She traipsed around her château just

Josephine posing on the running board of one of her luxury cars, a promotion present from the manufacturer. She endorsed cocktails, bathing suits, lipstick and Bakerfix. *Agence France-Presse*

like she always lived that way. I think she thought she was Napoleon's Josephine."

Visitors to Le Beau-Chêne saw a different woman from the Casino de Paris star. At home Josephine wore simple skirts, white blouses with Peter Pan collars, and canvas sandals. Without eye makeup and Bakerfix, she looked like a teenager. Sometimes she dismissed the servants and cooked for the guests herself, serving soul food and homemade beer, which she had learned to make in St. Louis.

Italian dramatist Luigi Pirandello, who had caused such a stir in intellectual circles with his play *Six Characters in Search of an Author,* became a regular at Le Vésinet. Pirandello told Josephine that he needed to study her closely because he planned to write a play about her, but the play never materialized. In time, like so many in the revolving cast at Le Beau-Chêne, he drifted off.

During this period torch singer Libby Holman arrived in Paris to see Josephine. She was traveling with her fiancé Zachary Smith Reynolds, son of tobacco king Richard Joshua Reynolds. After Libby married Smith, she was accused of murdering him, thus becoming a central figure in one of the most sensational trials of the 1930s.

A dashing bisexual with a dark olive complexion, a legacy of her Sephardic ancestry, Holman was a fixture in Harlem nightclubs, drawn to the milieu by a fascination for blacks. She prowled the ginmills of Lenox Avenue and Broadway restaurants dressed in a man's suit and a bowler hat. Enormously appealing, she found lovers worthy of her passions—among them Jeanne Eagels, Tallulah Bankhead and, later, Montgomery Clift. According to Holman's biographer Milt Machlin, Josephine's name belongs on this celebrated roster.

The two women met during the opening days of *La Revue Nègre.* Though they did not spend much time together, Holman developed a deep personal identification with Josephine. A few years later, she decided that she wanted to portray Josephine in a stage role.

Though enormously successful as a torch singer (Brooks Atkinson described her voice as a "dark purple flame"), she always thought of herself as a dramatic actress. Holman decided that Josephine's life story would provide an excellent vehicle for her to triumph on the stage. Before arriving in Paris, Holman visited London and hired Noel Pierce to write the play, which was to be called *Dusk.*

Josephine was a gracious hostess to Libby Holman and Smith Reynolds, even traveling with them to Deauville where gendarmes arrested Holman on the beach for wearing a skimpy bathing suit. Unfortunately for Holman, *Dusk* failed to generate enthusiasm from backers.

When Duke Ellington came to Paris to play at the Salle Pleyel, Josephine dispatched her Rolls Royce to bring him to Le Beau-Chêne. He was beguiled by her warmth and simplicity. Ellington felt immediately at home with Josephine's "honest-to-goodness hospitality" as she "heaped goodies on me as though I were really somebody."

Another side of Josephine's domestic life was less attractive. "She could be very bossy with her employees," says Hélène Guignery, "even cruel sometimes, especially if she thought they were fooling around, not doing their jobs."

Fortunately Pepito was emotionally equipped to live with the many changes in Josephine's personality. She alternated between periods of cool serenity and fits of hot temperament that came over her like a summer squall. She could be working in her garden or sitting on the oriental rug in the living room playing quietly with her dogs, when the slightest irritation—a wrong word spoken or a disturbing gesture—set her off. "She was always in a crisis," says Josette Reboux, a servant. "I never knew what started them. Sometimes there would be one per day; other times two per day or only one per week. Sometimes a crisis would last a week. They were like seizures that took hold of her." Josephine was high-strung and was always ready to fight at a moment's notice.

At Le Beau-Chêne, under Pepito's devoted aegis, Josephine worked with tutors on her singing, dancing and acting. She wanted to do everything well, but she was flighty. If left to her own devices, she would not and could not submit to the discipline necessary to excel at anything. She liked to stay up late and was abnormally restless, eager to leap over all obstacles to get what she wanted.

When fame touches the young, it may bless them and curse them at the same time, for those who are celebrated often lack the grit to go back and begin an apprenticeship in a profession. Yet Josephine was making progress with her singing. Between 1931 and 1935 she cut over a dozen records, including "J'ai Deux Amours," "La Petite Tonkinoise," "Suppose!" "Love Is a Dreamer," "Si J'étais Blanche (If I Were White)," "Ram-Pam-

Pam," "Sans Amour" and "You're Driving Me Crazy." "J'ai Deux Amours" alone sold over 300,000 copies.

Pepito was practical-minded. He understood what one must do to get from here to there. At his urging Josephine began to take ballet lessons. As always, Pepito enlisted the best teacher he could find, in this case George Balanchine. He brought Josephine to the point where she became sufficiently proficient to dance a ballet number in *La Joie de Paris,* the Casino de Paris revue of 1931. But the daily rigor of specific ballet routines was alien to Josephine. She, who liked to walk barefoot, found toeshoes confining.

Determined, Pepito forced her to adhere to a schedule. When they traveled he saw to it that she practiced forty-five minutes each day on an improvised *barre* made of the backs of a row of chairs. If Josephine rebelled, he locked her in her room.

It is not surprising that Pepito alternately adored and despised this creature of his imagination. He loved her three times over; as his woman, as his creation and as his child. He was enthralled by Josephine's total self-centeredness and her ability to enslave people by her charm. Once she had ensnared someone into her orbit, she had to dominate them. While Pepito exercised his power managing her career, supervising her daily activities and regulating the household, Josephine was in control. Although he was an intelligent, imaginative and, by turns, merciless businessman, Pepito lacked a commanding center. Creating Josephine was his self-assigned role in life.

Without Josephine he was nothing and he knew it. Her energy and ambition were unlike that of anyone Pepito had ever known. She had been his springboard from a degrading life to that of a theatrical impresario.

Josephine realized that her accomplishments were largely the result of Pepito's tutelage, and her dependence on him and his approval of her ran deep. But while Pepito existed for Josephine, she existed for the world.

She needed Pepito to reassure her constantly that his fantasy woman—the woman he had turned her into—would continue to enthrall the crowds.

Josephine not only supported Pepito but delivered her enormous earnings over to him. Having grown up in a household where her mother supported her stepfather, and having lived in a neighborhood where prostitutes gave their earnings to pimps, she accepted it as part of the natural scheme of things that a woman works for her man.

Josephine's disposition was not suited to thinking through financial problems. She lacked a sense of money, and whenever she had any it was gone. "I can remember walking along the street with Josephine," says Hélène Guignery, "and if she saw a beggar, she opened her purse and handed him money without looking to see how much she gave him."

But Josephine's problems ran deeper than that. She barely knew how to add and subtract. One can only imagine what she must have felt when presented with a contract, phrased in tautological legalisms and involving intricate financial splits.

So Josephine and Pepito played out a *pas-de-deux* of their interlocking dependencies. Although she could be despotic with him, shunting him into the background when it suited her purpose, he would always see her as a willful child, his protégé, his creation. When Josephine went into a tantrum—smashing whatever came to hand—Pepito had only to talk about business and she would become soft and malleable.

Gradually, despite her reliance on Pepito, Josephine began to withdraw from him emotionally. She was outgrowing the need to have Pepito for a mentor. Now she saw him more and more as a policeman keeping her under surveillance.

Pepito was becoming increasingly irritable about Josephine's spending sprees and, in particular, the large amounts of money she would lavish on her wardrobe.

Clothes had happy associations for Josephine. They reminded her of the afternoons she had spent playing dress-up in her grandmother's outfits, and how her grandmother praised her and said how pretty she looked. Josephine linked clothes with love; buying things covered a hollow.

Tensions came to a head over a minor incident. Josephine bought a hat at Maggie Rouff. Pepito told her to return it because it was too expensive. Josephine went back to Maggie Rouff and charged ten hats. Pepito locked her out of the house and did not let her in until the next morning.

As such quarrels became more frequent, Josephine and

Pepito stayed in their own corners, wary of each other.

Then, too, Pepito was seventeen years older than Josephine and not of a particularly strong physical constitution. Josephine, for her part, needed constant release of her excess energy.

She was ready for a man her own age, and she did not have to look far. A chorus boy at the Casino de Paris caught her eye. His name was René Victor Eugène Ducos, but he would soon be known on the Paris kiosks as Jacques Pills of Pills and Tabet, a highly successful singing duo in France during the 1930s and 1940s.

Handsome and elegant, Jacques Pills possessed a natural refinement and was loaded with talent. He was the same age as Josephine, twenty-seven. He had a wonderful smile and, like Pepito, the winning ways of a con artist.

Jacques was the son of an officer who had been stationed in a small town in Les Landes, a region in southwestern France. As a youth he studied pharmacy, but the prospect of spending his life as a Madame Bovary cohort in a provincial village drugstore did not appeal to him. Rejecting the assured status of a routinely dull but comfortable life, Jacques signed on at the Casino de Paris, where he was hired by Varna for *Paris Qui Remue*.

To Josephine he was a charming adolescent, evoking all her warm, maternal feelings of tenderness and protection. With Pills, Josephine had the opportunity to have a protégé as she had been one to Pepito.

From the beginning Josephine could see that Pills was not interested in marrying her. He had great affection for her, but in the presence of a woman so adorable and despotic, he was faintly afraid. Yet Pills was an opportunist, and Josephine could open many doors for him. She was a stepping-stone in his career.

At the same time Josephine was trying to come to terms with her feelings about motherhood. As she advanced into her late twenties, her yearning to be a mother became an obsession. She wanted to have a baby more than anything in the world—more than anything, that is, except relinquishing her stardom. How could she reconcile these two goals?

Josephine began to reach out to motherless children in an effort to fill this gap in her life. Through George Guignery, a second-generation resident of Le Vésinet whose roots in the community ran deep, Josephine became involved with the St. Charles orphanage several blocks from her house. Started by the village of Le Vésinet after the Franco-Prussian War, St. Charles was originally a home for children of soldiers killed in Alsace-Lorraine.

Each year Le Vésinet sponsored a benefit called "Les Gosses à la Mer," "The Kids to the Sea," similar to the Fresh Air Funds for disadvantaged children in the United States.

Josephine worked as a committee member for the 1931 "Gosses à la Mer" benefit. She donated clothes, furs, jewelry, antiques and knickknacks from Le Beau-Chêne to be auctioned off.

Not long after the bazaar, Josephine announced to the "directrice" that she would be godmother to each and every child in the orphanage, which meant she would undertake partial responsibility for about fifty children.

Josephine had swings and slides installed in the garden of Le Beau-Chêne for the orphans who, when they came to visit, were also free to play with the animals. The monkeys fascinated the children, who delighted in chasing them around the house. They skimmed up the curtains and settled on the ornate pelmets, chattering with rage or fear, their droppings striping the blue satin with brown while the children shrieked with pleasure.

For the holiday season Josephine decorated a giant tree in the hall of the villa. On Christmas Eve she gave a party in which she presented each child from St. Charles with a present.

Josephine reveled in her role as Lady Bountiful to the orphans. Because there were so many of them, she did not have the responsibility of a one-to-one relationship. "Josephine was a wonderful playmate to the children of St. Charles," says Hélène Guignery. "But she never disciplined them. If a child did something she didn't like, she told one of the servants to speak to him."

Josephine loved her orphans as she loved her animals. The love of small creatures represented pure love, unalloyed with the jealousy, mutual blaming and exploitation she found in adult relationships. A young child—and the younger the better—could not singe her with insults or nag at her the way Pepito did.

Josephine's longing to be a mother filled her life and left people confused. Jacques Dubarry, a pediatrician now in his sixties, remembers when he was a young intern studying in Bordeaux and Josephine came to town for a benefit performance. He was puzzled by the split in Josephine: a woman with a bubbling, carefree air, heavily charged with sexuality and abandon, yet also hungering to take on the nurturing role of motherhood.

Josephine had come to Bordeaux to help raise money for the children's wing of the Hospital of St. André, where Jacques Dubarry was completing his internship. After the show Dubarry and several friends, all medical students, invited Josephine—to her delight—to spend a few hours carousing with them. Before she left the theatre, she rang up Pepito in Paris to report on her performance, adding that she was just about to turn in for the night.

Josephine joined the interns in the back room of a café in the student quarter. "We all drank a lot, including Josephine," says Dubarry. "She was in great form. At the end of the meal, in the midst of the empty bottles on the table, she sang us her repertoire, accompanied by one of the students who played the piano."

After Josephine finished singing Vincent Scotto's "La Tonkinoise," the students sang a pornographic version back to her. "Oh, how filthy!" she said, letting out a robust laugh. With her strong memory, Josephine quickly picked up the words. *"Veux-tu baiser en levrette . . . sur le plumard . . ."*

The evening ended with Josephine giving everyone a Charleston lesson. "What an unforgettable experience when you are twenty-five years old," says Jacques Dubarry, "to have Josephine Baker dance with you."

The next day, when Dubarry and his comrades showed up at Josephine's hotel, they found her somewhat morose. She wanted to go to the nursery of the Hospital of St. André to see the newborn babies before returning to Paris.

A young nun in charge of the baby ward walked with Josephine down the long rows of white cribs. Josephine turned from bed to bed, patting one child, kissing another, picking some of them up and feeling their bottoms to see if they were wet. Suddenly she turned to the nun and in a voice that filled the nursery said, "I can't have a baby!"

After the interns saw Josephine off on the train back to Paris, they speculated about the possible medical reasons for her dilemma. Had she had a hysterectomy? Did she have a venereal disease? Perhaps she had inherited syphilis?

Whether there was something gynecologically wrong with Josephine has never been clear. During her fertile years she suffered from severe menstrual cramps, sometimes so painful that she could not move. This is unusual for women who are physically active. Her pregnancy at age thirteen was terminated by either a miscarriage or an abortion; back-alley "scrapes," or "biting the bitter apple" as they called it in St. Louis, often resulted in a botched job, permanently injuring the patient's reproductive organs.

Yet Josephine would serve as godmother to hundreds of babies. In fact, if an opportunity arose, Josephine did not wait for an invitation but volunteered for the job.

One evening the director of the Pernod liquor company came backstage with Bernard Tamisier, whose wife Henriette had gone into labor that day. Introducing Tamisier, Josephine's friend said, "This man's wife is in the process of making a baby."

"And me," answered Josephine, "I'll be the godmother."

When word came the next day that the baby was a boy, Josephine went to the hospital and told the astonished Tamisiers, "The baby must be called Richard after my brother Richard who lives in St. Louis. I love him very much."

Dumfounded, the Tamisiers said, *"D'accord!"*

Josephine later wrote a note to Henriette Tamisier saying how much she loved children and how she suffered because she could not have a baby. "It isn't anything physical," wrote Josephine. "It's because God doesn't want me to have a child."

Henriette Tamisier worked as a teacher in a small village

outside Paris. It was decided that the baptism would be held in the village church. Josephine invited Jacques Pills to be her escort at the christening, hurting Pepito even further.

Noticing the poverty of the country priest as she talked with him before the christening, his wan face and shabby clothes, Josephine whispered to Henriette Tamisier, "I'm sure he isn't eating." Whereupon Josephine gave the priest money not only for food but for a new cassock and surplice as well.

Josephine was not just a titular godmother to Richard Tamisier. On Sunday afternoons, with Richard in diapers, the Tamisiers came to visit Josephine in her dressing room at the Casino de Paris. Josephine played with Richard between acts; once, while holding Richard on her lap, he wet through his diapers onto Josephine's long red satin dress. Instead of changing, Josephine walked on stage to sing "J'ai Deux Amours." Before she began, she called the audience's attention to the stain on her dress, announcing with pride, "My son did this."

Despite overpowering maternal instincts, Josephine never had a child. Why? For one thing, Josephine was frightened of what pregnancy would do to her body, the major instrument of her success. It might leave stretch marks, varicose veins and ripples of flab where once there had been nothing but taut satin skin. Like a professional athlete at her prime, she felt that her body would be marketable for just so many years.

"She talked about having a baby a lot," says Marcel Sauvage. "So I finally said, 'Josie, if you don't want to have a baby with Pepito, then just pick out some good guy and get on with it.'"

"'No,' she said. 'I can't have a baby now. Maybe later on when nobody wants to look at me. Everything is in my legs.'"

So much of Josephine's approval from men came either because she was a sexual object, as Simenon had treated her, or because she could make a lot of money for a man, as she had done for Pepito. If she had a baby and lost her exotic appeal, who is to say the man would not leave her?

The public can be very cruel with their sex queens, often trying prematurely to write them off as too old for the job. Josephine began to face this problem before she was out of her twenties.

In the spring of 1931 Paris held "L'Exposition Coloniale," a splendid extravaganza spread out on the great lawn of the Champs de Mars and across the Seine on to the Trocadéro. Natives from Guinea, Chad, Morocco and Dahomey, from the islands of Guadeloupe and Martinique, and as far away as Cambodia and Laos strolled the streets of Paris day and night, enthralling the fashion-obsessed Parisians with the splendid colors of their costumes.

The Colonial Exhibition Committee elected Josephine "Queen of the Colonies," a title that carried considerable honor. Josephine was ecstatic, for she felt she had truly been adopted by France. But when the committee's choice was announced in the papers, the news was greeted by a cyclone of protest. France's President Gaston Doumergue, Minister of the Colonies Paul Reynaud, and the General Commander of the Exposition, Henri Olivier, all received letters of complaint, to wit: Josephine was a product of Harlem, scarcely a French overseas possession. She did not speak proper French or any of the native African dialects. What's more, she had taken the curls out of her hair and oiled it as smooth as a Caucasian. On that issue *The New York World-Telegram* ran the headline, QUEEN, WHERE IS YO' KINK? Finally, the objection that hurt her most was that she was too old for the job. Her critics argued that Africans marry young, often at twelve or thirteen. "Therefore, an African woman of Josephine's age would be a grandmother."

"I'm twenty-seven and why should I be ashamed of it?" Josephine replied. "I look young and I feel young. That's all that matters."

Despite her crowing, Josephine feared she was passée. She worried constantly that her triumphs were flukes. The same year as the Colonial Exposition, a Danish journalist, Joergen Bast, cabled his newspaper the *Berlingske Tidende:* "She's a little girl with two big eyes and when she stands in front of the footlights, you can see that she is already getting crow's feet. These are the eyes of a deer. They get afraid and they get hard. It's like she's on a slave auction block trying to find out how much she's worth."

Though Josephine would repeatedly go through periods

when her confidence as a woman and as a performer was shaken, her phenomenal courage was a trait that grew steadily stronger as she matured. Her sangfroid in a crisis was controlled and measured. On September 12, 1931, Josephine was traveling the Orient Express from Budapest to Paris when a TNT bomb exploded on the track as the train crossed a viaduct a few miles west of Budapest. The blast was said to have been set off by Communist terrorists demanding better conditions for railroad workers.

The locomotive and nine cars crashed into a ravine to a depth of more than 100 feet. Twenty people were killed outright, over one hundred seriously injured. As the panicked passengers in Josephine's car sat frozen with fear, she rose to her feet and calmed them by singing, "J'ai deux amours, mon pays et Paris. Par eux toujours, mon coeur est ravi."

THIRTEEN

"She was a master of mob psychology. It was as if she said to herself, 'I've taken these suckers this far, I may as well take them all the way.'"

—Ben Carruthers, writer

At the end of September 1933, as soon as Josephine's engagement at the Casino de Paris came to an end, she departed for England to play in a revue that consisted of loosely patched together numbers from her Casino performance. Pepito reasoned that an eighteen month tour of England and the Continent would produce an enormous amount of revenue, capitalize on fresh audiences and, not least important, separate Josephine from Jacques Pills.

Before leaving Paris, Josephine had the sad duty of committing Chiquita to the Jardin d'Acclimatation, a small zoo located in the Bois de Boulogne. Chiquita had grown from a spirited cuddly pup to a horny adolescent. He became temperamental, felt fenced in. He did not know any other leopards and so his sexual interests took aberrant forms. He craved silk stockings. He licked and clawed at women's legs trying to get at the mesh.

One night Chiquita escaped over the wrought-iron fence at Le Beau-Chêne and crawled through an open window into the bedroom of a wizened dowager who lacked a sense of adventure. *"Mon Dieu. Quels cris!"*

The *voiture cellulaire,* the paddywagon, arrived in a panoply of sirens. Josephine did her utmost to charm the policemen,

187

promising to keep Chiquita under closer surveillance, but the leopard's fate was sealed.

Sometimes when she drove through the Bois, Josephine stopped off to visit Chiquita imprisoned in his fake jungle habitat at the zoo. But as time passed, her visits became fewer and fewer. If anyone inquired after Chiquita, she lowered her eyes and explained, "He died."

Josephine's first stop on the tour was London, and it was also her first performance in the British Isles. She played at the Prince Edward Theatre in October 1933, a scant eight years after her Paris debut. And yet, to Londoners, she was a period piece: Josephine Baker of the 1920s, the dancing toy of the Negro vogue in Paris.

The British had their "Roaring Twenties," but as with most things British, conservatism cast its pall over the primal urges of Flaming Youth. When the shimmy hit London in 1921, introduced by Mae Murray, it was condemned as vulgar. Chorus girls were warned by a Harley Street specialist that "girls who sacrifice their nerves and beauty to the shimmy will be claimed by old age."

In 1926, when Florence Mills and the Blackbirds played at the Palladium, the Charleston stunned the audience. The Reverend E. W. Rogers, Vicar of St. Alden's, Bristol, warned, "Any lover of the beautiful will die rather than be associated with it. . . . It is neurotic! It is rotten! It stinks!"

Josephine was determined to show the British that she was not just a passing fancy from another decade. At the same time, she wanted to win them over. To do this she modified her dancing. The savage number, thus tamed, became merely ugly, and she never recovered from her bad start.

Accustomed to the elaborate sets of the Casino and the Folies, Josephine felt handicapped by the scanty makeshift props her company transported from city to city. The revue cried out for the froufrou of the Paris music hall.

After reading the so-so reviews following her first performance, Josephine received a small group of reporters in her bedroom as she breakfasted on orange juice and Danish pastry. "What is this about the lukewarm reception? Why, I never remember having received so much applause before. In Paris, even when they like you they don't bother to applaud. By comparison, last night's reception seemed marvelous to me. Of course, I realize that the performance left a good deal to be desired. Through no fault of mine, the show was ragged, and we set at once to put it together."

To help salvage the revue, Josephine poured more energy into the rehearsals, transmitting her vigorous spirit to the company.

Josephine was able to fall instantly to sleep at any time of the day or night and to wake up at will. Plagued with nightmares and insomnia, she could not sleep a full night through, so perhaps this trait was nature's way of compensating for normal sleep. Suddenly, in the middle of a rehearsal or any other activity, she would fling herself down on a bed or a couch or a chair, close her eyes and go immediately to sleep. Twenty minutes later, exactly, she would awake refreshed.

Despite lackluster reviews, the show came out ahead, grossing $15,000 the first week, $13,000 the second and $11,000 for the remaining two weeks.

Josephine next toured the Continent from the bleak outposts of Finland to the Acropolis. She was immediately popular in Athens and Cairo. Mussolini, considered a racial fanatic, banned her from ever playing in Italy. He then inexplicably relented, whereupon the entire royal family turned out to applaud her in Rome.

As with her first tour, Josephine's reception in a country depended pretty much on how the citizens felt about blacks. Once again, the Scandinavians loved her. When she stepped off the airplane in Copenhagen in July, holding one of her monkeys and wearing a full-length leopard coat, bouquets of flowers came at her from every side. Said Copenhagen's leading daily, the *Berlingske Tidende*: "What has she got, this Josephine? We have our own Marguerite Viby who sings better. We have our Royal Ballet who dances better, and Armstrong is bigger than she is, but Josephine comes and conquers everyone. Last night Tivoli's concert hall was boiling. Josephine Baker was better last night than she has ever been before. She is the most fantastic show lady that has ever been seen here."

On Josephine's return to Paris, Albert Willemetz, director of the Bouffes Parisiens Theatre troupe, invited her to star in *La Créole,* an Offenbach operetta he planned to revive for the 1934 season.

"Does Monsieur Offenbach want me for the part?" asked Josephine.

Offenbach, whom Rossini called "The Mozart of the Champs-Elysées," had been dead since 1890, but Willemetz felt that one of his operettas, full of melodic delights, frivolity and verve, was ideally suited to Josephine's flamboyant temperament. The light, innocent melodies of *La Créole,* composed in 1875, a quarter-century before Josephine was born, were just the right vehicle for her aura of sensuous naïveté and her high, airy, half childlike, half thrushlike voice.

Since *La Créole* was not considered one of Offenbach's best operettas, Willemetz and his partner George Delance reworked the libretto to insure its success and to tailor the role to Josephine. They borrowed words and songs from Offenbach's other works, added a children's corps de ballet, and generally pumped life into the outmoded work.

Josephine was delighted with the character. She told one interviewer, "I intend to *be* a Créole, just like the *other* Josephine, Napoleon's wife."

Ironically, there was a strange association of bad luck attached to Offenbach's name; so much so, that when opera people spoke of him they crossed themselves. Yet, for Josephine, being cast in his operetta represented one of the luckiest breaks in her career.

The show was booked into the Théâtre de Marigny, off the Champs-Elysées, where Offenbach had launched his troupe in 1855. Josephine was thrilled at the idea of appearing in an actual theatre, not in a music hall. "I took a role. I carried the role in a play."

During rehearsals Sacha Guitry, the French actor and playwright, often dropped by to watch Josephine rehearse. He helped her with her acting, showing her how to fully realize the character of "La Créole." It was an enormous boost to Josephine's ego to have an authentic actor take an interest in her for professional reasons. "He knew that I was a comedian and not a colored frog. . . . He, more than anyone, helped me to understand the performer's craft. Act on stage the way you do in real life; keep the theatre constantly in mind when you're not performing and forget about the critics."

La Créole opened on December 15, 1934. Most of the critics gave Josephine high marks for her performance. *Variety* said: "The revival of Offenbach's 'Créole,' starring Josephine Baker, finally consecrates Miss Baker as a full-fledged French headliner. Opening day of the show cinched its success, and all credit is being given to the star, not to the operetta."

Vanity Fair was also complimentary, saying of Josephine: "With the chameleon-like quality of her race she has managed to take on the artistic coloring of both sides of the Atlantic and remain herself. In her eager climb from colored chorus girl to Parisian leading lady she has learned how to sing, move, act, and dance classically in the best Boulevard tradition."

Josephine's unbridled enthusiasm for the part and her ability to grasp the lighthearted spirit of *La Créole* enabled her to make the transition from ostrich plumes to farthingale without an awkward moment. "It was a happy time," she said. "I wore costumes which reminded me of the long dresses with trains and the leg-of-mutton sleeves I had borrowed from my grandmother when I played dress-up. I could laugh in this role, sing, prattle, make faces, dance, cry like a bird, howl, at my pleasure."

During the run of *La Créole*, Pepito negotiated with film producer Arys Nissotti for a movie specifically tailored to Josephine's personality and multifarious talents. *ZOUZOU* was the result, a frothy musical about a laundress who becomes a Parisian music hall "vedette"; the film costarred the great French actor Jean Gabin.

One of the bonds between Josephine and Pepito was that they both entertained outlandish fantasies about how to keep Josephine in the public eye. Nowhere was this more apparent than in the promotional buildup for *ZOUZOU*.

Pepito hyped the film with an urgency and desperation he had never shown before, out of fear that he might lose Josephine. She was his investment; he did not want to leave her and start from scratch.

Yet, despite this display, Pepito was not himself. He did not look well and his energy was low. What neither Josephine nor Pepito knew at the time was that he had cancer of the kidneys, which was slowly eroding his body.

Two designers, Jeanne Beauvois and Marcel Rochas, each named dresses for Josephine—"La Créole" and *"ZOUZOU."* A Josephine Baker shoe, brown lizard skin, was mass-produced and marketed in Paris and the provinces. Bakerfix was still going strong; in addition, Josephine lent her name to a cosmetics line. These products, sold in Great Britain as well as France, were designed to transform the porcelain-skinned British and the ruddier complected French into tawny sirens.

But it was with bananas that Pepito showed his master stroke. Stickers, like today's Chiquita labels, were printed with the message, "Josephine Baker is *ZOUZOU."* Troops of lackeys were dispatched to fruit merchants all over the city in an effort to persuade them to create imposing hills of bananas in front of their stores all bearing the label. He paid doctors to submit articles to the Paris papers endorsing the nutritional aspects of bananas. For the premiere he even tried to get movie house owners to dress their ushers in banana skins, but no one took up that idea.

An English publicist, James V. Bryson, helped Pepito put out the *ZOUZOU* newsletter for distribution to movie theatres in England and France. Bryson apparently liked the job. "Not since the 'Hunchback of Notre Dame,' when I left for America to exploit Victor Hugo and Lon Chaney, have I had such an opportunity as I have today," he wrote.

While Josephine's career was going well, her private life was not. Jacques Pills was now a name in Paris and no longer needed Josephine to give him a boost. He stopped calling her, and he went out of his way to avoid her. If one is to get ahead in life, one has to act alone, not be a leaner. And there was no democracy in a love relationship with Josephine. If you offered your hand to her, she would take your arm and the rest.

As much as Josephine talked about love, she could only give so much of herself. Her self-absorption gave her a power, and she needed to ration that energy for her stage performances.

So Josephine and Pills went their separate ways, each involved with their own work, with their pride and their ambition. But since they moved in the same circles, there was never a definite break.

Ironically, although Josephine got over Pills, he could not forget her. Years later he walked into her dressing room in a theatre in Rio de Janeiro and said, "If you don't marry me, I'm going to marry someone else."

"Who?" asked Josephine, nonplussed by his belated proposal.

"Edith Piaf."

And so he did. And they lived unhappily ever after—for a while. Piaf's capacity for pulling men into her maelstrom and then weakening them by the sheer force of her emotional needs was at least the equal of Josephine's.

However, in the early 1930s, when Pills jilted *her*, Josephine was deeply hurt. It was alien for her to play the deserted woman. She had no shoulder to cry on. Pepito was much too tormented by her infidelity, not by the fact she had slept with someone else—he was well aware of her track record—but that she had fallen in love with the person. Bricktop and Josephine now moved in their own spheres, and Josephine's other women friends hero-worshiped her so, it was impossible to let them know she had been kicked in the teeth.

Josephine's reaction, as always, was to hide her feelings in public and proceed with the glittering parade, putting herself on display, adding to the legend of "La Bakaire." About this time she persuaded one of her admirers, the Maharajah of Kapurthala, to stage a luncheon for her at the Ritz Hotel. She had never set foot in the Ritz, a white American stronghold on alien land.

For Josephine, this was a momentous occasion. Having traveled around the United States as a teenager, with its rigid color line in hotels, to be received at a hotel like the Ritz would represent a victory. She was determined to carry it off with style and dignity.

Located on one of the most beautiful squares in the world, la Place Vendôme, the Ritz was originally the Hotel de Gramont, built in 1705 for Anne de Gramont who, according to Saint-Simon, was "an old trollop" and a kleptomaniac to boot.

If any hotel represented luxury in Paris, the Ritz was it. Five hundred employees were on call for two hundred guests.

Those who were fussy about servants could bring their own; sixty servants' rooms were set aside for this purpose.

Josephine could not have picked a more appropriate sponsor for her debut at the Ritz than the Maharajah of Kapurthala. He was a slender, cultivated man in his sixties, clean shaven except for a moustache. His most striking feature was the red-hot gaze in his eyes. He resembled a Medici. In full regalia he was quite a sight. He owned the world's largest topaz, four inches of amber fire worn as a belt buckle. He also owned an ornament for his turban made of three thousand diamonds and pearls.

The Maharajah had one of the few houses in the Bois de Boulogne and traveled regularly between Paris and Kapurthala, a small kingdom in northern India bordering on the Himalayas.

He had his own army, concubines by the dozens, and a private jungle in which elephants, tigers and leopards roamed. He was a splendid anachronism as well as a good sport.

Though the picture of confidence in maturity, a troubled youth had caused the Maharajah to be a voracious eater. He weighed 270 pounds in his teens, most of which was fat lumped around his middle. One story about his adolescence circulated in Paris, embellished no doubt in the retelling, concerned the difficulty he had in copulating due to his excess weight. Despite the best efforts of inventive courtesans, the Maharajah could not give much satisfaction. Finally, an elephant trainer in the Maharajah's employ came up with a unique solution: a bed with a ramp to allow the female reclining on her back to more easily support the Maharajah's great weight. The prince and his retinue found relief at last. The Maharajah eventually slimmed down and earned a reputation on the Continent and in the East as a competent lover.

Josephine was an elegant success at the Ritz. She wore a tailored black dress, a colossal silver fox fur and a close-fitting turban decorated with flowers. The gathering included André de Fouquières, a Parisian Beau Nast, and a collection of actresses and minor nobility.

The Maharajah of Kapurthala concluded that, like royalty, she was a presence. "One must be born a princess to know how to act like one," he told her, "but you are the exception that proves the rule."

The luncheon went over without a flaw. When Josephine returned a few weeks later to take tea with the Duchesse de Rohan, there was no flurry or comment.

Josephine's forays into society received as much attention in the American press as any of her artistic achievements, which may account, at least partially, for Irving Berlin's wonderful song about her: "I've Got Harlem on My Mind." It was sung by Ethel Waters in the 1933 smash hit musical *As Thousands Cheer*. The song begins:

> *I go to dinner with a French marquee*
> *Every evening after the show.*
> *My lips are saying "Mon Cheri"*
> *But my heart is singing heigh-di-ho.*

Josephine did indeed have Harlem on her mind. She was homesick, not just for Lenox Avenue, the Cotton Club and Small's Paradise, but also for the rest of New York. "I've longed to go back, if only for just one evening, to walk along Broadway and look at the lights."

While the people of France opened their hearts to Josephine and made her one of their own stars, the fact remained that she was still an American. And despite the raw deal her country had given her, her roots were in America. For too long she had been cut off from these.

Pepito pushed for an American tour. Jake and Lee Shubert offered Josephine a contract to appear in the 1936 version of the Ziegfeld Follies, for which the Shuberts had already assembled an impressive array of talent: Vincent Minnelli was doing the costumes, George Balanchine creating the ballets, Ira Gershwin and Vernon Duke composing the words and music, and Fanny Brice and Bob Hope were leading the cast.

Josephine realized that working with such a celebrated entourage could only enhance her comeback. But the Shuberts were regarded as somewhat sleazy. Lee Shubert subscribed to an old Willie Hammerstein adage: "The best seats in a theatre for a producer are seats with asses in them." And the Shuberts' productions were geared to that philosophy. The Brothers Shubert had started producing plays as far back as 1901. They enjoyed considerable success by supplying the lowest common denominator to popular musical theatre, first with Americanized operettas, then with inanely plotted musical comedies, and finally with tacky revues.

A few days before she left for America, Josephine made her first public political statement in support of Benito Mussolini.

Frustrated by the British and French who controlled the Mediterranean, this "Sawdust Caesar" was determined to restore Italian grandeur. "A virile people," he said, "have a right to empire." In the fall of 1935, his troops invaded Ethiopia, a country rich in raw materials but with an impoverished population and medieval political and economic institutions, including slavery.

Josephine told a surprised group of reporters at Le Beau-Chêne: "I am ready to travel around the world to convince my brothers that Mussolini is their friend. If need be, I will recruit a Negro army to help Italy." Then she added, "Haile Selassie is an enemy of the people. He maintains slavery, which Mussolini is determined to stamp out."

Josephine was infatuated with Mussolini. She had been introduced to him when she performed in Italy two years before, and she felt their short encounter somehow gave her a link with his destiny.

Il Duce was a swaggering braggadocio who, like Josephine, had spent much of his life on stage. "The crowd loves a strong man," he would say, "the crowd is like a woman." Just as his adoring followers had confused appearance with reality, so too had Josephine. She had been seduced by his superficial intelligence and his extraordinary ability to ride the emotional wave of the day.

Black American newspapers had given heavy coverage to Mussolini's Ethiopian adventure and were absolutely aghast at Josephine's stand. The Italians indeed "freed the slaves," but as their campaign bogged down, Il Duce's troops sprayed mustard gas on the Ethiopian defenders.

Haile Selassie, the Lion of Judah, was an idol to many Americans of color. They perceived him as the courageous David pitted against the fascist Goliath. The attack on the tiny kingdom of Ethiopia moved the Negro communities in the United States as no other foreign event ever had before. Ad hoc committees were formed to raise money and gather medical supplies for the African nation. Years later Emperor Haile Selassie said: "We can never forget the help Ethiopia received from Negro Americans during the terrible crisis. . . . It moved me to know that Americans of African descent did not abandon their embattled brothers, but stood by us."

Josephine ultimately paid a high price for hero worship as Mussolini's dreams turned to ashes. But these regrets would come in the future.

The day before she sailed, Josephine presided over a book signing of *Une Vie de Toutes Les Couleurs* at Flumerton's Bookstore near l'Opéra. This was her third autobiography, written in collaboration with French journalist André Rivollet.

Josephine played the "femme de lettres" to the hilt, as in a somber-checked tailored suit and matching hat she greeted a hundred or so of her admirers. She was the very picture of the composed author.

But when a friend, standing in line to have her autograph a book, asked Josephine how she felt about going back to America, Josephine dropped her professional mask and looked wide-eyed and vulnerable. "I'm so excited," she said. "I'm all puffed up like a frog. Pepito's heard that New York is a wonderful place, all new and friendly. But I'm afraid I'll feel like a stranger. I don't know what will happen."

On the morning of her departure, Josephine felt sad at leaving Le Vésinet. She knew this trip represented a turning point in her life. Her beautifully groomed Pekinese sat on her bed as Josephine packed the last things in her Vuitton luggage. In the driveway she bade farewell to the staff and took a final glance at her garden, her flowers and her pets.

Pepito had booked them on the *Normandie*, which had just completed its maiden voyage. The liner was not only the longest and fastest, but was the most luxurious and glamorous ship ever built. At Le Havre the police let her park her Bugatti on the pier; when she walked up the gangplank the captain himself gave her a bouquet of flowers.

As the *Normandie* swept toward America, Josephine could not wait to arrive in New York. She chatted endlessly with Pepito, who had notified the newspapers and wire services; still Josephine wondered if they would come to see her. From Europe it was hard to gauge how well known she was in the United States.

Coming into the harbor, the Statue of Liberty evoked memories of her departure in 1925. She remembered how lacking in self-confidence she was then and how eager she had been to escape the shame of her childhood.

While the ship was docking, Josephine looked down at the people on the wharf and was shocked to see so many black faces, until she realized they were maids and porters. Josephine also saw a cluster of about thirty reporters calling up to her. "What do you think of Joe Louis? Do you consider him more important than Einstein?" "Do you know the president of France?" "Are you going to see Roosevelt?"

After the press conference and the crush of customs, Josephine and Pepito took a cab to the Hotel St. Moritz, which seemed to be just the right place. Facing Central Park South, the St. Moritz was famous for its continental atmosphere and its Café de la Paix, a sidewalk restaurant so reminiscent of Paris.

The manager stood at the front desk and greeted them cordially. He indicated to a bellhop to take their bags upstairs, where Pepito had reserved a large suite for Josephine and a smaller one for himself. The manager then turned to Josephine and said, "Here at the St. Moritz, we have many guests from Southern states and we cannot afford to alienate them. You can stay here, but you are going to have to stay out of the lobby. The service entrance is in the back."

Josephine knew she had come home.

FOURTEEN

"The Legend has come home."

—*The New York Times*

For Josephine, returning to New York meant a confrontation with her fantasies. She yearned to be a star in her native land, to make a hit on Broadway and then go on to Hollywood and become the first black woman to shatter the movie color line. She dreamed of playing leads not only in musical comedies but in romantic roles.

It had been ten years plus one month since Josephine left America. Could people forget the slipjointed kid dressed like a pickaninny from *Shuffle Along,* and would they accept her as a sophisticated continental woman, an intimate of the great?

To cover her insecurities, Josephine played the grande dame before the rabble. Wisely, instead of making an issue of how she had to use the back door of the St. Moritz, she made use of her luxurious suite to greet the world, flanked by her two Pekinese, a confused bustle of maids and Pepito, ever the debonair Roman "count."

To build herself up, she treated Pepito like a lackey in front of the press. *"Vite! Vite! Pepito. Cherchez les sandwiches pour tout le monde."* Her attitude inspired all sorts of quips in the newspapers about how she led him around on a leash with her dogs. "Josephine didn't like anybody who was good to her," says Bricktop. "She would always put that person down."

199

One reporter, anxious to clarify certain stories about Josephine, came away resigned to the fact that it is better not to let daylight in on magic. "Of the Josephine Baker legend you can believe what you want to believe. You have to, because if you ask questions she smiles very pleasantly and—very courteously (and shrewdly, too)—leaves the legend to itself, which is how a legend grows."

While rehearsing for the Ziegfeld Follies, Josephine enjoyed New York. She went to the premiere of *Porgy and Bess,* which she loved. "London would be mad about it," she told Lucius Beebe, "and I'd like tremendously to sing the feminine lead part there myself."

And then came the incident with Beatrice Lillie (Lady Peel in private life).

After *Porgy and Bess,* Josephine attended an extravagant party given by the publisher Conde Nast for George Gershwin. Beatrice Lillie, an enormously popular comedienne at the height of her career, was also there.

Bea Lillie swept in and, as usual, was surrounded by a mob of adoring friends and sycophants. Then Josephine breezed through the doorway, stepped out of her white mink coat and let it drop to the floor. A butler ran over and picked it up. Forgetting Bea Lillie for the moment, everyone turned to gaze at the most recent dazzling arrival.

Josephine was wearing a buttercup-yellow satin gown, slit in front to the waist, and white lilies in her hair.

"Who dat?" Lady Peel said.

Josephine's calculated metamorphosis into an international cosmopolite did not always produce the proper effect, such as the evening Larry Hart of Rodgers and Hart invited her to a dinner party. Josephine, sensitive about her poor English, decided to speak French. Since many of the guests spoke French and the menu was in French, Josephine slipped into her favorite role, the great French lady *bien élevée.*

Unfortunately, Larry Hart's maid, Mary Campbell, was a black spitfire who did not put up with any guff from her employer or his friends. So when Josephine asked her, *"Donnez-moi une tasse de café, s'il vous plaît,"* Mary's humor turned foul. She yanked the plates off the table and returned to slap a cup of coffee under Josephine's face.

"*Merci*," caroled Josephine, somewhat startled.

"Honey," Mary bellowed, "you is full of shit. Talk the way yo' mouth was born."

Before the Follies opened, Josephine traveled to Chicago where she saw her second husband, Willie Baker, and made arrangements to divorce him. Willie, working as a waiter, was rather pathetically quoted as saying, "I'll take her back if she'll have me."

Josephine also traveled to St. Louis to see her family for the first time since 1921, when she had brought Willie Baker home to meet them. They were impressed with the changes in Josephine: "She was classy," says her brother Richard. "More high-strung, but very happy."

While she was away there had been three deaths in the family. Grandmother McDonald, who adored her and was the only one of the clan to recognize Josephine's unique qualities, died in her sleep shortly after Josephine left for Paris. And then little Willie Mae, so pretty despite her missing eye, bled to death. The third was her stepfather, Arthur Martin.

In 1934, the year before Josephine's return to the United States, Arthur's life ended under peculiar circumstances. Since the time Josephine left St. Louis, he had worked sporadically at odd jobs but could not keep any position for long. The deep depressions and fits of temper that had plagued him for years became more intense. Finally he became so out of control that Josephine's mother, Carrie, was forced to have him admitted to the municipal mental hospital in St. Louis. Several years later, a policeman knocked on Carrie's door and said, "Your husband is dead. He broke the glass in the window in his cell and he ate it."

Josephine's real father, Eddie Carson, was still alive and in good health. With the onset of the Depression, a number of the nightclubs in the Chestnut Valley district had closed down so he was no longer able to work full time as a drummer. Yet he had found a civil service job with the city government, and played in his spare time with the Pythian's Society band.

When Josephine first went to Paris, Eddie tried to keep up

with her through a musician he knew at the Folies-Bergère. Never forgetting that Eddie abandoned her when she was a baby, Josephine had mixed feelings about keeping in touch, although she did send him a publicity photograph of herself inscribed "To my Father."

During her St. Louis visit, which lasted only five days, Josephine took Carrie house-hunting in the best colored neighborhood in St. Louis. They found a white stone house that pleased Carrie. But when Josephine offered to pay $20,000 in cash, Carrie backed off. "When you come back, we'll talk about it," she said.

"It was hard for Mama to realize that somebody could have that much money," Richard explains.

The Ziegfeld Follies opened at the Winter Garden Theatre on April 20, 1936. All of the principals in the show received smashing reviews—except Josephine. Fannie Brice, Bob Hope, Judy Canova and Eve Arden simply dazzled the reviewers, while they had a field day trouncing Josephine. Brooks Atkinson in *The New York Times* commented coldly, "Miss Baker has refined her art until there is nothing left of it." *The New York Post* dismissed her "dwarf-like voice eclipsed in the cavernous Winter Garden." Ira Wolfert of *The American* called her singing "curious." Her voice reminded him of "a cracked bell with a padded clapper," yet he went on to say, "Still I like it. I'm fond of Chinese music." *Time* magazine was savage:

Josephine Baker is a St. Louis washer-woman's daughter who stepped out of a Negro burlesque show into a life of adulation and luxury in Paris during the booming 1920's. In sex appeal to jaded Europeans of the jazz-loving type, a Negro wench always has a head start. The particular tawny hue of tall and stringy Josephine Baker's bare skin stirred French pulses. But to Manhattan theatre-goers last week she was just a slightly buck-toothed young Negro woman whose figure might be matched in any night club show, and whose dancing and singing might be topped practically anywhere outside of Paris.

Josephine could not very well blame her flop on the show's creative cast; so Josephine turned on Pepito, making him the scapegoat for her failure. If Pepito had negotiated a better contract, she reasoned, she would have received top billing and the Shuberts would have been forced to treat her like a star. She ignored the fact that it was Pepito who hired a claque to applaud wildly whenever she came on stage, prompting Walter Winchell to comment, "Critics aren't fooled by noise."

Never one to wallow passively in defeat, Josephine rented Barbara Hutton's former residence at 125 East Fifty-fourth Street and converted it into a cabaret geared to the "silk stocking" district. Here, in her own nightclub, Josephine thumbed her nose at the color line by having two white male dancers nibble her ankles and kiss her neck as she ran through her repertoire of French melodies.

Josephine then hired Alice Delano Weekes, who jumped at the chance to appear as a hootchy-kootchy dancer. Weekes was President Roosevelt's cousin and the daughter of John A. Weekes, head of The New-York Historical Society and a governor of the Union Club. *Variety* tagged her "a blue-blooded hip twister." Josephine paired Alice with "Truckin'," her Harlem doorman in a Zouave uniform who had a yen to get into show business.

Crushed by Josephine's continuing attacks, Pepito finally abandoned her and sailed back to France, resolving to make a new life for himself. But there the weakness and physical exhaustion he had felt in New York became worse. A doctor's examination confirmed that he had cancer of the kidneys. He died several months later, alone in an apartment he was renting off the Champs-Elysées. To the end he was consumed with the idea of saving Josephine from her own excesses, most especially her irresponsibility regarding money. He left everything he owned to Josephine, telling a friend, "She's going to need it."

Pepito's death freed Josephine. Because he had been so controlling, she never felt completely in charge. Yet, at the same time, she was left rudderless. Together they had formed a private world; he represented one of the very few people who had known her with all her defenses down.

As much as Josephine was capable of loving anyone, she had

loved Pepito. She would never again find a man so totally in her corner. Years later she had his remains removed from a crypt in Neuilly to the small graveyard on the grounds of her château in the Dordogne, where she buried him next to her mother. In her final years, although she remarried twice after his death, she kept his framed photo on the desk in her office. If anyone inquired, she would say, "He made me."

In the meantime, Josephine, in New York, was determined to straighten out her own affairs. Her contract with the Shuberts ran till September, but she wanted out and so did they.

The next development in her career came as a surprise. Paul Derval, her old boss from the Folies-Bergère, sailed to New York specifically to convince Josephine that she should star in his 1937 revue. A Colonial Exposition was planned for that year, and with tourists flooding to Paris, Josephine would be right back in the spotlight.

They talked terms in Josephine's dressing room at the Winter Garden, amid posh surroundings that gave no indication she had bombed in New York. Walls and ceilings were draped with a rich sky-blue satin. Underfoot was an ermine rug, while on her dressing table, skirted with an exquisite white lace, was a fresh arrangement of lilies of the valley.

"As I began to talk about the contract," recalled Derval, "I sat down in a white satin chair, whereupon Josephine began to scream at the top of her lungs. I assumed that she was just getting worked up for her usual outrageous salary demands. I kept talking and she continued to yell. As it turned out, she was having a fit because I was sitting on top of her Chihuahua, a fluff ball in ribbons who was sleeping in the chair."

Josephine threw him out. "A gentleman never sits down in the presence of a lady until she invites him to do so. Pepito taught me that."

Pepito also taught Josephine how to seize the moment to jack up the price on a deal. Instead of accepting the 40,000 franc advance Derval proposed, she said she would take no less than 42,500. "That will cover the veterinarian's bill."

Josephine returned to Paris a lonely woman. Left to her own devices, her featherbrained proclivities got the upper hand. In addition to performing at the Folies-Bergère, she opened a new Chez Joséphine at a nightclub called Le Frontenac off the

Champs-Elysées, where she spent long nights raising Cain with the tourists who had flocked to Paris for the Colonial Exposition.

During this frenzied period Josephine turned for affection to Frederic Rey, the star nude dancer at the Folies. A twenty-two-year-old Austrian with silver-blond hair and a body of virile perfection, Frederic, née Franz, had started out as a protégé of Mistinguett. As a plucky youth of seventeen living in Vienna, he presented himself to her backstage at the Ronach Theatre where she was performing. "I am crazy about the music hall," he said, pleading, "take me with you."

Never one to leave a good body alone, Mistinguett invited

1936. Josephine gives a street concert in Paris. *Keystone*

him to journey with her to Paris, where she would help find him work.

Unwilling to wait around for Rey to obtain a visa, Mistinguett sequestered her Adonis in a wicker basket stuffed with plumes. As the story goes, he did not look up until the Eiffel Tower came into view. Delirious with joy, Rey cried, *"Bonjour, la Tour."*

Five years later, partnered with Josephine in nude love scenes at the Folies, they developed more than a professional relationship and were soon sleeping together. Love was never mentioned. Josephine simply wanted to ease her lonely nights. "If she needed a certain man around, then she felt she had to go to bed with him," says Rey, who is now in his late sixties and still dancing in Paris music halls.

In amour, Rey found Josephine to be more a gymnast than a sensualist: "It was like making love to a boy. She was not soft and cuddly. She was in charge, in the driver's seat. She decided what to do and how to do it."

After they ceased being intimate, they remained close. Josephine adored Rey and treasured their friendship until her death. Josephine had a knack for turning swains into loyal allies. This was perhaps because she did not take coitus too seriously. More important, she never talked about the performance of her lovers.

While her affair with Frederic represented a passing adventure to Josephine, the next man in her life aroused a deep passion. Probably even Josephine did not realize how hard she could fall or how hurt she could be.

His name was Jean Lion. They met in the spring of 1937 at the Pavillion Dauphine in the Bois de Boulogne, where they had both dropped in for tea after horseback riding in the park.

"It was *coup de foudre*, love at first sight," says Albert Ribac, who introduced them. Ribac was one of Lion's business partners and an acquaintance of Josephine.

Jean Lion was a golden boy. Tall, blond and athletic, with roguish eyes and the easy confidence of a born charmer, he was the sort of man who is almost too good-looking. If he had not been so ambitious and successful, he could have been just another boulevard dandy. "Jean was the toast of Paris," recalls his old friend Jacqueline Stone. "Every mother wanted him for her daughter—and for herself."

Josephine with her horse, Tomato, in the Bois de Boulogne. *AGIP*

Jean represented many things that Josephine had missed in Pepito. He was only twenty-seven, four years younger than she, and not inclined to be domineering, or so it seemed to Josephine. Pepito had taken business much too seriously to ever let himself go. Josephine was ready for someone gay, charming and handsome. Jean Lion appeared to be the answer.

Whereas Pepito looked somewhat dissolute, with the pallor of the nightclub, Jean Lion was a vigorous sportsman, an early riser. "Josephine loved to watch him ride," says a friend of Lion's. "It was stirring for her to watch a sexual man atop such a sensuous animal."

Jean was a change-of-life baby, the adored and pampered "afterthought" of bourgeois Jewish parents from the small village of Crèvecoeur-le-Grand, located about 100 kilometers northwest of Paris. His mother loved him in a totally uncritical way, treating him like a young prince who deserved the very best. Such boundless maternal love endowed him with what F. Scott Fitzgerald called a "heightened sensitivity to the prom-

Multimillionaire sugar broker Jean Lion taught Josephine to fly and even proposed to her up in the air.

ises of life." Like Gatsby, Jean Lion believed in the green light.

A precocious talent for business enabled him to become a member of the Paris bourse, the French stock exchange, by age eighteen. And at twenty-seven, he was already a millionaire several times over. As the president of Jean Lion and Company, he bought and sold sugar on the world market. "Josephine had a lot of money on her own," says Bricktop, "but this guy was rich as all outdoors."

Josephine set out to win Jean, strategically plotting ways to monopolize his time. Her life remained as chaotic as ever, reaching the point where her career itself was at stake.

Out of the blue, Paul Derval received a doctor's certificate stating that Josephine was taking a leave of absence due to illness and had left Paris for a rest. Furious, Derval hired a replacement. Several days later Josephine called him from Vendée on the western coast of France.

"What are you doing there?" asked Derval.

"I'm hunting with Jean. I shot a fox and I'm going to give the pelt to Madame Derval!"

Jean regarded Josephine as a plaything—but not completely. He respected her because she was self-made, and he felt her fame and great popularity in France would serve to advance his career. Jean toyed with the idea of entering politics and figured that Josephine's extraordinary popularity with the French people would be a tremendous asset. He thought in terms of the French Senate or possibly becoming the mayor of Paris.

Jean was crazy about flying and, while wooing or being wooed by Josephine, he gave her lessons; she actually got her pilot's license. In a gesture that characterized his derring-do, he proposed to her up in the air.

The next day Jean breezed into his office on Avenue Emmanuel III and greeted his two partners, Albert Ribac and Maurice Sallioux, with the question: "What would you say if I told you that I was going to marry Josephine?"

"Why would you want to do that?" asked Albert Ribac. "You are already sleeping with her."

"I think it would be crazy to marry her," Maurice Sallioux said. "She's an actress, she's colored, and she's older than you are."

Anxious to give his friend time to reflect on such a big step, Albert Ribac suggested: "As a farewell to your bachelorhood, why don't we sail around the world? Why not enjoy the women of Singapore and Saigon while you're still free?"

Jean did not tell Josephine about his world trip. Instead, he postponed the date of the wedding, explaining to her that he had to spend several months in his New York office. Since Josephine was committed to play out her run at the Folies-Bergère, there was no possibility of her joining him.

Before leaving Paris Jean wrote Josephine several love letters, carefully dating them one week apart to cover the period when he was supposed to be in New York. Then he wrapped the letters in a package and sent them to a business associate in New York, who mailed one each week to Josephine.

The secret trip became a great joke with Jean's friends. The canard, of course, was at Josephine's expense. Though fortunately she never found out about it, she was aware that she could not trust him.

"She was in love with him to the point of craziness," says

Jacqueline Stone, a friend of Jean Lion's. "She had to have that man, and she was willing to do anything to get him."

Their madcap courtship culminated in a festive—and unusual—fall wedding. Though Jean Lion's parents vigorously objected to him marrying a Negro ("They almost died," says Bricktop), the family agreed to let the ceremony take place in their village, Crèvecoeur-le-Grand.

The entire village was invited to the ceremony, and most of them came. Josephine arrived at city hall for the ceremony dressed in a black hat and a full-length sable coat. Standing on the steps of the building, she made a little speech to the crowd that was touching in its simplicity. "Haven't we all got a heart? Haven't we all got the same ideas about happiness? Please tell me. Isn't it the same for every woman? Isn't it love?"

Jammy Schmidt, mayor of Crèvecoeur-le-Grand, spoke next, obviously delighted to be in the spotlight. "Heretofore, the prominence of our village has been confined to a fifteenth-century château and our famous black chicken hatcheries. Now it will be known as the place La Belle Baker chose for her wedding." Schmidt then read from the Napoleonic Code on marriage, rolling out the words with a guttural flair. The wedding was punctuated by unusual fanfare as local firemen sounded trumpets and a group of hunters fired shotguns into the air.

The newlyweds set up housekeeping in an apartment on the rue de la Trémoille off the Champs-Elysées, though Josephine held on to Le Beau-Chêne in Le Vésinet, just in case things did not work out. Houses represented security to her in a way that men never could.

Although Jean's family finally succumbed to her charm and his mother even spent long weekends at Le Vésinet, Josephine's marriage did not give her the comfort she craved. She felt that she was on trial—and she was. No matter what Josephine was to the world, Jean Lion expected to be the star in their marriage. After all, he was a Frenchman.

Jean wanted a *maîtresse de maison*, a job for which Josephine was totally ill equipped. He looked to her to supervise his wardrobe, wind his watch, fill his fountain pen, and to plan meals and seat people properly at dinner parties. A simple chore such as writing thank-you notes became a nightmare for

Josephine; she could not spell in French much less compose a proper letter.

Josephine continued to dance at her cabaret, which meant that she and Lion were operating on different schedules. "I used to return home from my club at five in the morning," said Josephine. "One hour later Jean was on his way to the factory. I slept until late in the afternoon. I dined early before going on to my club, and often Jean had not come back from his office. Two people could not go on like that and expect to stay together."

Josephine promised to retire, and she even went on a goodbye tour of the Côte d'Azur and North Africa. But showmanship was in her blood, and she simply could not turn her back on the stage. One evening, to Lion's horror, she danced nude, painted head to toe in gold, at a dinner party given by Mrs. Reginald Fellowes at her mansion in Neuilly.

Daisy Fellowes was immensely rich, heiress to the Singer Sewing Machine fortune. In heartfelt credit to the company that

Josephine in racing silks takes the lead against French jockey Semblat in a 1937 exhibition match at Tremblay on the outskirts of Paris. *Keystone*

underwrote her lavish lifestyle, she was known to cross herself every time she saw the Singer trademark.

Josephine's behavior baffled and hurt Jean. Not only would she not "dwindle into a wife," she wanted to dominate every situation. Lion confided to a friend, "If she doesn't get her way, she screams."

Josephine was in deep conflict. She loved Jean. And she loved the idea of a husband. She valued the credibility that marriage gives a woman, the certitude, the feeling of having a place in society. But in marrying Jean she came face-to-face with her fantasies about abandoning the stage and leading a normal life.

Josephine had been responsible for her own survival for too long to place her destiny in someone else's hands and mold herself to a new image. As Simone de Beauvoir said, "To catch a husband is an art, to keep him a job." The only job that Josephine knew was that of performer.

Josephine and Jean were trying to make an impression in two different worlds. Josephine valued the raffish nightclub crowd that applauded her exhibitionism. She did not feel alive unless she was on display. "If she received two people she had to show up as a star," says Jacqueline Stone. "She even had to perform in front of her animals."

Jean was keenly aware of social nuances. He wanted to be accepted in French society. Coming from a middle-class Jewish family, an *arriviste,* with no university education, he skirted the circle that mattered to him. Since he lacked the normal prerequisites for a place in a power elite, he was determined to attain his goal through money and style.

The disparity in their ambitions showed itself clearly at Maxim's, Jean Lion's favorite restaurant. To this day Maxim's is the most elegant, exclusive and celebrated in France. The burnished brass and mirrored walls, the red-plush banquettes and vintage wines, give it an air of sumptuous perfection, just the tone Lion wanted to convey to his business associates.

Jean Cocteau called Maxim's "a theater where a new show opens every night, where every woman plays the part of her life." Josephine saw her role as prima donna, stage center in the Grande Salle rather than sitting unnoticed in one of the private dining rooms upstairs that Jean Lion preferred. The electricity in the air was too much for her. She table-hopped, talked too loud and waved to acquaintances across the room. One night the maître d' condescendingly addressed Jean as Mr. Baker. The incident triggered one of their bloodiest rows.

While Jean carried his possessions out of Le Vésinet, Josephine stood in the driveway crying, "I'll kill myself." Then she pleaded, "Please don't leave me. I promise I'll change."

There were more fights, truces, fiery reunions. Each time Josephine lost ground.

Josephine had been so starved for love in her formative years that no single man could fill her needs. She required the adoration of no less than twenty million Frenchmen. In a moment of candor, she told a startled reporter, "Marriage is only good for one thing, and that's having babies." Not long after that extraordinary statement, Josephine discovered she was pregnant. She began to knit bibs and booties, just as she had done back in St. Louis when, at thirteen, she learned she was pregnant the first time.

But Josephine suffered an early miscarriage. Once again the baby clothes disappeared, and not long after that she discovered that Lion was having an affair with an American woman who was married to a French aristocrat. The Lions separated.

Crushed by Jean's rejection and dreading the thought of being alone once more, Josephine rushed into an affair with Claude Meunier, a millionaire whose fortune came from his family's chocolate company.

Like many theatrical people, Josephine had trouble differentiating between manufactured emotions and her true emotions. She wanted to know the intoxication of love, the joys of motherhood, of tears and laughter, but most of all she did not want to be bored. She felt the pain of a failed marriage and a lost baby, but she lacked the capacity to be introspective.

In the spring of 1938, Claude Meunier took Josephine for a vacation in the Dordogne valley, a region in south-central France known for its richly forested hillsides, spectacular rock formations, prehistoric cave paintings and—perhaps most fondly—for its truffles and foie gras.

Near the town of Sarlat, in the hamlet of Milande, Josephine looked up an acquaintance, the ship's physician from the *Nor-*

Les Milandes, Josephine's fifteenth-century chateau in the fertile Dordogne Valley. It was here that she achieved her dream of a "village of the world"—gathering children of different races, religions and nationalities; raising them together to show that mutual understanding between different peoples was not a utopian fantasy. *H. Roger-Viollet*

mandie whom she had met in 1935. He owned a charming fifteenth-century castle called Les Milandes.

The doctor gave Josephine and Meunier a tour of the château, explaining that he was trying to rent it because his American wife preferred to live in the United States. Enchanted by Les Milandes, which had fifty rooms surrounded by hundreds of acres of rolling land, Josephine decided to rent it on the spot. Since it had no heat or electricity, she decided not to occupy it right away.

The winter of 1938 was exceptionally bleak. Sitting in a Montparnasse cinema, Josephine was moved to tears by a film showing poverty and malnutrition in the slums of Paris. The next day she hired a truck, filled it with coal, tripe, pigs' feet, potatoes, bread and toys, and had her chauffeur drive through the tenements as she stood in back heaving the contents to the amazed and grateful residents. One friend later questioned her motives: "It was like throwing bread before chickens," he says. "She liked to see people grovel before her."

Josephine and Maurice Chevalier christen elephants at the Cirque d'Hiver. *AGIP*

On November 9, 1938, in Germany, during a night of horror, synagogues, Jewish homes and shops went up in flames. Men, women and children were shot and clubbed to death while trying to escape.

"The Night of the Broken Glass" radicalized Josephine, who remembered the stormtroopers hurling ammonia bombs at her and shouting "Go back to Africa" when she had performed in Germany and Eastern Europe in the late 1920s. She decided to join the International League Against Racism and Anti-Semitism.

In 1939 Hitler crushed Poland and Europe was at war. The fall and winter of 1939 were known in France as "La Drôle de Guerre," the Phony War, as Hitler's army made no move to attack the Maginot Line. The French, for their part, showed little appetite for leaving their cellars and bunkers to attack the Germans.

Nor were there any air attacks, only leaflet droppings. Artillery barrages were light, infrequent, and did little damage.

The same month the Allies declared war against Germany, September 1939, Josephine opened in *Paris-Londres*, a Casino show in which she was given equal billing with Maurice Chevalier.

Josephine drove herself mercilessly during the day. She reported to work at the Red Cross relief center on rue de Châteaudun, an ancient alley full of bums in the shadow of l'Eglise de la Trinité. She did everything from comforting homeless families to helping prepare the pot-au-feu for the hungry. On her day off she flew supplies for the Red Cross into Belgium. She wrote hundreds of letters to soldiers at the front and, at Christmas, sent 1500 presents to them, each with an autographed photo of herself.

Josephine performed with Maurice Chevalier for the French troops posted along the German frontier. Most of the applause went to Josephine, which enraged Chevalier. With his jealousy aroused, he refused to treat Josephine as a legitimate artist. "She just gets up there and wiggles her rear end," he told the press.

Though driven to the point of exhaustion with work, Josephine could not forget Jean Lion. When "La Drôle de Guerre" started up, he had enlisted in the army as a pilot. While stationed on the German frontier, he received a serious concussion in a jeep accident. Josephine obtained permission to go to the front and visit him daily for two weeks in the hospital. It was then that she realized she could not win him back. "I can't believe it. I've lost him forever," she told Albert Ribac, who had accompanied her. Two years later they were divorced. The judge who presided over the case said: "Here are two people who never had a chance to get to know each other."

In the late spring of 1940, shortly before the German assault through Belgium to Paris, the fever of war was everywhere.

One afternoon George Guignery, driving his car along the road from Le Vésinet to Paris, spotted Josephine walking. He stopped to offer her a lift but she declined, explaining that she preferred to hike the 25 kilometers. "I must see how long it will take me by foot," explained Josephine. "When the Germans take over Paris, we won't be able to get gas anymore. I must be able to get to town on my own in order to be able to look after the sick."

Josephine's ardent patriotism came to the attention of an ambitious young officer in Le Deuxième Bureau, the French military secret police. Jacques Abtey was an attractive man in his early thirties. Of Alsatian origin, he had the sandy blond hair and blue eyes associated with that region.

Abtey's job was to recruit people to work undercover for the Allies. Daniel Marouani, a theatrical manager who had joined the Deuxième Bureau, urged him to enlist Josephine. *"C'est une femme courageuse!"*

Knowing Josephine's reputation as *"une grande amoureuse,"* Abtey had reservations about recruiting her for such work. He was reminded of Mata Hari, the Eurasian double agent who, like Josephine, made her first public entry into Paris as a professional dancer. Poor Mata ended up before a firing squad of French soldiers in the Paris suburb of Vincennes, crying courageously, *"Vive l'Allemagne,"* as they riddled her with bullets.

Doubtful about Josephine's qualifications, Abtey nevertheless visited her at Le Vésinet, coming away with a quite different impression. He was bowled over by the sheer force of her patriotism.

"France has made me what I am," Josephine told Abtey. "Wasn't I the darling of the Parisians? They have given me everything, especially their hearts. Now, I will give them mine. Captain, I am ready to give my life for France. You can make use of me as you will."

Because of her stand on Mussolini five years before, Josephine was a welcome guest at the Italian embassy. Knowing this, Abtey asked Josephine to use her connections to discover as much as she could about the imminent entrance of Italy into the war. Within a week Josephine produced some extremely useful information.

Abtey was persuaded that Josephine would bring to her work the same extraordinary drive and enthusiasm that had underscored her theatrical career. And so Josephine went to war.

FIFTEEN

The last time I saw Paris
Her heart was young and gay
No matter how they change her
I'll remember her that way.

—Jerome Kern and
Oscar Hammerstein II

As the Germans advanced toward Paris, Parisians fled en masse. According to police estimates, only 700,000 inhabitants—out of five million—were left in the city by June 13. Josephine and Abtey agreed to meet at Les Milandes, 521 kilometers to the south.

Josephine joined the exodus of panic-stricken persons fleeing the capital. She drove her Packard, taking her maid, Paulette, two Belgian refugees, and three of her dogs. Knowing that gasoline would be impossible to obtain en route, the gas she had hoarded had been stored in champagne bottles.

They inched along Route Nationale No. 20 toward the Dordogne and Les Milandes, part of a seemingly endless caravan of vehicles. In autos, on foot, on bicycles, a frightened and leaderless swarm of citizenry struggled south, their pitiful belongings hanging from motorcycle racks and baby carts.

Shortly after dawn on June 13, Hitler's jubilant troops, led by the 9th Division, entered Paris without a shot being fired. The French leadership, such as it was, decided not to fight in the streets and risk all that was priceless and irreplaceable in the capital.

Josephine's beloved city was in the clutch of the Germans, who unfurled the swastika over the Arc de Triomphe and goose-stepped down the Champs-Elysées. Four long years would pass before Josephine would set eyes on La Ville Lumière once again.

Josephine was part of a small select group of the truly brave. When she joined the Resistance in 1940, it scarcely existed except in the propaganda of the British and the Free French. Most of the population of France was simply too stunned by defeat to think of resisting.

But after a slack period marking the entrance of the Nazis into the capital, the city stirred again. By July 15, only a month later, 65 percent of the commercial enterprises were back in business. The fashion houses continued to have openings. The cafés were filled. Many of the restaurant menus, printed in German, displayed cards saying "forbidden to Jews." The cinemas and music halls opened their doors, although the Sarah Bernhardt Theatre was debaptized because Sarah was Jewish. Said one German official: "You certainly have a gay air for the conquered."

Josephine's early commitment to defending France is particularly noteworthy in view of the large numbers of French performers, artists and intellectuals who marched through the antechambers of the collaboration.

"Vive la paix honteuse!" cried Jean Cocteau as he joined the Nazis sipping Dom Perignon at Maxim's. Actor, dramatist, producer Sacha Guitry, whose spellbinding plays delighted the French before the war, fell into easy friendships with the Germans. He was even reported to have dined with Hermann Göring. Tino Rossi, Jean-Louis Barrault, Fernandel and Danielle Darrieux all accepted scripts that had been carefully censored by German authorities.

Two Nazi favorites were Josephine's comrades and rivals from the music hall—Mistinguett and Maurice Chevalier. "La Miss" made a triumphant comeback at the Casino de Paris, rising from the ashes of the Third Republic to wow the Germans with "the most famous legs in the world." Chevalier also continued to perform, singing his songs and telling his old jokes over German-controlled Radio Paris. *"Ça sent si bon, Paris,"* he crooned. "Oh, how good Paris smells."

A very real part of Josephine's patriotism was prompted by revenge, for German regulations forbade the appearance of Negro and Jewish entertainers in the cabarets, music halls and theatres of Paris.

Josephine spent an anxious summer at Les Milandes with Jacques Abtey, hiding members of the Free French on their way south while all the time worrying that Nazi sympathizers, disguised as refugees, would betray her.

Abtey was married, with a family, and even today he remains discreet when speaking of their relationship. But to those who saw them together, it was obvious that he worshiped her.

At night they hovered around a rickety radio as the announcer spoke of two zones, one occupied by the Nazis, the other free.

Eighty-four-year-old Marshal Pétain was running unoccupied France. This legendary hero of World War I, aided by a handful of defeated generals, had jettisoned the Third Republic and replaced it with a fascist dictatorship similar in many respects to that of Hitler's Reich.

The dim voice of the BBC could also be picked up. And here from time to time an obscure general named Charles de Gaulle, until recently a mere colonel, addressed the French people in a passionate voice, urging them to resist. From the beginning Josephine was a confirmed Gaullist, and she never wavered in her support of "le Grand Charles."

Word came from Free French headquarters in London that Josephine and Abtey should make their way to Lisbon, Portugal—neutral territory—and from there establish contact with London. As a camouflage, Josephine was told to line up performing engagements and have Abtey travel as her secretary.

Josephine left Les Milandes in the care of the villagers whose tiny hamlet bears the same name. Fearing the Germans would confiscate her priceless paintings, crystal and flatware, the villagers removed Josephine's possessions from the château and kept them for her until after the war.

In Marseille, Josephine and Abtey met Captain Paillole, their Riviera contact, who delivered the disheartening news that their visas would be held up for three weeks by the consulate in Portugal. Lamented Josephine, "They sure aren't passing them out like Métro tickets."

Undaunted, Josephine phoned an admirer, who was also the ambassador of Brazil, and requested transit visas through Spain and Portugal on the pretext that she and Abtey were heading for Rio de Janeiro. To protect Abtey, who might be suspect traveling as a free agent, Josephine arranged to have his papers stamped "Accompanist to Josephine Baker." A most courageous gesture.

Josephine's popularity was so strong in Europe that her appearance in Lisbon merited front-page coverage. The articles intimated that she was "well preserved," which Josephine did not find amusing. "It's terrible to grow old," she said.

Lisbon was the social and political capital of England's historic ally, governed by a right-wing oligarchy jealously guarding its precious and profitable neutrality. Awash with double-dealing, rumor, malice and deceit at every level of government and society, this ancient city became the conduit for stranded notables and a haven for double agents and conspirators. Lisbon in 1940 was a destination, a place to convene and to scheme, and, at a price, a point of departure.

Josephine flitted from one embassy party to another, playing the sexy dingbat, all the while eavesdropping on the conversations of high-placed diplomats who found it hard to talk about anything except the war. Afterward, using invisible ink, she made detailed notes on her sheet music.

Years later Captain Paillole told Abtey that "the destiny of our Allies and consequently the Free French was written in part over the pages of 'J'ai Deux Amours.'"

In late November 1940, Free French headquarters in London sent word that Josephine and Abtey were not to come to Britain but instead were to return to Marseille and help build up a solid network of spies.

An announcer on a Portuguese radio station bade Josephine farewell with the message: "If you should see Hitler, tell him we are waiting for him with impatience—to send him to Saint-Hélène."

In Marseille Josephine was thrown back into the "pagaille," the confusion, of a divided France. The word was on everyone's lips, the only word that seemed adequately to sum up the situation. Again and again it was "quelle pagaille" as people talked about the army's rout and the new Vichy government.

The newspapers, reduced to two or at most four pages, carried column after column of classified advertisements in which families scattered by the war attempted to reunite.

Although she was now an official member of the Free French Forces, Josephine refused to accept a salary for her work—money that could be put to better use in the war effort. But this left her with a problem. Jean Lion had imbued Josephine with the French bourgeois maxim that the best thing to do with one's money is put it into real estate or gold; certainly sound advice for a spendthrift like Josephine, except that she now had little cash on hand.

To economize, Josephine rented a modest, unheated room in a hotel near the Gare St. Charles, which she claimed was "filled to the gills with whores." From her window she could see a tragic swirl of humanity. All day long soldiers and refugees streamed to and from the railroad station, up and down the Boulevard Dugommier and the Canebière, in and out of cafés and restaurants of the Vieux Port, packing the front and rear platforms of the streetcars, pushing, shoving, jostling.

The winter of 1940–41 was bitterly cold. Wearing her overcoat to bed at night, shivering, Josephine developed walking pneumonia. Yet she drove herself mercilessly during this bleak period.

To raise money, she persuaded the management of the Municipal Theatre in Marseille to stage a revival of Offenbach's *La Créole*. In ten days Josephine had relearned her lines, coached other members of the cast with theirs, and scrounged around for costumes. The production premiered on Christmas Eve, 1940, the coldest holiday in years.

By January 1941, as rumors circulated wildly that the whole of France would soon be occupied by the Germans, Jacques Abtey and Josephine were ordered to move their base of operations to North Africa.

When Josephine flew to Casablanca, leaving the producers of

El Glaoui, the Pacha of Marrakesh. A feudal ruler with a large harem, El Glaoui sheltered Josephine in his exquisite palace during World War II. *H. Roger-Viollet*

La Créole high and dry, they sued her for 400,000 francs. Even though she produced an X ray showing that she had pneumonia and thus required a warm climate, she was still forced to pay 100,000 francs.

Before departing she asked Frederic Rey, who performed with her in *La Créole* and was heading for Casablanca by boat, if he would first go back to Les Milandes and fetch a few of her pets. She missed them and reasoned that the animals would help disguise her real mission. After all, how many undercover agents travel with two monkeys, one Great Dane, two white mice and a hamster?

Josephine arrived in Casablanca five days after Jacques Abtey. This medieval port of luxury, filth and decadence was then ruled by Vichy functionaries and a vacillating, self-serving local aristocracy. Its calm superficial beauty contrasted sharply with the tension and intrigue running through the city. In this atmosphere of fear and confusion, Josephine and Abtey quietly met with the Free French, becoming part of the vast information network of the Resistance movement.

As an entertainer, Josephine was free to travel from North Africa to Spain and Portugal, and back. She proved to be an excellent pipeline for vital information. Years later, when she was awarded la Légion d'Honneur, her citation noted that she possessed *"un sang-froid remarkable."*

While awaiting orders to return to Spain in May 1941, Josephine visited Tangier. Here she met El Glaoui, the Pacha of Marrakesh. Of all the men conquered by Josephine's charm, none was more intriguing or devious than El Glaoui. A lean man with falcon profile and feverish black eyes, he was over sixty when Josephine met him. Yet this autocrat par excellence remained a passionate and sensuous prince.

The Pacha had started out as a member of the comparatively unimportant Glaoui tribe, but like his brother El Mandani was ambitious. By following the ancient ways of the Berber chieftains—assaulting their neighbors, sequestering their lands and women—these extraordinary brothers eventually dominated the Atlas Mountains that bisected Morocco. When El Mandani died in 1918, El Glaoui became even more powerful. He was known as "le Grand Seigneur" and "King of the South." By the time Josephine knew him, he owned vast tracts of land and half the water rights in the Marrakesh region. His absolute authority extended over 660,000 Berbers. That he outwitted the Vichy puppets and supported de Gaulle was of immense importance to Allied strategy in North Africa.

El Glaoui was a notorious lecher with a large harem. Since he and Josephine were scrappers, connivers and intensely charismatic individuals, it was only natural they should become *très amis.* Another bond was that El Glaoui's mother, Lalla Zora, was a black woman of Ethiopian origin.

Josephine and Abtey moved to Marrakesh where the Pacha had a luxurious palace. El Glaoui, dependent as he was on the largesse of the French and anxious to help in every way, was an important contact for their undercover operations.

To Morocco's liberal minority, El Glaoui was the Devil incarnate whose princely style was sustained at the expense of the tribes he ruled. By maintaining his feudal rights, he stood in direct opposition to the progressive views of the Moroccan nationalists. Scorning them, El Glaoui was a dedicated medieval lord.

In the vast salons on the ground floor of his palace, in opulent scented rooms of silk and velvet, he presided at splendid feasts. During the war years his personal guests included Winston Churchill, Archie Roosevelt and General Mark Clark.

Cocktails were served from an American bar. Guests sat on the floor for dinner around elaborately carved tables. Black slaves in lavishly embroidered white costumes served mutton, vegetables, fowl, fish and pastries. All food was eaten with three fingers of the right hand.

After dinner the Pacha's dancing boys and girls, bedecked with bracelets and rings, swayed in passionate rhythms. General Clark said of the Pacha's floor show: "The performance was fascinating, although quite strange to American ears. The singing and music sounded a bit like a combination of female tobacco auctioneers with a background of fire engines. The dancing was a melding of palsy, St. Vitus dance and a mild form of jitterbugging."

Josephine was impressed by El Glaoui's exquisite manners and thoughtfulness. He introduced her to Marrakesh, capital of his personal domain, where she saw snake-charmers, sword-swallowers and fire-eaters. She met the Berber dancers from the mountains and the black Gennaoua dancers from the Sudan. She was also welcomed into the homes of two other prominent Moroccans, Moulay Larbi el Alaoui, first cousin of the Sultan of Morocco, and Larbi's brother-in-law Si Mohamed Menebhi.

At a time when Josephine's friendship with El Glaoui was still fresh, she became pregnant. It has never been clear who the father was. Regardless of paternity, El Glaoui took an active interest in the sad events that followed.

Late in her pregnancy Josephine gave birth to a stillborn baby, delivered at the Comte Clinic in Casablanca. Labor was followed by a high fever and an incipient infection.

Dr. Henri Comte, director of the clinic, performed an emergency hysterectomy. Josephine awoke from the operation in critical condition, her fever still out of control. Dr. Comte strove to combat the infection with sulpha drugs, but she remained desperately ill. She had an enormous wound in her stomach.

Two days after the operation, the head of the Red Cross in Casablanca sent over a girl to work as Josephine's private nurse. Her name was Marie Rochas. She was the daughter of a French army officer and had just completed her nurse's training; this was her first job.

Marie hovered over Josephine's bed, determined to save the star's life. "My grandmother used to talk about her, raving about her beauty and vitality, but in that bed I saw a woman who was bone thin. Her arms were scrawny. Her skin was spotty and wrinkled. She had fits of crying that were pitiful. It wasn't the physical pain that made her unhappy. It was the hysterectomy.

"I tried to comfort her. I said, 'You can go back to France after the war and everyone will still love you.'

"That only made her cry harder. She said, 'But will they remember me? Will they remember me?'"

Josephine was obsessed with the loss of her reproductive powers. Her dream of having a child of her own was gone forever. "Years later," said Marie Rochas, "when I read that she adopted all those children, I understood. To adopt one or two children is normal, but twelve! That's frustrated motherhood."

During the darkest part of Josephine's illness, Jacques Abtey hardly left her side. Sleeping on a cot next to her, he helped Marie Rochas change Josephine's sheets and bathe her. When the pain got so bad at night that she could not sleep, he held her hand and they prayed.

For the next six months, from December 1941 through June 1942, Josephine's condition fluctuated radically. She was in such a weakened state that she caught infections easily. She developed peritonitis as well as blood poisoning.

Abtey was in despair. "She was doubled up with her legs up to her head and bust," he remembered years later. "Her face was tight. Her skin was waxy, as if she were dead."

Since Josephine's condition was clouded in secrecy, the rumor spread in Casablanca that she was dead. A UPI stringer wrote up the rumor as a verified news item, and the story was printed throughout Europe and in North and South America. Her obituary in the *Chicago Defender* contained the ironic line: "Miss Baker had few associates within her own race even though some of her closest friends were Negroes."

Just when Josephine's seemingly inexhaustible supply of courage had reached its lowest point, she received word that El Glaoui was at last coming to visit her. He announced his visit by flooding her room and adjacent terrace with giant baskets of flowers.

The announcement of the Pacha's visit had a miraculous effect on Josephine. If this was a death-bed call, she reasoned, then she would play it for all it was worth. She was too proud to have him remember her as a dried-up waste.

Josephine had arrived at the Comte clinic with sixteen trunks. These lined the corridor outside her room.

Marie replaced the hospital linen with Josephine's satin sheets. She removed Josephine's hospital gown and dressed her in a see-through peignoir. Then she brushed Josephine's frizzy hair away from her face and placed a yellow orchid above her left ear.

"It took me two hours to do her makeup," says Marie, "because of the blotches on her skin." She wore no jewelry except for a simple pair of diamond earrings the Maharajah of Kapurthala had given her in the early 1930s.

Even at such moments, Josephine's sense of theatre did not desert her. She instructed Marie to apply makeup herself and stand next to the bed. "You are blond and blue-eyed. I am dark. The Pacha will find the contrast *très drôle.*"

When El Glaoui arrived and took Josephine's hand in his fingers, her face flushed with color and for the first time in a long while, she smiled.

"It was like a stage performance," Marie remembers. "Josephine surmounted her pain and for a brief afternoon looked up at the Pacha as if he were the only man on earth."

The Pacha insisted that Josephine recuperate at his palace in Marrakesh. She promised to come as soon as she was stronger.

SIXTEEN

"Josephine Baker is the greatest woman God ever blew breath into."

—An American GI

In the late spring of 1942, Maurice Chevalier was passing through Casablanca. Hearing that Josephine was very ill, he dropped by the Comte Clinic to see her.

For Chevalier, Josephine made no attempt to primp. Of all the French who played hanky-panky with the Germans, none was more often the target of Josephine's wrath than the "man in the straw hat," France's goodwill ambassador around the world. Josephine considered Chevalier a shallow opportunist, notably deficient in heart and soul. "He is a great artist but a small man," she told Jacques Abtey.

When Chevalier walked into her room at the Comte Clinic, Josephine greeted him with a barrage of insults, calling him a "coward" and a "traitor"; her vehemence reached the point of near hysteria. After he left, Marie Rochas gave her a sedative to calm her down. Later, Josephine told an Associated Press reporter, "Chevalier is to the stage what Laval is to diplomacy. His type of propaganda, trying to put Nazism over to the French people, is worse than a speech by Hitler."

Chevalier countered Josephine's stinging attack by describing her in interviews as a wasting has-been. "Poor thing. She's dying penniless."

For a "penniless" woman, Josephine lived quite well. When

228

her health was on the upswing, she was permitted leaves of absence from the Comte Clinic. She would stay in the homes of either Si Mohamed Menebhi, one of the prominent Moroccans who had taken her under his care, or at the sumptuous palace of El Glaoui in Marrakesh.

The Pacha gave Josephine a wing of the great house connected to the palace. She had an immense bedroom walled and floored with Moroccan tiles and carpeted with magnificent Berber rugs. Her entourage included personal servants and an escort for her carriage, which was pulled by matching bays. In the afternoons she traveled to market wearing the traditional Moroccan djellabah, the long cloak and hood that for centuries has protected Arabs from heat and cold.

Despite constant medical surveillance and the solicitous attention of friends, Josephine suffered several relapses that required rehospitalization in Casablanca as well as three more operations to remove intestinal blockages.

At one point her health was so precarious that Si Mohammed Menabhi distributed bread to three hundred beggars—the destitute, the blind and the maimed—asking them to pray night and day to Allah that Josephine would be cured. Gradually she started to mend.

Most of Josephine's visitors at the Comte Clinic were people she hardly knew. Under the guise of visiting an international celebrity, members of the Resistance met with Jacques Abtey in her hospital room. Here they made plans and exchanged messages. The French protectorate of Morocco was then controlled by Vichy, which of course would support the Germans if the Americans landed in North Africa. Abtey and his workers expected the Americans to invade North Africa using the coastal cities as a base of operation against the Germans. They were accumulating voluminous information on troop concentrations, naval units, supplies of gasoline and ammunition, as well as details about airports where resistance would be heaviest.

On November 8, 1942, the Americans landed near Casablanca. Josephine hopped out of bed and, dressed only in pajamas, ran out on her balcony, ecstatic with joy. "That's the Americans for you," she said to Abtey. "Europe doesn't know their force or their will. They'll win the war for us."

The Casablanca landings, like those at Oran and Algiers, were made on beaches flanking the city. The resistance of the French led to bloody fighting as the French fleet turned its guns on American forces. Three days later the fighting was over; the Axis defense had collapsed.

Ollie Steward, a war correspondent for the *Afro-American* newspaper, landed with the troops. Hearing that Josephine was alive despite the wire service death notice, he called on her at the Comte Clinic.

He fou..d her in good spirits. Propped up with pillows, gazing dramatically out the window toward the Atlas Mountains, she seemed ebullient yet uncharacteristically reflective. She startled Steward by the urgency in her voice. "I cannot locate my mother. She's moved since the war started. She must still be in St. Louis, but where? Where? If you could trace her through your newspaper, I would be eternally grateful."

Josephine had to let Carrie know she had survived, had endured. As much as Josephine prided herself on her independence, she still needed her mother in a way that was almost childlike. She wanted Carrie's blessing for the risks she had taken, and her understanding for the mistakes she had made.

A week after the landings, the deceptive calmness and tension prior to the Allied assault was transformed. North Africa teemed with soldiers in the early days of 1943—French, American, British, Moroccan and Colonial troops. But in Casablanca there was little for the bewildered and lonely men to do.

As soon as the Americans landed in North Africa, their commanding officers realized that they had a major social problem on their hands. In Morocco, at that time, it was forbidden for men and local girls to meet on a casual basis. Should a respectable woman be found even conversing with a strange man, the scandal could lead to sudden death to one or both parties. Naturally the men were homesick, not only for women without veils but for all those little reminders of America: a morning paper, especially the comics; friendly smiles and handshakes; a hot dog and a Coke.

To help solve the problem, Sydney Williams, a black sociologist from Chicago serving with the American army in

Casablanca, organized an interracial canteen called the Liberty Club, sponsored by the Red Cross. Hearing from Ollie Steward that Josephine was alive, he asked her to baptize the club with a performance. She agreed.

At thirty-six, weakened by illness, Josephine was understandably nervous. The wound in her stomach still had not healed completely; if she stood up too long she saw spots. However, it was obvious after one song that the old magnetism was still there. Supported by a red-hot band, Josephine was sensational.

On the great day, generals and GIs stood elbow to elbow in the Liberty Club. Latecomers peered through air vents in the roof.

At the end of her triumphant performance, Josephine dramatically announced that she was putting herself at the disposal of the American forces.

During this early period of the occupation of Morocco, relations between the French authorities and the Allies, including de Gaulle's forces, were delicate and often hostile. In most instances local French administrators and large landowners had supported Pétain's Vichy government. Some were ardent fascists and remained so; others, where loyalty wavered, now felt humiliated, betrayed and guilty. For tactical reasons, American commanders were compelled in some instances to consort with Vichy. This compounded the problem and further poisoned relations between the various sides.

When Sydney Williams took Josephine to the residence of a Frenchman in Casablanca where there were both American and French guests, the tension was apparent.

After dinner Josephine, aware of the strain among the guests, seized the moment to act. Without warning she stood up and began to sing the "Marseillaise." Taking the cue, the Americans joined in. Upon hearing the stirring lyrics and martial tones of their national anthem, many of the Frenchmen started to cry.

After the last line Josephine raised her hands over her head and in a gust of exuberance cried, *"Vive la France."*

The Frenchmen rose to their feet and chorused, *"Vive l'Amérique."*

Reflecting upon that evening and many others in which Josephine single-handedly broke down social barriers, Williams surmised, "She is one of the most remarkable women alive. She was a balance between the French and British and Americans on one hand, and the Arabs and Negro GIs on the other. She was always doing something for somebody."

Invigorated by the Allied presence, Josephine was now determined to play a role. With Frederic Rey, who had been working in North Africa as an entertainer and an undercover agent, she planned an exhausting tour of the army camps to entertain the men. Jacques Abtey saw it as a vehicle for his continuing intelligence work; Si Mohammed Menabhi agreed to go along and act as interpreter. Setting off in three jeeps containing supplies, costumes and a few props, the happy band began their journey across the scorching North African desert.

The long, narrow desert battlefield stretched from Axis headquarters at Tripoli to the British stronghold at Alexandria, 1,400 miles to the east. The Germans, Italians and British had spent themselves to hold this desolate strip of land simply because neither side could afford to let the other have it. For the Allies the Western Desert was a critically important buffer protecting the Suez Canal and the Middle East oil fields, both of which the Axis powers wanted. In addition, whoever controlled the North African airfields controlled the strategically vital Mediterranean.

Though rail-thin and plagued by recurrent abdominal pains, Josephine found the arduous desert life exhilarating, a tremendous release from the claustrophobia of her hospital room. She was bounced about in the jeep, performed under fire, and became lost in sandstorms. At night she slept in a bedroll with Abtey; from the distance she could hear the wailful cries of the jackals savaging the dead.

"It was very cold in the desert," remembers Fred Rey, who slept next to them. "The temperature dipped below freezing. Josephine neither complained nor showed fear. Once in Libya, a pack of coyotes started to circle us. We were all huddled together in a pile. Suddenly Josephine sat up and yelled to them, 'Don't eat us!'"

Despite such hardships, she looked happier and gayer than

she had in years. But she was appalled by what she saw. This was the closest Josephine had ever come to war. She was particularly moved by the cemeteries, little hills of sand marked with crosses, many bearing the word "Unknown."

Everywhere she looked she saw the ugly wreckage of battle—the twisted, broken trucks, tanks, cars and squashed-out planes gutted by high explosives, charred by fire, stark in the bright desert sun.

By the time they reached Benghazi on the frontier of Egypt, they had been driving through the desert so long they almost mistook the vision ahead of them for a mirage. Here was a group of British officers, sitting erect, lightly protected from the searing sun by an open-air tent, calmly sipping tea.

"Join us," said one of the officers in greeting. In her thirst Josephine gulped the tea, only to realize that it was made with saltwater. She spat it out and said, "May I please have a beer?"

Josephine performed several times a day before as many as three or four thousand troops. For these men sick of heat, dust and sand fleas, cut off from towns, with no place to go except perhaps to the Mediterranean once a week for a swim, Josephine Baker was a heady symbol of romance and escape. "I wanted to bring them the breath of Paris," she said, "the breath of France."

On a makeshift stage supported by oil drums, Josephine danced everything from ballets to the Samba, sang everything from "I'm Dreaming of a White Christmas" to "My Yiddish Mama." She switched costumes in a nearby tent.

Entertaining the soldiers was a stirring experience for Josephine: "Often I knew the men would be sent into battle before they knew. To see them in front of me so full of life and enthusiasm, and knowing that many of them wouldn't come back alive, was the hardest part of the tour."

One night while doing a show 20 miles outside of Oran, Josephine was eating a sandwich during a break when German tracer bullets hit the crowd. She fell belly down and continued to eat. Just then a soldier crawled over to her in the dim light, calling, "Miss Baker, Miss Baker." He handed her a dish of ice cream for dessert.

Josephine traveled with a trunk full of publicity photos that she autographed and handed out to soldiers after shows and when she visited hospitals, a duty she performed throughout the war.

These hospital rounds were a salutary experience, for most of the wards in the desert were makeshift tents that provided little shelter from the relentless heat and the Kasham, the pitiless desert wind. Sitting and chatting with the men, Josephine tried to relieve their boredom, homesickness, pain and discomfort. She was singularly lacking in the dullness and pretense of many actors and actresses offstage. She shed the mask of the entertainer. She was herself, and she was adored for it.

Josephine's visits to American army camps remained cruel reminders that racism was alive and flourishing in the armed forces. Jim Crow laws pervaded every aspect of military life. By the end of 1942 nearly half a million Negroes were in the Army, but only 5 percent served in combat units. The balance were assigned to construction units or served as mess attendants and stewards. Behind this policy was an attitude of mindless bigotry.

A 1936 report from the National War College, from which virtually all the top army leaders graduate, reveals the nature of the stereotype that pervaded the thinking of the army's senior officers.

As an individual the negro is docile, tractable, light-hearted, care free [sic], and good natured. If unjustly treated he is likely to become surly and stubborn though this is a temporary phase. He is careless, shiftless, irresponsible and secretive. He resents censure and is best handled with praise and ridicule. He is unmoral, untruthful, and his sense of right doing is relatively inferior. Crimes and convictions involving moral turpitude are nearly five to one compared with convictions of whites on similar charges. . . . Their emotions are unstable and their reactions uncertain. Bad leadership in particular is easily communicated to them.

During Josephine's shows the white soldiers took the seats in front and the blacks stood at the back. Josephine would then insist that the blacks have equal rights for seats. The performance over, she would head straight for the black troops.

Black Pfc. Johnnie M. Hilliway, stationed in Oran, North Africa, wrote to his sister Gladys in Chicago: "She really put on a heck of a show, on or off stage, for the boys. I thought they were going to 'eat her up'. . . .

"She asked us to write to folks back home and tell them she is very much alive. Boy! You bet she is!"

Josephine's act was so good that it soon became known in the Western Desert as the hit of North Africa. Staff Sergeant Walter Terry, dance critic of the *Herald Tribune,* was stationed in Cairo and filed a story reporting that Josephine sang and danced "brilliantly" in a series of sold-out performances. "Audiences literally screamed themselves hoarse at La Baker, whose sufferings had apparently harmed her not at all, but rather added increased shimmer to her voice, strength to her dance, and radiance to her effervescent personality."

Noel Coward crossed paths with Josephine at Shepheard's, the smartest hotel in Cairo. He wrote in a diary he kept of his Middle East tour: "She is doing a wonderful job for the troops and refuses to appear anywhere where admission is charged or where civilians are present. She says firmly that entertaining the fighting service is her self-appointed war effort and that she has no intention of being side-tracked from it for any reason whatever."

Between 1943 and 1944 Josephine performed in Jerusalem, Corsica, Sardinia and Italy. In June 1944 Josephine had one last skirmish with death before war's end. While she was riding with Abtey in a small plane off the coast of Corsica, both engines in the aircraft lost power and the plane dropped into the sea. The lucky passengers were rescued by a small boat patrolling the coast.

Josephine's propaganda mission raised 3,143,000 francs for the Free French Forces. She was rewarded for this by being made a member of the Ladies Air Auxiliary, "les filles de l'Air" as they were affectionately called.

After the liberation of Paris on August 25, 1944, Josephine returned to France, reentering the city of her dreams in the natty blue Air Auxiliary uniform complete with gold epaulets. She was so proud of this that she would occasionally appear in it until the day she died.

Some members of the Free French felt that Josephine was overplaying her war role. She had often been seen in public with El Glaoui, and there were rumors that she received her Air Auxiliary status simply because she was the Pacha's *"petite amie."* It was known that he had a lot of pull with the Allied top brass.

"She came back to Paris more French than Louie XVI" says Alain Romains, who also worked for the Free French in Africa and was awarded la Légion d'Honneur. "I said to her, 'It was very nice of you to save France for us, Josephine.'"

Yet in October 1946, while she was recuperating in Paris from another intestinal operation, Josephine was awarded the Medal of the Resistance with Rosette. At the ceremony General de Gaulle's daughter, Madame de Boissieu, conveyed the best

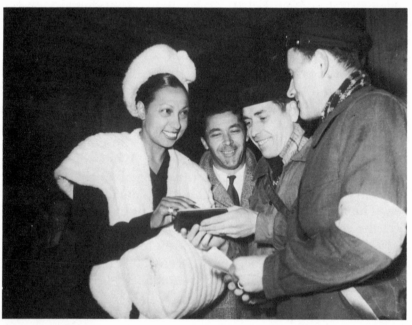

1948. Josephine, always gracious in greeting her admirers, signs autographs at the Gare Austerlitz. *AGIP*

wishes of her father, who also sent along the following hand-written letter:

Colombey-les-Deux-Eglises   14/10/46

Dear Mademoiselle Josephine Baker,

It is with all my heart and knowledge that I send you my sincere congratulations for the high distinction of the French Resistance which you have received.

Not long ago I fully appreciated the great services you have given in the most difficult moments.

After that I was more touched by the enthusiasm with which you have put your magnificent talent at the disposal of our Cause and for all who followed it.

My wife and I are expressing our fervent wishes for your rapid and complete recovery.

While I am waiting to have the honor of seeing you again, I beg you, dear Mademoiselle, to accept my respectful homages to which my wife wants to add her very sympathetic greetings.

C. de Gaulle

Although the war had deepened Josephine's character, it had also left scars. After so much upheaval and uncertainty in the past four years, stability was now of paramount importance to her. Josephine wanted to get married.

Contemplating her fourth union, Josephine was far more cool-headed and realistic than she had ever been before. Jean Lion, the husband who came closest to fitting her romantic ideal, would not bend to her will; he had dreams of his own. Clearly she needed a more pliable sort.

In this frame of mind, she began to see Jo Bouillon, an orchestra leader she had known slightly over the years. When Josephine was commissioned to follow the French First Army through liberated countries performing for the soldiers, she invited his orchestra to accompany her. This was a fitting beginning for her relationship with Bouillon; he would always be the backdrop, the admiring fan eclipsed by the star.

Jo Bouillon considered Josephine a first-rate entertainer who

Josephine with orchestra leader Jo Bouillon, who was to become her fourth husband. *Keystone*

could be just as successful again as she was before the war. Josephine was well aware that many people considered her passée, and that some even doubted she was alive. The wire service announcement of her death had received such widespread coverage that for years Josephine was in the ironic position of having to refute the article. As late as 1964, when she attended a jazz conference in Paris, a man came up to her and said, "Are you Josephine Baker?"

"Yes."

"Didn't you used to be dead?"

Josephine was forty-one years old, the onset of middle age. The thought of exhibiting herself nude in a revue now frightened her. "After thirty-five years of age, a person shouldn't appear nude, not in public nor to their lover," she told Michael Gyarmarthy, the artistic director of the Folies-Bergère.

While her face lacked the strong bone structure so vital to

beauty once the bloom has gone, it was nonetheless appealing. She still looked the gamine. Bettina Bergery, an American who worked for Elsa Schiaparelli, noticed a melancholy that had not been there before the war. "Her skin got lighter and her humor darker."

Vulnerable as she was about the passage of her youth, Josephine wanted a man around to give her moral support. Jo Bouillon appeared suitable for marriage. He was a fine musician who had an orchestra with a national reputation. Since he performed every night with la Radio Française, his name was *"très dans le vent"* in show business circles. Though not rich, he had good business sense.

Bouillon also had a genuine love of nature and thus could act as the overseer of Les Milandes, which Josephine planned to turn into a large tourist complex complete with hotels, soccer field, swimming pool, restaurants and, of course, a small zoo. But most important, Josephine wanted to adopt children, and she had to have a husband for this.

For his part, Bouillon could profit from an alliance with Josephine. There was a faint tinge of *collabo,* or collaborator, attached to his name, since he had performed in Paris during the Occupation. Yet entertainers must eat, and he was keeping the spirit of France alive by playing French songs, so it did not seem a fair accusation. Nonetheless, marrying a war heroine like Josephine could only benefit him.

Bouillon took genuine delight in her company. The substrata of psychic pain was not apparent at first. She came across as a happy lark.

Bouillon was known to be shy with women. His lack of interest in the opposite sex troubled many of Josephine's friends. "I said, 'Baby, forget it,' " Bricktop recalls. "You can't fit a round peg in a square hole."

Bouillon, now forty, had never been married. His engagement to Josephine caused lifted eyebrows among his friends as well. "A man fashioned by nature the way Bouillon is cannot possibly have a successful happy marriage with a woman of Josephine's temperament and passionate feminine instincts," said a musician who had known Bouillon intimately for years.

Josephine and Jo Bouillon were married in her private chapel at Les Milandes. *Agence France-Presse*

Despite her misgivings, they were married on Josephine's birthday, June 3, 1947, at her chapel at Les Milandes. The entire village turned out for the ceremony.

Josephine made no bones about this being *un mariage de raison.* As she told George Guignery, her longtime friend at Le Vésinet, "I need work. He has an orchestra. We can travel together and he can get bookings." What Josephine did not realize is that bonds made in a spirit of pragmatism can be just

Josephine, forty-three, triumphs again at the Folies-Bergère. Here with dance partner and former lover Frederic Rey, she stars in "Beauty and the Beast." *H. Roger-Viollet*

as painful as those forged in the white heat of passion.

In order to raise money to convert Les Milandes into a tourist center, Josephine sold her château at Le Vésinet as well as her apartment house on rue Bugeaud, which Pepito had bought for her. She also went back to work at the Folies-Bergère, where she startled Paris by singing Schubert's "Ave Maria," followed by a vigorous mating dance in which she played "Beauty" to Frederic Rey's "Beast." She also embarked on an extensive tour singing and dancing in Europe and in North and South America.

While performing in the United States with Jo Bouillon and his orchestra, Josephine visited St. Louis and urged her family to come live with her at Les Milandes. She wanted them to bask in the sunshine of her success.

Carrie had remarried and her husband did not want to move to a country where he did not know the language. She left him with great reluctance. After she had gone, he told a friend, "We loved each other dearly, and her daughter came along and took her away just like that."

Margaret and her husband Elmo joined Carrie. Richard would come four years later. For the trip, Carrie and Margaret each purchased new sets of false teeth. Carrie did not get a good fit. "Well," she reasoned, "maybe they're not meant to fit. After all, they're not mine. They are false."

Hoping to please Carrie with her skills as an entertainer, Josephine invited her mother to watch a performance in Bordeaux. What Josephine did not realize was that in the long years since she had seen her mother, Carrie had become deeply religious.

Carrie was appalled at Josephine's peek-a-boo displays of bosom and leg. In her dressing room after the show, Carrie fell on her knees in front of Josephine and wept. "Tumpie, you never told me you were one of those painted women!"

Though she still played the scarlet bird of paradise when she cavorted onstage, Josephine was also becoming more religious. She now said her prayers before retiring at night, and even arranged to have the village priest celebrate Mass each Sunday in the chapel at her château. Afterward, Jo and she were often invited to neighboring homes. He was accepted more easily than Josephine. Certainly the fact that he was French helped, but as one of their neighbors added: "You could relax with Jo. You couldn't with Josephine. She was exhausting. Also, when you saw her out of the artistic milieu where she had been trained, she didn't come across as very bright. She lacked the education necessary to hold up her end of the conversation."

It was highly appropriate that Josephine should choose the Dordogne area for her castle. This district, perhaps more than any other, evokes the historic and aristocratic values of France. Located in the south middle region of the country, it was the original inheritance of Eleanor of Aquitaine, claimed, conquered and dominated alternately by the families and vassals of the Plantagenets and Valois. Fortified villages, bridges, rivers, caves, soaring cliffs and broad lush valleys characterize this dramatic, beautiful area.

Above all, the Dordogne is a land of castles. Many of them, even today, are the seats of their proud patrician owners to whom the peasants and bourgeois still pay traditional respect. Josephine's emergence as the proprietor of a commercial resort was greeted with a mixture of wonder and disdain.

Whatever anyone thought of Josephine's grand scheme, it was a boon to the local economy. Les Milandes soon became a center of industry. Josephine and Jo Bouillon hired the farmers to till the soil and to help construct buildings.

Both Josephine and Jo Bouillon were complete neophytes at running a farm. Their separate ways of approaching the challenge indicated early on the conflicts that would divide them so deeply in the years to come.

Bouillon was practical, shrewd with money, and had the narrow, solid feel for small change so often found in *la petite bourgeoisie*. He was also intelligent, blessed with an eagerness to learn. He spent long hours in Perigord's municipal library steeping himself in the rudiments of agriculture and horticulture.

Josephine believed she could run Les Milandes by force of whim. She refused to accept the idea that a farm has a rhythm of its own dictated by the cycles of nature and the eating habits of the livestock. She planted tomatoes in October, expecting to have a crop for Christmas "when nobody else has them." And when the undersize tomatoes shriveled on the vine, she bought plump ones from the merchants in the nearby village of Sarlat, who quickly realized that they could make a good living off Josephine.

She did not want her hens pent up in a coop, insisting "they must be free." So the hens laid their eggs under the cabbage and lettuce leaves in the vegetable garden, and the eggs attracted vermin which destroyed the crops. She studiously hosed down her pigs "so they will look all pink and pretty," yet they were not fed on a regular basis because there was such a rapid turnover of help.

Josephine on her farm. *Black Star*

The cows suffered because they were not milked regularly. When Michael Gyarmarthy traveled down from Paris for the official opening of Les Milandes as a tourist center, Josephine asked him to lend a hand milking the cows because the farmer who handled the job had just quit. A born cosmopolite of cushioned comforts, Gyarmarthy recoiled at the idea, whereupon Josephine inveigled him into stringing up lights in the barn. By nightfall the name of each animal sparkled in flamboyant neon letters above their stalls: Jeannette, Rosette, Pervenche, Julie, Honorine. . . . Josephine clasped her hands with joy, exclaiming, *"Quelle merveille!* This is absolutely the model farm."

Living in a countryside steeped with reminders of the Middle Ages, Josephine and Jo gracefully assumed the medieval role of responsibility toward the serfs. The small farmers who lived in the shadow of the castles worked the same land farmed by their ancestors. The tradition of peasant to liege lord exists to this day.

Josephine fitted easily into the role of chatelaine and, in the beginning, the natives were grateful. She brought plumbing and electricity to the hamlet. If anyone in the village was sick, Josephine often sat up with the person herself; if they required hospitalization, she picked up the bill.

Zizi Padavoni, a teenager when Josephine and Jo Bouillon opened Les Milandes, worked for them as a laborer. When it was time for him to do military service, they gave him two hundred dollars as a going away present. The gesture, he said, was typical of the generosity and goodwill characterizing Josephine and Jo Bouillon's early days at Les Milandes. "They had a kindness and a radiance that penetrated the whole village."

SEVENTEEN

"Josephine Baker has it all—class, talent and ding-dong."

—Walter Winchell

World War II was the catalyst that brought out Josephine's political and humanitarian dimensions, and permanently altered her character. Gone forever was the dizzy flirt of yesteryear; Josephine was now a woman of substance. But it was not just the war that forced Josephine to become *"un personnage."*

Entertainer Bobby Short said of Josephine's metamorphosis: "There's an old Negro expression called 'the change.' It's a word that's applied to people who've led 'the sportin' life.' In Negro lore, 'sportin' life' meant just what it did in *Porgy and Bess.* It's the world of pimps, gamblers, whores, and show business.

"A woman decides to do 'the change' when one day the phone stops ringing, or men don't make passes anymore, or they realize that the ploys of their youth just won't work. Then they turn to Jesus. And they decide to be a force for good in the world."

Josephine did "the change."

Far more than most people, Josephine needed the assurance that she weighed in the scheme of human affairs, that she had all the qualifications to be taken seriously. Marshaling her

246

energy and courage, she now directed them against the cause closest to her heart: racism.

When Josephine arrived in the United States for a series of performances with Jo Bouillon and his orchestra in 1948, she was still haunted by the treatment of black soldiers during World War II. Here was a war that had been fought against a monstrous racial threat, yet black soldiers were treated as inferiors, as lesser beings than the German POWs they guarded.

Now that she was back in the United States, segregation once again became a personal reality. According to Jo Bouillon, they were refused reservations at thirty-six hotels in New York City because Josephine was black. They finally found a room at the Hotel Gladstone on 114 East 52nd Street.

The incident stirred Josephine's deepest feelings of anger. While at the Gladstone she phoned Roger Féral, the editor of *France Soir,* and suggested to him that she write a series of articles on segregation in the United States. Féral went for the idea.

Josephine left Jo Bouillon in New York and traveled through the American South dressed in old clothes, pretending to be an anonymous Mrs. Brown. She wanted to find out what it felt like to be an average Negro living under Jim Crow laws. Years before Freedom Rides, Josephine sallied into the fray. "She was much tougher than all those sit-in cats you saw on TV," says producer Jack Jordan. "She used the drinking fountains, the lunch counters and the ladies' rooms. They threw her ass out in the street and she walked right back in."

Back in France, Josephine decided she would return to the United States and strike an all-out blow against discrimination. "My music hall career must be secondary now," she told her friend Bruno Coquatrix. "I'm going to dedicate my life to helping my people."

In 1951 America was not ready for the black firebrand from Paris. In retrospect, that is what made Josephine's achievements so extraordinary. She beat all the big-name civil rights leaders of the 1960s to the punch—and she paid dearly for her courage.

During the early postwar era, Americans were not activists.

The 1950s ushered in the "Affluent Society" in which a large segment of the white population began to experience ever-increasing prosperity. It was a time when consensus was the goal and nonconformity a sin. It was also a chauvinistic era marked by accusations and loyalty oaths. The daily reality of the cold war caused people to be hysterically afraid of the Soviet Union and of Communist subversion in the United States itself.

The year before Josephine arrived saw the conviction of Alger Hiss for perjury, the arrest and trial of Ethel and Julius Rosenberg as atomic spies, and the outbreak of the Korean War. On TV, Senator Estes Kefauver conducted his criminal investigations, revealing the extent and power of organized crime. America was victorious, supremely powerful and magnanimous to her allies and former enemies. Nevertheless, at home she was a curious mix of paranoia, materialism and self-satisfaction. Social issues did not predominate.

Blacks lived in worried silence. With the close of the war, the high hopes and benefits they expected in recognition of what they had done at home and in the field seemed to vanish. They were in a holding period, submerging tumultuous emotions of bitterness, despair and anger. But beneath the deceptive passivity lurked a fierce race consciousness. When a young woman in Harlem was asked how Hitler should have been punished if he had lived, she replied, "Paint him black and send him over here."

In Miami, where blacks were daily humiliated by Jim Crow laws, including exclusion from local beaches, Josephine became one of the first to perform before a mixed audience. She was also the first known black to become a bona fide resident in a Miami Beach hotel. And she was the first to dance as a guest at a Miami Beach nightclub. At the end of the opening show, she said to the audience: "This is the happiest moment of my life. I have waited twenty-seven years for this night to sing to my people."

Josephine received superb reviews. One was from Walter Winchell, who wrote in the *New York Mirror* (January 17, 1951): "Josephine Baker's applause [at Copa City] is the most deafening, prolonged, and sincere we ever heard in forty years of show-biz. A one-gal show, with exquisite gowns, charm, magic and big-time zing. In two words: A star. P.S. And her legs are as lovely as Sugar Ray Robinson's. Gets $1,000 a day after a twenty-seven-year absence abroad. She won't appear anywhere if members of her race are not admitted."

Josephine was flooded with telegrams from blacks all over the country. Philadelphia's Reverend Marshall Shepard summed up the superb irony of it all: "Isn't it singular, even shocking, when one considers that in Miami Beach preachers for years have been expounding the doctrines of love; but the lines of segregation stood just as firm as ever. But at the command of one little brown girl, the walls of segregation came tumbling down."

Wherever she went, Josephine carried on her lessons in democracy. She called on white business leaders and asked, "Why haven't you hired any colored people?" In Chicago she visited the annual convention of the National Association of Television Broadcasters and insisted upon a conference with the organization's president. She then urged him to raise the number of blacks in the NATB. She toured department stores in the Loop, talking with owners and managers about racial quotas in their hiring policies. She also met with the heads of Chicago's First National Bank, International Harvester, the Illinois Central and the Chicago Association of Commerce and Industry.

In San Francisco, during a hit run at the Golden Gate Theatre, she took on the Chamber of Commerce, the City of Paris department store and Oakland's Key System Transit Company.

Not all of Josephine's lectures were received with good grace. Frank Teasdale, president of Key Transit, delivered a lengthy tirade about the company's buses being worth millions of dollars. He also spoke of lives and property.

"How can so many Negroes qualify to drive trucks in the Army but not drive your buses?" Josephine asked.

When Teasdale blamed lesser officers of the firm and said that he made it a policy never to interfere with them, Josephine walked out on him.

Perhaps the most remarkable event of her American tour was a relatively minor incident in Los Angeles, because it shows the kind of uninhibited action she exhibited to prove she was a free person. Sitting in the dining room of the Biltmore Hotel in Los Angeles, Josephine overheard a Texan at the table next to her announce, "I won't stay in the same room with niggers."

Josephine got up from her chair, called the police and demanded the man's arrest. The police told her that since they did not hear the remark, the only way they could arrest him was under a California law providing for a citizen's arrest. Josephine promptly arrested the Texan. In court he was fined $100 or ten days in jail. The man paid the fine.

Josephine became personally identified with two well-publicized civil rights cases. The first was the crusade to "Save Willie McGee." Four times the thirty-eight-year-old truck driver had been slated for execution. He was convicted of raping a white woman while she lay in bed with her small daughter. Many people, including Albert Einstein who rallied to his defense, felt that McGee had been framed.

The day he was finally executed, hundreds of white Mississippians stood on the lawn of the Laurel, Mississippi, courthouse. When the lights of the courthouse dimmed, showing that the electrocution switch had been pulled, they broke into cheers knowing he was dead. The police paraded a coffin through the crowd to show that justice had been done.

Josephine, who had been at Willie's wife's side up to the time he died, paid for Willie's burial.

The night after the execution, Josephine was appearing at the Fox Theatre in Detroit. Just as the show was ready to go, Josephine walked to the footlights and addressed the almost all white audience. She said that she would go on that night but her heart was not in it. "They have killed one of my people, Willie McGee. He was executed. I feel very deeply about it. I feel very deeply for my people, just as you feel very deeply about yours." Then she related some of the events of the McGee case and harshly denounced the judge and the court, but even more the iniquitous system that had doomed Willie McGee.

During a five-day engagement in Philadelphia, Josephine made a surprise visit to the Mercer County courtroom in Trenton, New Jersey, where the longest and costliest trial in the state's history was taking place. In the summer of 1948 six black men were sentenced to the electric chair, accused of beating a seventy-three-year-old white man to death with a soda bottle in the back room of his novelty shop.

The "Trenton Six" became a cause célèbre because the men were rounded up in a police dragnet that swept through the black neighborhoods of Trenton. The evidence against them was largely circumstantial. The defense claimed the men had been forced to sign confessions after a brutalizing five-night interrogation period in which they were given narcotics and threatened with violence.

Josephine arrived unannounced at the trial. She sent a note to defense counsel Raymond Pace Alexander, in which she asked permission to address the six defendants. "I want to bring a little cheer to the men," she explained.

Presiding Judge Ralph Smalley adjourned court for ten minutes while Josephine talked to the accused in their cells. She told them to "keep their chins up and to have full confidence that justice would prevail."

John MacKenzie, one of the six, had been entertained by Josephine at the 19th General Hospital in Le Mans during World War II. He was so moved by Josephine's talk that he burst into tears.

Though four of the Trenton Six were freed after a new trial, Collis English and Ralph Cooper were sentenced to death. The NAACP appealed the verdict. Two years later, in 1953, Ralph Cooper entered a plea of no defense and made a confession incriminating himself and his codefendant. Cooper, it was believed, had been forced to do this to gain his freedom. Collis English died in prison from a heart attack.

On a gloomy wet Sunday, May 20, 1951, Harlem in all its finery turned out to honor Josephine—100,000 strong. Jo Bouillon flew over for the event, carrying two Dior dresses for her to wear on the great day. Only Joe Louis had ever pulled such a crowd in the black capital. Sponsored by the NAACP, "Josephine Baker Day" began with a twenty-seven-car motorcade moving slowly up Seventh Avenue. Sitting on top of a cream-colored convertible, Josephine waved to the vast throng watching from fire escapes, upstairs windows and along

Harlem's avenues. Many of the bystanders wore dress clothes and top hats. "I love you, love you, I love you," Josephine said, throwing kisses to her thousands of admirers. Bouillon concluded, "My wife should have been a chief of state."

A contingent of 1500 Girl Scouts presented her with roses in front of the Hotel Theresa at Seventh Avenue and 125th Street. The mayor of New York, Vincent Impelliteri, gave a cocktail party in her honor. That evening 5000 people poured into Harlem's boiling hot Golden Gate Ballroom to pay her tribute. Backstage, as Josephine dabbed the sweat on her arms with a Turkish towel, Nobel Peace Prize winner Ralph Bunche, later Undersecretary-General of the United Nations, and certainly the most influential black in America, told her, "This is literally the hottest reception you'll ever have."

Among those paying tribute to Josephine were Fredric March, Gypsy Rose Lee, Duke Ellington, Billy Daniels, Buddy Rogers and Walter White, head of the NAACP.

By midnight, moved beyond words and fighting back tears, Josephine expressed her one regret: "Mama should be here."

Josephine's time had come. Buoyed by her victory in Miami, she embarked on a campaign to turn the country's racial customs and codes topsy-turvy. Just by being herself—bold, basic, outrageous and beguiling—she accomplished more in one grand sweep across the United States than all the black American entertainers combined.

Her approach was fresh, a cool breeze of proud impertinence. She stood on the platforms of railways stations; she visited people who were lecturing on racial equality. For starters, she issued a press release stipulating that black stagehands and musicians must be hired for every show in which she appeared. She also insisted that she would only perform in cities where she received accommodations in first-class hotels. She meant it. She turned down a $12,000-a-week engagement at the Chase Hotel in St. Louis because the hotel refused to abide by her policy of nondiscrimination. When the Biltmore, the Henry Grady and the Georgian Terrace in Atlanta turned her down, she canceled her engagement there, drawing national attention to a Georgia law which stipulated that any white hotel granting accommodations to Negroes would be liable to revocation of its innkeeper's license.

The incident drew the wrath of the Ku Klux Klan. Josephine began receiving threatening phone calls, prompting her to tell the press, "I am not afraid of the Ku Klux Klan or any other group of hooded mobsters. I'll meet them in the South or anywhere else they like. But I will not go to Atlanta because I have not been assured that they will grant me the rights they grant to any other citizen of this country of my birth."

Professionally, Josephine succeeded beyond all expectations. She broke box office records in city after city. She revived vaudeville in towns where it had not only been sleeping, but dead. She grossed over $100,000 on the tour.

Earl Wilson described her as "the most exciting personality in the last twenty years." Paterson Greene of the *Los Angeles Examiner* said, "If an orchid could sizzle, it would be something like Josephine Baker." Louella Parsons reported: "I agree with the person who said, 'There's no use trying to describe her style because she is ten thousand women in one.' " Hortense Morton called her "the most exciting thing to hit San Francisco since the Golden Gate Bridge."

What was really important to Josephine was that she was being taken seriously as a civil rights pioneer. She received the NAACP's Most Outstanding Woman of the Year Award for 1951, and her activities were praised on the floor of Congress. "Josephine Baker's contribution to the nation," wrote Ted Yates in the *Chicago Tribune*, "believe it or not, can be summed up as the best public race and press relations stunt of the century—if not for all time."

With a heady feeling of confidence, Josephine returned to New York to play a short engagement at the Roxy. Her two-week run, which grossed $55,000, was sold out every performance.

Ironically, Josephine's rival Mistinguett, now a feisty eighty-three, was opening at the Martinique Club on West 57th Street. "She didn't draw flies," as they say in Harlem. Columnist Robert Ruark dealt the final blow, "As an old legman, I buy Baker's gams over Mistinguett's every time."

Josephine's $150,000 wardrobe attracted the attention of Seventh Avenue. Designers sat in the audience sketching her Paris originals because Christian Dior, Balenciaga, Pierre Balmain and Jacques Griffe all created for Josephine.

Josephine singing at the Roxy during her smash hit comeback in 1951. Said *Ebony:* "The legend named Josephine Baker has come home again to her native land to score an artistic triumph that show business historians will probably call the most remarkable of our times." *Alfred Eisenstaedt,* Life *magazine*

Her clothes filled six trunks and forty-eight suitcases; eight additional boxes contained thirty-six pairs of shoes and a few hats. It took four taxis to haul the luggage from the airport to the hotel.

Tamara Goutrevich, who had been chief costume designer with the Grand Ballet of Monte Carlo, took charge of the wardrobe assisted by Josephine's two maids.

The Roxy management converted its huge basement storeroom into closet space for her clothes. It assigned her a double dressing room offstage, and built her a dressing alcove for quick changes.

The costumes, which she received free as advertisements for Paris couture, became an integral part of her act. In *The Wonderful World of Musical Comedy,* Stanley Green wrote: "She was Nefertiti and the Queen of Sheba all poured into one Balenciaga gown. With her eyelids twinkling with sequins, her fingers, wrists, throat and ears aglow with diamonds, and her hair braided into the most artfully cascading ponytail, she would sweep among her adoring subjects like some bronze bird of paradise to be engulfed by her adoring subjects."

Josephine proudly showed off her wardrobe to anyone who passed by her dressing room. She told one visitor: "See, they have everything—built-in corsets, foam rubber falsies. They practically stand up by themselves, like Christmas trees."

Josephine's wardrobe was the talk of New York. A television poll conducted at the Stork Club named her "The Best Dressed Woman of 1951."

Then, a few nights later, Jim Crow cast its vote at the Stork Club.

Her friends from Paris, Mr. and Mrs. Roger Rico, were in town for the season. Rico was pinch-hitting for Ezio Pinza in *South Pacific.* On October 16, when Josephine joined the Ricos at the Stork Club for a midnight snack, she sailed into one of the more celebrated confrontations of her career.

Sherman Billingsley, proprietor of the Stork Club, was "the lord of snobdom." A former convicted bootlegger and now the host-darling of café society, Billingsley knew his clientele: "People will pay more to look at each other than for food, drink or service." To support his theory, he managed to pull in such crowd pleasers as Randolph Churchill, the Duke and Duchess of Windsor, Franklin Roosevelt Jr., Joseph P. Kennedy, Lord Beaverbrook, J. Edgar Hoover, Bernard Baruch, Andrei Gromyko and Senator Joe McCarthy.

Walking through the Cub Room to join the Ricos, Josephine passed Walter Winchell and Jack O'Brien, a reporter for the *Journal American.*

When the waiter took the order, Josephine asked for a steak and a bottle of wine. Half an hour later she had not been served. "She waited for almost an hour even though we received our dinners," Mrs. Rico said, "and none of the waiters, including the one who had taken the order, would come near us. They pretended not to hear when my husband called.

"We finally forced our waiter to come to the table and asked about Miss Baker's order. He said they had no steaks. We asked about the crabmeat cocktail and he said they had no crabmeat. We asked about the bottle of wine and he said they were still looking for one. When we said we would order something else, he went away again."

At this point Josephine went to call Billy Rowe, the only black deputy commissioner in the New York City Police Department.

On the way she passed Walter Winchell. Even though he said later that he waved as she went by, Josephine claimed that Winchell looked right through her. He left a few minutes later.

Josephine went immediately to the home of Walter White, head of the NAACP, to discuss ways in which they might call attention to the case.

The next day Josephine gave the *Daily News* an interview about the incident that included an attack on Winchell. He was "the great liberal," she said, and yet "he did nothing to have his friend Sherman Billingsley intervene and see that I was accorded proper treatment."

Winchell was furious and replied on his Sunday night news broadcast, "Jergens Journal," which reached millions of people: "I am appalled at the agony and embarrassment caused Josephine Baker at the Stork Club. But I am especially appalled at the efforts to involve me in an incident in which I had no part."

Considering the power of the Winchell press, it is surprising Josephine should have chosen him as a target for her wrath.

Walter Winchell was, at his worst, an opinionated self-serving gossip who, if crossed, was a vicious adversary. Ethel Barrymore summarized the sentiments of many people when she said, "I don't see why Walter Winchell is allowed to live."

Josephine's stand on the Stork Club had a tremendous public response. It was front-page news in New York papers as well as many newspapers throughout the nation. *The Chicago Defender* ran the headline: STORK SUPPLIES FORK BUT HOLDS STEAK ON LA BAKE! The incident was covered thoroughly by all sixteen Paris dailies, where it was referred to as *"l'Affair du Stork."*

By her act of defiance Josephine aroused the public conscience. Fatima cigarettes, sponsors of the weekly Stork Club TV show, reported that in major cities their salesmen were not renewing orders, asserting that sales had dropped off due to "the Baker incident."

Josephine's lawyer, Arthur Garfield Hays, mobilized the liberal community. Hays was one of the founders of the American Civil Liberties Union; he had worked on many famous cases including that of the Scottsboro Boys and the Scopes "Monkey trial."

With Hays in her corner, an impressive list of organizations rallied to Josephine's defense, among them: The American Newspaper Guild, the New York State Liquor Authority, the American Guild of Variety Artists, the Alcoholic Beverage Board and Actor's Equity.

Sugar Ray Robinson and Joe Louis offered financial aid in suing the Stork Club, but Robinson would not join Josephine in her damnation of Walter Winchell. He explained: "I know of too many things that Walter has done for people of all races and all creeds."

Winchell considered Josephine the ingrate of all time because she was not only slandering his name, she was also defaming his favorite roost. Many nights he spent writing his column on a banquette in the Cub Room of the Stork Club: "Winchell's News Service," table 50 in the left-hand corner as you enter the room. It was in that spot that Grace Kelly told Winchell about her engagement to Prince Rainier. And it was here John Steinbeck approached him and told him: "We all think you are doing a fine job for your country. Don't stop. Your enemies are the enemies of your country."

With a vindictiveness seldom equaled in his career, Winchell set out to destroy Josephine. He called her "pro-Communist," "anti-Semitic," as well as a "dangerous woman" who "hates colored people as much as she hates Jews." He particularly relished attacking her war record: "While our boys were over there stopping bullets, Josey-Phoney Baker was living it up, making oodles of dough in Paris, wining and dining the Nazis' and Mussolini's bigwig generals."

Her relatives found the "pinko" tag amusing. Brother Richard said, "Imagine Josephine a Communist. When you think of the way they dress in Moscow."

For Josephine the incident was emotionally draining and professionally disastrous. The year had begun so triumphantly, but now no one wanted her. She was simply too controversial. Nightclubs and theatre engagements were canceled; the chance to do a book with Flo Ziegfeld on her life was called off. When she sat down in a restaurant even in Harlem, people around her would often change tables.

On December 26, 1951, Ernie Hill of *The Chicago Daily News* ran the following item:

> Edith Sampson, noted Negro attorney of Chicago, said she is tired of hearing Jos. malign the U.S. and praise France for its handling of race problems. Called her "mentally dishonest" in praising France. "She should stop and consider what France is doing to some 45,000,000 in its African colonies. French colonialism is a blot on the world's conscience. Education and health facilities are meager. These people suffer much more than does Miss Baker in Atlanta or in New York. In the United States we are at least attempting to eradicate barriers. When France tries to do one tenth as much in the colonies I will be willing to listen to Josephine Baker."

As Josephine's ideas came under increasingly bitter attack, many black people did not want anything to do with her. When her own people rejected her, that hurt the most.

Carolyn Carruthers, Josephine's private secretary at the time, affirmed Josephine's limited grasp of the accusations being hurled against her. "I don't think Josephine ever even voted. If you read her speeches you'll see that her ideas were simple, like

Sunday sermons. She had one idea, that all men should live together as brothers."

When a Hollywood reporter tried to find out just how far left Josephine was, she shook her head, "I don't even know what a Communist is."

Black producer Jack Jordan, who spent a lot of time with Josephine, offered the most plausible explanation for her contradictory political stands: "Josephine was a doer. She absorbed by hearing. I never saw her read a book."

Her political views were a mixture of naïveté, a messianic will to make men love one another, and a desire to get back at America for not accepting her as the instrument of its deliverance from racism. This helps to account for Josephine's extraordinary behavior in Argentina in 1952.

Traveling with Carolyn Carruthers, Josephine's Buenos Aires sojourn began in September 1952 at the first bloom of the mild Argentine spring. The trip was scheduled for six weeks, but Josephine became so embroiled in Argentine politics that it lasted almost six months.

Two months before her arrival, Eva Perón, the beautiful and intimidating wife of dictator Juan Domingo Perón, had died at the age of thirty-three. La señora Presidenta had been at the height of her glory; the entire country, save for her enemies, was prostrate with grief.

Josephine was fascinated by the legend of Eva Perón. She had no interest in learning about the ugly realities behind the Cinderella story. What mattered to Josephine was that Eva came from nowhere to become the most powerful woman in the most powerful country in Latin America.

Eva was an illegitimate child from the pampas who wore broken shoes and darned socks. Like Josephine, she had quit grade school in order to work and help support her family. But she became a lush honey-blonde with a dazzling smile. She used all the arts of the courtesan to climb to the top, where she sat in the presidential palace as consort to the dictator.

What Josephine did not know was that Eva, Saint of the Working Class, Lady of Hope, Protector of the Forsaken, took from the rich and gave to the poor, then stole from the poor. She squandered the public purse on clothes and jewels, spending $40,000 annually buying dresses from the same couturiers in Paris as Josephine. It was said that her collection of jewelry was one of the most valuable in the world.

Juan Perón was an impractical, shortsighted tyrant, mostly bluster and big plans. Nevertheless, by aping his idol Mussolini's bombast and public giveaways, he became immensely popular with the masses and remained so for years.

Under the Peróns Argentina was a fascist state, a refuge for Nazi war criminals, protected by a Gestapo-trained secret police. The Peróns dominated and bankrupted the nation.

With Eva's death, Juan Perón was destitute and weakened. He was the windbag whom Eva had propped up during her life. She had been the dynamo supplying him with energy. Now, in his period of mourning, he passed his days in unparalleled lechery, sleeping with high school girls in the quinta of the presidential residence in Olivos. Many of the teenagers were petrified by the middle-aged dictator. His subsequent interest in Josephine was psychological (the weak drawn to the strong) and political, not physical.

When Josephine opened at the Ciné-Opera Theatre, Perón was in the audience. Afterward one of his assistants came up to her and said: "The General wants to meet you. Be ready tomorrow morning at 11:30."

Josephine enthusiastically agreed, telling Carolyn: "We must go. It would be rude if we didn't."

They were driven to La Casa Rosada, the pink Government House on the Plaza de Mayo, where President of the Republic Perón conducted his official business.

Josephine found Perón to be a fine figure of a man, handsome and straight-backed, *"un bien pedazo de pan,"* as Argentinians say. She was complimented by the fuss he made over her, more so still when he said: "My wife followed your career through the newspapers. She admired you very much."

Perón undoubtedly saw Josephine as an ideal propaganda tool in his cold war with the United States. The "Yanqui" had never been very sympathetic to the Peróns; his anti-American rallies in the streets of Buenos Aires did not help.

Following her meeting with Perón, Josephine carried a bouquet of flowers to the General Confederation of Labor

In 1952 Josephine visited Buenos Aires where she
became an outspoken supporter of dictator Juan Perón. At Casa Rosada, the government house, President Perón poses with Josephine, her secretary
Carolyn Carruthers, and his Subsecretary of Information, Raul Apolo. *Wide World*

headquarters where an altar with a statue of Eva was set up in
the lobby. Eva's body was on the third floor, where Pedro Ara,
the famous Spanish pathologist, was experimenting with a special embalming fluid that would turn her corpse into something
like a waxen effigy. The body was kept under constant surveillance, hidden from those who believed her to be a saint and
who might steal her body as a source of miracles. Josephine
called Eva "my sister . . . an illustrious wife untimely dead."

Despite the warnings of her friends in Buenos Aires,
Josephine fell into a kind of symbiotic relationship with Perón.
Like Evita, Josephine's direct manner and simple ideas com-

plemented Perón's bombast. At the same time, her vocabulary was remarkably similar to Eva Perón's. They both were fluent in the glib expressions of humanitarianism—freedom, dignity, heart and love—which they intoned over and over again until the words took on hypnotic effect.

Whether Josephine knew that she was being used is not clear. Carolyn Carruthers recalls: "The General was very nice to her. He was not a bad person as far as guests were concerned." Perón showered Josephine with gifts and money.

At the General's behest, Josephine agreed to speak at the Eva Perón memorial rally. Addressing a group of Argentine workers, the *descamisados,* or "shirtless ones," Josephine spoke with such conviction that she easily brought her audience under her sway. She called Argentina an "enlightened democracy," and she praised God because He was wise enough to create men like Perón, whom she called "a sincere and understanding person," one who aspires to "liberty and justice . . . an extraordinary man."

The Government Press Office, which employed more than a thousand people, undoubtedly had a hand in what followed. Three articles by Josephine appeared in the Argentine newspaper *Critica,* and numerous others about her ran in the public press. In all of them Josephine is sharply and mindlessly critical of the United States, which she called a "barbarous land living in a false, Nazi-style democracy." Many of her remarks were directed against the race problem: "As the entire world knows . . . in the Yanqui democracy, the Negro has no rights whatsoever"; and "I have personally seen many lynchings and men and women killed like animals."

She even took potshots at Dwight Eisenhower, who had just been elected president: "Black people will suffer as they have never suffered. . . . May God have pity on them."

Josephine's tirades were given wide coverage in the United States. Congressman Adam Clayton Powell Jr. called a press conference in his New York office to charge that Josephine had "done great damage" to the cause of Negro rights by her "deliberate distortion and misrepresentation" of the racial situation in America. Powell concluded his statement by declaring that since Josephine had allied herself with "the communist press," she had "completely abolished . . . any good she may have accomplished in previous years."

In Washington the Immigration Department did not take kindly to her anti-American comments. They issued a statement saying that if Josephine cared to reenter the United States, she "would have to prove her right and worth."

Josephine immediately responded with a declaration that would haunt her for years. On the day she made the statement, Carolyn Carruthers had taken a break to visit some of the small villages in the pampas. Driving down the Avenida de Mayo on her return in the evening, she saw a tickertape in lights dancing around the top of a building. The headline ran: "JOSEPHINE BAKER SAYS 'TO BE BARRED FROM THE UNITED STATES IS AN HONOR.'" Carruthers was heartsick and furious. She remembers thinking, "Jesus, I can't even take a day off without her getting into trouble."

In order to get through the lobby of the Plaza Hotel to their room, Carolyn had to fight her way through a mob of reporters determined to interview Josephine. "It looked like a revolution."

When Carolyn unlocked the door to their suite, Josephine was sitting in the middle of her bed nervously buffing her nails. The phone rang.

"You answer it," said Josephine.

It was Ted Posten of *The New York Post* calling from New York. He had acted as one of Josephine's champions during Winchell's smear campaign, and he was floored by Josephine's vituperative remarks.

"What the hell is going on down there?" he asked Carruthers.

"Josephine's right here."

"For God's sake don't put her on. She'll be three hours and Dorothy Schiff is paying for this call."

Josephine weaseled out of any explanation for her actions. She told Carruthers, "You know how the press exaggerates."

"Yes," said Carolyn. "And I know how you can talk, too."

In retrospect, Carolyn Carruthers thinks that Josephine's responses were dictated by caprice or her mood of the moment. Said Carruthers, "She had at least six separate personalities. Some mornings I'd look at her in bed as she was waking up and

I'd wonder, 'Who is she going to be today?'"

Then too, Josephine could fib with disarming sincerity because she greeted each situation with the freshness of a child. She was a great respecter of the dramatic possibilities of any event and therefore did not really hold herself culpable for her more extravagant remarks. "Everything was just a performance for her," Carolyn surmised, noting that her political antics proved to be a great drawing card to the box office. "She liked to see the theatre full."

Josephine saw Perón as a tool to put across her philosophy of brotherhood. At her request Perón set up a World Cultural Association to combat prejudice, and he appointed her president of it. Argentina was hardly a hotbed of prejudice. The country was more than 95 percent Roman Catholic and had perhaps 5000 blacks in the overall population.

As the country's leader in social reform, Eva's official title had been First Samaritan. Now that she was gone, Perón asked Josephine to assume some of her duties. The Eva Perón Foundation had been founded to build schools, hostels and hospitals, all on a most extravagant scale. What he wanted was someone to do as Evita had done; tour the places, specifically the hospitals, accompanied by much fanfare, to draw attention to his benevolence.

Perón planned for Josephine to visit only those hospitals that gave a good impression. They were the new hospitals. Although supposed to serve the poor, they catered to favored Peronistas. The older hospitals were left without funds and even abandoned. Some were in desperate need of drugs and food.

The situation was worsened by a shortage of trained nurses. In official parades hundreds of smartly turned-out nurses, all with lipstick and nail polish to match, marched briskly by. And yet in the hospitals, Josephine could not help but notice their scarcity. In the free wards she came across families camped out around a patient's bed to ensure adequate nursing.

Josephine toured psychiatric and maternity hospitals, local health care centers and a leper colony. Everywhere she went she was appalled by the lack of equipment and the miserable living conditions.

Heady with the power of her job, Josephine came down hard on her underlings. Ramón Carillo, Minister of Health, bore the brunt of Josephine's criticism. He recounted his experience in a pained but obsequious letter to Perón:

> The Señora Josephine Baker, invoking the authority of Your Excellency, submitted us to a series of brow-beatings which we accepted stoically, like gentlemen, because she was your official guest. . . . It suggested itself to us that, in her acts and social views, she was trying to imitate the most reverend Señora Eva Perón. It is true that the Señora Eva Perón called me hundreds of times to make me aware of the deficiencies in our services. She always did so with tact and energy, but with perfect knowledge of how our department operates, and also with respect. Even though she had the high position of wife of Your Excellency, she never treated me like the Señora Baker did—not that this is to accuse Señora Baker of anything, for we are always at Your Excellency's service for the good of the Perónist movement.

Josephine could no longer ignore the sinister crimes of the Perón regime. In cafés, in drawing rooms, throughout the city, there was a sublife of secret fear, a Kafka-like discomfort in the atmosphere. She began to listen to the tales of midnight arrests, disappearances, tortures and murders. When a friend of Jo Bouillon's, who lived in Buenos Aires, urged Josephine to go to an insane asylum that was not on Perón's official list, Josephine agreed.

"The people were treated like animals," recalls Carolyn Carruthers. "They were rolling around on the lawn in rags, eating their own filth."

It was then that Josephine, disillusioned and sickened but probably no wiser, decided to leave Argentina.

EIGHTEEN

"In St. Louis we were the peasants."

—Josephine

Bruised by her political skirmishes with the United States during her stay in Argentina, Josephine returned to France with a renewed sense of purpose. She vowed to take her patch of earth there and transform it (as much as the French government would allow) into a sovereign state, her own "Capital of World Brotherhood." Despite her humanitarian goals, democracies and plebiscites held no allure for her. Josephine saw herself as queen of a feudal empire.

Because she thought herself a monarch, she regarded everyone around her as her subjects. She had her own flags; wrought-iron grilles over the basement windows contained the initials JB; and she even opened a fake post office and had stamps printed to make Les Milandes seem like a country. Of course the République Française did not recognize the stamps as valid, but they gave Josephine the illusion that she was a sovereign.

The Dordogne region is a hotbed of castle ecologists, conservative landed gentry, many of whom have inherited the property of their forebears. Several of the castle owners opened their fortresses to tourists either as a business investment or just to pay for upkeep, but Josephine's ideas were considered *"de trop."* Her flashy touches galled them. The heart-shaped swim-

266

Richard Martin, Josephine's brother, worked at Les Milandes as chauffer, gas station attendant and waiter.

ming pool, the neon silhouette of Josephine above the door of the theatre in the amusement park, the native village reminiscent of the Congo, the Jorama Wax Museum with its series of exhibits dramatizing landmarks in Josephine's life (such as her 1950 audience with Pope Pius XII)—all were looked at askance.

Les Milandes boasted another configuration that scandalized the old guard. Josephine commissioned a sculptor to chisel a likeness of her as the Virgin Mary surrounded by a flock of children. Muttered one grande dame in the neighborhood, "Modesty is not Madame Baker's forte."

The Chartreuse, Josephine's showcase hotel, provided some startling decorative notes. The second-floor bedrooms, dripping with organdy and pastel chintzes, were dedicated to French women famous in history or literature. Each door was inscribed with a name, a charming sisterhood of the bed, including La Pompadour, Du Barry, Camille, Agnès Sorel, La Montespan and Madame Sans-Gêne. The nameplate of the most luxurious chamber read, simply, Josephine. But she assured visitors that Josephine Bonaparte, not Baker, had been the inspiration.

On the third floor each bedroom was named for a different country, presumably to express the theme of global brotherhood. Each relentlessly carried out a national decorative motif. The red, white and blue USA room boasted a set of Western saloon doors that swung open on the bidet.

At first, when there was plenty of money around and the dream of Les Milandes was still fresh, Josephine was generosity itself. She wanted to share everything with her family.

When brother Richard arrived in 1952, he was greeted with open arms. A compactly built man with the same mysteriously luminous skin as Josephine, Richard had just left his second wife and a successful trucking business in St. Louis to begin anew in Josephine's fairytale kingdom. For Richard, the best part of moving to France was "bein' able to walk down the street with a white woman and not bein' scared of gettin' hanged."

Richard remembers his first day at Les Milandes. Josephine linked arms with him and took him on a tour of the town. As they wended through the narrow streets, Josephine pointed out the hotels, theatre, farm and rolling hills of her vast property. And she made it clear to him that what was hers was theirs. "Look what God has given us," she said. "To think of where we've come from and where we are today. I often think of the time when we were little kids and didn't have anything. I have often wished that we had this in America."

Josephine found jobs on the château grounds for her relatives. Margaret helped run the farm. Margaret's husband, Elmo, repaired and rented out the paddle boats that plied the Dordogne River. Richard started out as her chauffeur, but his loyal servitude as a driver moved Josephine to give him his life's dream—a gas station.

At Les Milandes, on the main road leading up to the château, she installed two Esso pumps and a small garage. Here for eight years Richard pumped gas for the steady stream of tourists who journeyed to Les Milandes during the 1950s while the project flourished. Josephine even built Richard a small house, where at night, standing in his front yard, he could stare up at her castle on the hill, ablaze with lights.

Summers, Carrie wore white linen dresses and sat in a rocking chair in the shade of an elm tree next to the château. Because she did not speak French, she spent much of the time in her own private world. The tourists photographed her and sometimes asked her questions. "I don't think Josephine had a beautiful body," she told one American. "Her legs were too long."

Now that Les Milandes was somewhat under control, Josephine was ready to embark on her noble experiment: the adoption of children of different races and creeds to prove to the world that everybody can live together in harmony. "If children can, grown-ups can, too."

Jo Bouillon claimed that early in their marriage Josephine became pregnant and then miscarried. "I braced myself for her tears," he writes in the book *Josephine,* "but she remained dry-eyed, aloof in her grief, silent, grave-faced, her hands pressed to her empty womb." In view of her hysterectomy in Casablanca, this would have been medically astonishing. What is equally remarkable is that Bouillon would not have heard about Josephine's operation since Josephine had given interviews on the subject to the French press. "I suffered a lot because I couldn't have children of my own," said Josephine. "I felt inferior because of that."

Josephine embarked upon motherhood with the same slap-dash spirit that underscored all her projects. In her forties, a time when many women are grandmothers, she traveled the globe looking for waifs, pieces of flotsam as she had been. In a sense she was adopting herself. "My babies will never be ashamed of their origins. They will be loved."

Between 1954 and 1965 Josephine adopted twelve children: Akio, a Korean; Janot, a Japanese; Jari, a Finn; Luis, a Colombian; Jean-Claude, Marianne, Noël and Moïse (Moses), all French; Brahim, an Arab; Mara, a Venezuelan; Koffi, from the Ivory Coast; and Stellina, a Moroccan born in France. There were ten boys and two girls. Josephine reasoned, "It's so much more important for men to get along than women."

In her search Josephine often visited rural villages looking for poor families who were having difficulty feeding and clothing their many children. She saw firsthand the dust of life. She watched children dying of dysentery, surrounded by filth, their vacant eyes without hope. And she heard the pitiful cries of babies too hungry to sleep, their bellies swollen from malnutrition. "One thing I never knew and she never told me," says Carolyn Carruthers, "was whether Josephine had to pay to get some of these kids. I wondered how parents could just give their children away."

In fact, because Josephine was a rich international star with a forceful personality, she was able to circumvent normal adoption channels. In some cases money did change hands. Josephine would also promise to give the children a good education and to write to the parents each week.

Many of the children had been abandoned: Akio and Janot were *"Konketsujii,"* Occupation babies who had been fathered by American GIs stationed in Korea. Noël was plucked from a garbage can in Paris on Christmas Eve. Brahim and Marianne were left under a bush in the midst of the Algerian War.

In 1955, when she adopted Gustavio Valencia, a Colombian boy from Homiguero near Bogotá, Josephine told his parents that she would not only stay in touch with them, she would bring Gustavio back to South America to visit them.

Josephine changed his name to Luis and never told him his last name. Nor did she ever take him to the village of his parents, who never saw him again. His father, who said he only agreed to give him up because he was so pressed financially, told a correspondent for the *Paris Herald Tribune,* "We never received so much as a phone call or a letter."

Josephine was determined to have as many nationalities in her family as possible, but not every country was as liberal and willing as she had hoped. The one country that flatly refused to give her a child was Israel. This struggling new nation needed all its sons and was not about to make an exception in Josephine's case. Undaunted, she found a Jewish child through "Legal Aid" in Paris and named him Moïse, or Moses. He was the only child to be thoroughly trained in the religion of his ancestry.

When Moïse set off for school each morning, Josephine tried to get him to wear his yarmulke, a skullcap worn by orthodox and conservative Jewish males. But Moïse rebelled because the cap set him apart from his schoolmates, most of whom were Catholic. Josephine saw to it that Moïse received a solid education in the Jewish faith by taking him one day a week for religious instruction to the home of André and Jacqueline Barasche, a young Jewish couple who lived in nearby Périgueux. Said Jacqueline Barasche: "Josephine told us her father was a Jewish tailor of Polish descent."

Josephine became so caught up in adopting children that she even adopted a Belgian baby of Hindu blood for Margaret, who was childless. At first Margaret had ambiguous feelings about instant motherhood, but she and her husband, Elmo, quickly grew to love the child, whom they named Rama. She became the center of their lives.

Since Josephine had the money for governesses, she saw no harm in adopting one child after another. This monomania of hers terrified Jo Bouillon. At the time they married, they had agreed to adopt four children. But Josephine could not be stopped. And to get the money to adopt the children, she continued to accept singing engagements around the world. She was away at least six months of every year. Because of this, the job of raising the children was left principally to sister Margaret, Jo Bouillon, the maids and the governesses. "She came and went like the wind," says Merle Trijoulet, who worked as an accountant at Les Milandes. "She would arrive on a Monday and leave Tuesday night."

Although Margaret was not particularly fond of Josephine's children, considering them untamed and disrespectful, particularly as they began to grow up, she still accepted her role.

Margaret had once been a strikingly handsome woman, several shades darker than Josephine with a soft round face and limpid eyes. But now she was fat with bad feet that caused her to waddle slightly. She had the air of authority of one who manages, who does the dirty work, who supports other people. "She's like Hattie McDaniels in *Gone With the Wind*," says Howard Saunders, who coproduced one of Josephine's tours. "She treated Josephine like Scarlett O'Hara. She knew that Josephine could be a raving bitch, but she loved her just the same."

Despite Jo Bouillon's alarm with Josephine's continuing adoptions, the promise of Les Milandes seemed very much alive. Between 1954 and 1959, the years of its great prosperity,

Les Milandes averaged 500,000 visitors a summer. There were constant parties and celebrations, fireworks displays, concerts by leading orchestras, performances by dance troupes, and lavish fetes at which cases of champagne were given away as presents.

While Josephine enjoyed the crowds of tourists who followed her about the grounds, she was fiercely protective of her children, whom she did not want to be considered *"bêtes curieuses."* But since she advertised Les Milandes in brochures, newspaper ads and on the radio as "the Josephine Baker Children's Camp, a bold experiment in human relations," people were curious to see how the experiment was working.

Just as she had done when she was a child in St. Louis, Josephine made Christmas for everyone. Her family, her employees, all the residents of the hamlet of Milandes partook in the feast, which Josephine went to great pains to prepare.

She spent thousands of dollars on toys for the children, and she gave every resident of the village a present as well. Brother Richard says, "Christmas was the happiest day of the year for her."

Josephine could not say no to the children. If she thought they were going to request something that she would have to refuse, she told them to ask the maids or the governesses for it.

When Josephine was at home she thoroughly enjoyed her role as mother. When the children were toddlers she would bathe them, dress them and cook for them. When they reached school age she drove them to nearby Castelnaud-Feyrac, an adjacent hamlet with a two-room schoolhouse, one room for children four to eleven years old, the other for the older children.

Whenever she could, Josephine would attend the school's *réunions scolaires,* the French equivalent of PTA. But she was often so tired from the hectic pace of her life that she fell asleep during the meetings. She also had trouble helping the children with their homework. Her mind would wander while the children dutifully recited their lessons.

The school at Castelnaud-Feyrac was taught by Monsieur and Madame Besse, who remember Josephine's children as being intensely loyal to each other and very proud of the château; the

Josephine takes a break during her 1956 farewell gala at the Olympia Music Hall in Paris. The New York *Herald Tribune* referred to her adieu as "merely a slightly exaggerated form of announcement that she is back with us again." Paris Match, *Pictorial Parade*

boys liked to pretend they were knights protecting the castle against invaders. The children were also very proud of Josephine. They did not know what she did for a living, but they knew she was famous. Because of this they felt privileged. Once when the King of Denmark dispatched a private plane to fetch Josephine for a party in Copenhagen, Marianne ran into the classroom and announced to her schoolmates, "The King has sent for Mama!"

Despite the pride the children took in Josephine's prominence, they missed her terribly when she went away. "Her children used to throw their arms around me and cling to me," remembers Madame Besse. "They had an enormous need for affection."

The children longed to have a real mother who would stay at home, and their feelings were obvious. "As I'm leaving," Josephine told a friend, "Marianne will stretch herself out on

Eight of Josephine's adopted children have their evening bath in a Stockholm hotel. Paris Match, *de Potier*

the front hall floor and scream her head off. She says to me, 'You're never here when I need you.' But I have to perform in order to support Les Milandes. I can't be in two places at one time."

Though true, Josephine did not like to admit that her career was her life blood. "She loved that stage more than anything else in the world," Carolyn Carruthers recalls.

Like so many entertainers, her "farewell engagements" came and went, yet she never really withdrew. The *Paris Herald Tribune* called her 1956 retirement show at the Olympia Music Hall "merely a slightly exaggerated form of announcement that she is back with us again."

When Josephine returned from her trips, the children and servants lined up to greet her. The field hands would march like soldiers up to the front of the château. For the children, Josephine's homecoming was a fête. They called her *Maman*

Cadeau, Mother Gift, because she always came back laden down with presents.

Josephine often chose these moments when everyone was together to deliver her lectures on economy. "We've got to sacrifice. We have to tighten our belts. We must pay our bills." At the same time, they could not help but notice the boxes of new clothes arriving with her luggage. Richard, who still worked off and on as her chauffeur, driving her around Europe for theatrical engagements, remembers: "When she wasn't on stage, she was in the department stores."

Shirley Hertz, who managed a number of Josephine's American performances, felt that Josephine spent much of her time with her two feet planted firmly in the air. "I don't think she ever tuned in to reality for twenty-four hours straight. If she made $10,000 on a booking, she'd say, 'We can go on making this money forever.'"

Mixed in with Josephine's glory years were the seeds of her demise. If Heraclitus was right when he said "character is fate," then much of the blame must be attributed to her. Josephine achieved her dream, to be the sovereign ruler of a domain. But living in a castle, high on a hill, she grew remote from the outside world.

Josephine developed a *"folie des grandeurs"* about Les Milandes. She wanted to expand her territory, to own everything as far as her eyes could see. With this goal in mind, she tried to buy up every house in the village of Milandes. Only two farmers held out.

Josephine's romance with power was particularly hard on her family. Richard never felt that he could walk into Josephine's château unannounced. He waited until he was summoned. "The only time I was inside the château was at Christmas."

Because Margaret played such a large role in helping to raise the "rainbow tribe," and because she was Josephine's confidante, she was able to come and go. But any assertion of independence on the part of Josephine's family was regarded with disfavor. Even Carrie was upset by Josephine's high-handedness. She confided to Richard, "I don't think Tumpie love us anymore."

When Margaret used her savings to open a tearoom on the

Josephine attends wedding of her brother Richard, who married the postmistress of Les Milandes. With her are three of her boys, Jari, Luis and Moïse. Paris Match, *Pedrazzini*

grounds, Josephine threw a fit. Margaret sold homemade pies and American-style ice cream, much richer than the French ice cream sold by Josephine's café across the path. It was a great hit with the tourists. Josephine put heavy pressure on Margaret to close down her business. "You're stealing my customers," she complained. But Margaret refused to give in.

Richard was most resentful of his sister's dominance. "She wanted us to live for her, to respect her as the mother and father. She wanted to be the boss for life."

Josephine's postmistress, Mary Louise Tamasier, was in her fifties when she worked at Les Milandes. It was there she met and married Richard, becoming his third wife. Although the marriage lasted only a few years, Mary Louise saw Josephine as both an employer and a sister-in-law. "In the beginning she embraced everybody, but then as Les Milandes grew bigger and the finances got out of control, she became more severe. She would point a finger at the nurse, the maid and the handyman and correct them in front of everybody."

Josephine's singular nature was not conducive to domestic bliss. Life in a castle, surrounded by servants, provided a climate for the dictatorial aspects of her character to get the upper hand. She began to regard Jo Bouillon more as one of her subjects than as a husband.

"Josephine wanted a man she could baby," says her close friend Charles Burney. "She wanted a pet she could bring up. Strong women don't want anybody to dictate to them. They have to be in charge."

Jo Bouillon was an intelligent man who had left music in midlife to manage a resort, and who now had the awesome task of helping to make Josephine's fantasy a reality. In the beginning Josephine needed Jo; as their lives meshed, this need turned to love. Their dependency on each other ran deep. She loved him as she loved her children, as an extension of herself. Sometimes, when they fought, she ran down the road to the farm where Carrie lived with Margaret and announced, "I'm going to sleep with Mama tonight."

In his capacity as Josephine's chauffeur, brother Richard had intimate glimpses of the marriage. "She was head over heels in love with Jo. What he do to make her love him so, I don't know and I wouldn't ask. But she was also cruel to him. She talked to him like he was a little kid. She made him miserable. He'd stay in his bedroom for two and three days. He'd hardly eat. And when he come out, he looked like death warmed over."

To some of Josephine's friends, this marriage was part of her need to create a problem so that she would have a challenge. "If you have someone who frustrates you," says Jack Jordan, "you are never bored. I think she wanted to prove that she could get him to be a man."

"*Qui tient la chandelle?*" Who is holding the candle? Only the two in the privacy of the bed ever really know. But one thing was certain. The tension between Josephine and Jo was not simply physical. Josephine was jealous of his popularity at Les Milandes and his close relationship with the children.

Jo Bouillon, the youngest son of a violin professor at the Conservatoire de Montpellier, had played the violin from the time he was a child. Now he wanted to pass this skill on to Akio, the oldest and brightest of their children, who demonstrated musical ability. Bouillon bought him a violin and started to give him lessons. Seeing them practice together, sharing something she could not be part of, so infuriated Josephine that she took Akio's violin and, lifting her leg, cracked it over her thigh.

As one such incident followed another, Bouillon, who described Josephine as "a woman with a personality like thunder," decided she was impossible to live with. He began to think of what he could do to get out of the situation.

In his capacity as manager of Les Milandes and consort to Josephine, Jo Bouillon drew a salary plus expenses for cigarettes, travel, liquor and any petty cash he spent on the children.

Bouillon hired a childhood friend to serve as manager of one of the hotels. According to Richard, the friend began to siphon off the profits for himself and shared this money with Bouillon. "They had two sets of books," says Richard, "one for the government and one for the house. And when Josephine came and asked for the books, they gave her the books for the government. Jo Bouillon was after her money, and he got it."

Whether it was Josephine's extravagance or Jo's shenanigans, Les Milandes began to go downhill. Where it had once been considered a breadbasket for the region, it was now wide open to thieves. Lack of supervision and the rapid turnover of employees made stealing an easy matter. Says Richard, "The workers came on motorcycles and left in cars." Josephine hired people on the spur of the moment without asking for recommendations. And she fired on whim, saying to a worker, "After today, I don't want to see you around here."

Everything was slipshod. Salaries were not paid regularly, providing the filchers with justification for their acts. Josephine sadly lamented, "It's not easy to find a peasant who is an idealist." Some of the workers even tried to extort money from Josephine. They claimed that Bouillon had made sexual advances to them and they wanted Josephine to give them money to keep quiet. One day a farm worker told Josephine that all of her sheep had caught a disease and died. Yet when she asked to see the carcasses, nobody knew where they were.

Josephine, once so trusting, now became suspicious of everyone, and the innocent suffered. A domestic Josephine had met on a trip to South America and invited to work for her in France could not count with French money. When Josephine sent her into town on an errand and she made a mistake with the change, she was fired. Another time, while Josephine was appearing at the Olympia in Paris, Bruno Coquatrix, the director of the theatre, noticed that she was piling her sedan with groceries before returning to Les Milandes.

"Why are you shopping in Paris?" asked Coquatrix. "Food is so much cheaper in the provinces."

"Because the merchants will cheat me," said Josephine.

Josephine was right. If the grocers in the nearby town of Sarlat knew that their produce was going to Les Milandes, they jacked up the price.

In 1957, after ten years of marriage, Bouillon left Les Milandes and moved to Paris. That same year Jean Lion died at the age of forty-seven of the Russian flu. "He went as only a rich man can go," says his friend Jacqueline Stone, "with the doctors standing in the corner arguing about the diagnosis." And two years later, while Josephine was en route from Rome to Istanbul, Carrie died.

Upon hearing the news of her mother's death, Josephine repeated a saying she heard as a little girl going to funerals in the Chestnut Valley. It was an homage paid to strong women in the black community who, against all odds, have kept their family together.

> *Mama fought the good fight*
> *The battle is over*
> *The victory is won.*

Josephine and Jo Bouillon reconciled briefly, out of a genuine concern for their children's welfare. But the trust in the marriage had been destroyed beyond redemption. Bouillon moved to Buenos Aires, where he opened a French restaurant.

Josephine refused to discuss her personal relationship with Bouillon explaining to a reporter for *Jet* magazine: "This will be a dignified divorce action and I do not intend for there to be any scandal connected with it. I will only say that the situation between Jo and myself had become unbearable. There are certain things that no decent, self-respecting woman can tolerate."

But they did not divorce. At the time they separated they had eleven children and Josephine wanted more.

Although Bouillon was not in favor of adopting more children, he nonetheless went along with signing the papers for Stellina, a beautiful Moroccan baby who was the daughter of a friend of Josephine's. And he continued to take an active interest in the children he had helped to raise, writing Monsieur and Madame Besse to get reports on their schoolwork and arranging to have several of the children visit him in Argentina.

In addition to her own marriage problems, Josephine had to keep a stern eye on Richard's domestic situation. The postmistress turned out to be a gold digger who thought that Richard would come into a sizable chunk of Josephine's money. Prompted by despair as well as desire, Richard moved in with Yvonne, a wild-eyed peasant, and began having children. He also took over at the gas station, running it his own way instead of Josephine's, which would end their relationship.

Josephine's way of loving, her insatiable need to protect and dominate, colored all of her close relationships. She pushed people too far, forcing them to take a stand, to either knuckle under or run for freedom. Richard, a renegade, chose to pick up and leave. Later he reflected, "She was always talkin' 'bout liberty, equality and fraternity, but she tell everybody what to do."

In the ten years from 1953 to 1963, Josephine had managed to go through over $1.5 million. By 1963 she was $400,000 in debt. In order to raise enough cash to keep going, Josephine went to Paris and pawned her jewels. "She didn't cry about it because she felt it was for Les Milandes," Carolyn Carruthers remembers. "She was a very stubborn woman. She was going to save Les Milandes no matter what it cost her."

At this vulnerable time in her life, Josephine was an easy mark for con artists. Hearing that Josephine was unloading her

Returning to a stage where she had triumphed twenty-one years before, Josephine stars in a benefit performance at the Egyptian Opera
House in Cairo. The proceeds were to go to the salvage operations of
the Nubian temples of Abu Simbel. In 1943, Josephine had given a
performance, on the same stage, for the Allied troops. London Daily
Express, *Pictorial Parade*

jewels, a fence approached her in Paris with an offer to help.

Josephine agreed to sell a large diamond. She drove with the fence to the Claridge Hotel on the Champs-Elysées, where a buyer for the jewel was supposedly waiting in the lobby. The fence parked in front of the Claridge under the chestnut trees. "You wait here in the car," he told Josephine, as he pocketed the diamond. "I'll take the jewel into my contact and bring back the money." They had agreed the fence would take 10 percent; Josephine never saw the fence or her diamond again.

Even in bleakest times, Josephine knew that she could always raise money on her life story. One person who hoped to do her biography was the extraordinarily talented rebel poet Langston Hughes. On January 8, 1963, his friend Arna Bontemps wrote him: "You are the ideal person to do the Josephine Baker book. I hope you waste no time getting to it. Her differences with the U.S. press (or a section of it) may hurt her personal appearances here, but I can't imagine this harming the book; it should help. The warm element of controversy combined with the warm element of sex and no strings and the French flavor! This could be your first best seller as well as a solid possibility for serialization, etc. So I urge again, let no grass grow etc." Unfortunately, for reasons which are not clear, the project never got off the ground.

Josephine blocked any negative thoughts from her mind. Rather than considering Les Milandes a defeat, why not look at it as a beginning? Instead of teaching a dozen children how to live in peace, why not five hundred? Now was the time to make her big dream come true. Les Milandes could become the International Brotherhood College, bringing together students in their mid- to late teens from all over the world. "Let's not think about a sorry tomorrow," Josephine told a reporter, "a tomorrow where people fight and kill each other when it's so unnecessary."

Her plans were vague: "We'll have a series of professors from different countries, of all colors and religions and all standards of life to teach the essentials of brotherhood. . . . The students must be able to have board and education without having to worry about the cost. . . . The future of the village will depend on the world's heartbeats."

1964. Josephine strolls with her Rainbow Tribe at Les Milandes. *Left to right:* Jari, Akio, Moïse, Noël, Marianne, Koffi, Jean-Claude, Janot, Brahim, Mara, Luis. *Keystone*

In August 1963, to stir up interest in her project, Josephine flew to the United States to participate in the March on Washington. She was not invited. She had trouble obtaining a visa, but that obstacle was removed by Robert Kennedy.

Over 200,000 blacks and whites took part in the march, the largest civil rights demonstration in United States history. It was a remarkable spectacle, one of disorganized order, with a stateliness that no amount of planning could have produced. Dressed in her French Air Auxiliary uniform, Josephine spoke to the crowd. And she listened attentively as Martin Luther King held the demonstrators enthralled:

... I have a dream that one day this nation will rise up, live out the true meaning of its creed: We hold these truths to be self-evident, that all men are created equal. ...

When we allow freedom to ring—when we let it ring from every city and every hamlet, from every state and every city, we will be able to speed up that day when all of God's children, black men and white men, Jews and Gentiles, Protestants and Catholics, will be able to join hands and sing in the words of the old Negro spiritual, "Free at last, Free at last, Great God a-mighty, We are free at last."

The March on Washington was both a turning point and a revelation to Josephine. Ten years before she had been one of a small number of brave elite who sallied into the fray. But now, a decade later, a whole army had joined the battle, led by a network of prominent blacks masterminding a national crusade.

The older civil rights leaders were wary of her. While they remembered her extraordinary valor in 1951, they could not forget her tasteless and absurd remarks during her brief espousal of Perón in 1952. The younger ones were not sure who she was. Undaunted, Josephine set out to find her niche in the movement. Naturally she saw her place at the top. In analyzing Martin Luther King's speech, Josephine told her nephew Richard, the son of her brother: "He wasn't strong enough. He should have put his foot down and demanded rights for black people. I could have done it better."

Josephine wanted to give a benefit concert for the civil rights movement. Jack Jordan found an angel who put up $15,000 to get the ball rolling. The concert was set for October 12, the proceeds earmarked to benefit SNCC, CORE and NAACP, as well as Josephine's Brotherhood School

Unfortunately, Josephine's history of anti-American statements, along with her notorious reputation as a fly-by-nighter when it came to paying people, made it difficult to find a public relations agency to handle her.

One of Josephine's economy measures, certainly frowned upon in show business circles, was to try to do her managers out of their commissions. Questioning her on this practice was not particularly enlightening. "He wasn't really my manager. He claimed he worked for me. . . . I'm not a *femme d'affaires,* I'm a humanitarian."

Josephine's cavalier attitude resulted in a rapid turnover in managers as well as a fair number of lawsuits. To work for Josephine was somewhat akin to following Moses as he crossed the Red Sea—hardly a singular experience. "She did in some of the best impresarios in the world," says a business acquaintance. "When she met you, she cased you for your vulnerable spots. She sized you up just as if you were an animal. It's as if she walked around you and said, 'Is the foreleg stronger than the backleg? Is he weak on the left side or the right?' You are her prey and you are helpless."

Finally John Morsell, one of Roy Wilkins's assistants at NAACP, called Henri Ghent, a former concert singer who wrote promotional material for Columbia Records. Morsell urged Henri to handle Josephine as a favor to the movement. He told him, "No top PR person in New York will touch her."

Henri was an excellent choice to promote Josephine. He is powerfully handsome with a shrewd instinct for people. The youngest of eleven black children from a dirt-poor Georgia family, he had traveled a path similar to Josephine's, using his talent as a classical singer to advance himself in the world. Henri had trained at the New England Conservatory of Music in Boston and performed with Fiedler and the Boston Pops before launching a fifteen-year career as a concert singer, most of it spent in France. There he became fluent in the language and developed a continental savoir faire every bit the equal of Josephine's.

Although Henri had been introduced to La Bakaire in Paris, he walked into her suite at the Hilton in New York wondering just how he was going to handle the fabled *"monstre sacré."*

In the corner of the room he saw a plain black woman huddled in an Indian shawl talking on the telephone. She was almost bald except for a thin layer of pure white fuzz. A black wig rested like a sleeping cat on the end table next to her. Beneath the shawl she wore a white flannel nightshirt that came to her knees. Her legs were wrapped in pink elastic bandages to protect her weary joints from getting chilled.

"At first I thought this must be some relative from St. Louis," says Henri. "Then I realized it was Josephine. Later she told me that she used lye to 'conk' her hair and it had destroyed the follicles."

Putting down the receiver, Josephine rose to greet Henri. Seeing that he was shocked by her appearance, she stretched out her arms and thrust her hips forward, doing a campy lampoon of her famous stage pose. "Show business is all illusion . . . all illusion."

Henri quickly realized that he was coming into Josephine's life at a shaky time. One moment she was a lost child, seemingly defenseless in her innocence, and the next a frightened middle-age woman who could still gear herself up for her public as a symbol of eternal youth. "She was so docile," says Henri, "so ready. I knew that she really wanted her public back. She hung on my every word without talking, but I could see her beadlike eyes running around a mile a minute."

To drum up publicity for the Carnegie Hall benefit, Henri called a press conference. "Her career needed an injection of something new," says Henri. "So I decided to present her as an artiste rather than just a music hall performer."

As the reporters filed into the room, Henri diplomatically suggested to Josephine that she speak only in French, telling her, "You sound so refined *en Français.*" Then he translated her remarks into English, editing out her stinging comments, downplaying any references to her verbal bonfires of the 1950s. "We say a lot of things in the heat of passion."

Seeing that the crowd was with her, Josephine became more confident. When a journalist asked if she knew in the 1920s that she was going to become a myth, Josephine threw her head back, laughed and said, "Yes!" There was a certainty in her voice, a deep pride about herself. She had acquired that assured language of the immortals, an awareness that her name would survive her death. As Coco Chanel once said, "Those on whom legends are built *are* their legends."

After the press conference Henri and Josephine journeyed up to Harlem to join friends for supper. As the taxi sped up Seventh Avenue, Henri could feel her intense relief. Putting her hand on his knee, she said, "Oh, Henri, it's so good to be home."

"Josephine ate as if there was no tomorrow," remembers Henri. "She sat there chewing on chitlins and cornbread, relishing every bite. I never saw an expression like the one on her face. She was so peaceful and happy. Down deep in her heart Josephine was never anything else but a black American."

The benefit was a great success. "She reminded me of an Arabian stallion," says Henri. "She *pranced* across the stage."

The next day Henri fired off telegrams announcing Josephine's triumph to the Paris newspapers; a New York success would rekindle interest in her by European promoters. It worked. Almost immediately Josephine's name was once more in the wind. Bruno Coquatrix talked about producing a musical called *La Dame aux Camélias* based on the book by Alexandre Dumas *fils*. It would star Josephine, who would play the lead in French in Paris and in English in New York.

People stopped Josephine on the street in New York to ask for her autograph, and old admirers surfaced. Buoyed by this adulation, Josephine reverted to her sassy self. One night as she sat in Chandler's restaurant with her close friend Florence Dixon, a man came up to her table. Bowing deeply, he held out his hand and presented her with a diamond stickpin.

"Miss Baker, I want you to have this."

"Thank you," Josephine said, barely looking up. Still ignoring the man, she turned to Florence and said, "Here, you take it."

Florence became annoyed at Josephine's insensitivity. "For heaven's sakes, Josephine, put it on!"

Henri was not impressed with the new frisky Josephine, especially since she had not gotten around to paying him. She became slippery as an eel when he brought up the subject.

Finally he confronted her in the lobby of the Essex Hotel. "Josephine had just moved over from the Hilton," he remembers. "She skipped out of there without paying her bill."

Josephine responded to Henri's request for payment by simply pretending he did not exist. It was not an overt gesture of ignoring him, it was more like a queen dismissing a subject. He says: "When she put on her prima donna act, she diminished the other person. You weren't aware that your legs had been cut from under you until you started to walk."

To Josephine's surprise, Henri held his ground—and then some. Shaking his fist in her face, he said: "I don't go for this star shit. Two weeks ago you were hungry. I gave you back the American public and I'll take 'em right back."

To bolster his stand, Henri phoned the *Amsterdam News* and asked them to publish an article saying that he planned to sue Josephine. Only after the article appeared did Josephine capitulate and pay him.

Henri looks back on the experience of knowing Josephine with deeply mixed feelings. "As an artist I kneel to her. As a person, dealing with her in business, I think it's fair to say I loathed her."

After a few quick phone calls, Josephine replaced Henri with Shirley Hertz, a successful theatrical publicist who had worked for Rosalind Russell. Though aware of Josephine's notorious mismanagement of money, Shirley genuinely admired her special gifts. "I've known many stars who had a glow," she says, "but Josephine had a fire the likes of which I have never seen."

Shirley Hertz acted as her PR agent in the spring of 1964, during which time Josephine played the Strand and the Brooks Atkinson with Geoffrey Holder. Carmen de Lavallade. She toured several cities in America and Canada.

Though not nearly out of the woods financially, Josephine was heartened by the steady flow of compliments from the critics. Judith Crist wrote of Josephine's performance at the Brooks Atkinson: "There's the flashing smile, the voice that's true and very sure, the hand to gesture nuances beyond sound, and the glamour—ah, the glamour! The eyelids match the mike, whether they're gold or silver or sequined, the mile-high hairdos, the skin-tight slit-skirted gowns and the figure-clutching jump suits are jeweled to a fare-thee-well, and the feathers and furs are dazzling and for dragging along the floor."

Because the problem persisted of how to keep the press from resurrecting Josephine's anti-American remarks, Shirley was very selective about whom she permitted to interview Josephine. "If a drama page critic called, I felt we were on safe ground. But if a paper assigned a reporter from cityside, I immediately became suspicious."

Josephine's canny ploys to outwit her creditors provided a leitmotif throughout the tour. Having little success in getting their hands on her earnings, they plotted to nab her wardrobe. "I remember being in a Philadelphia hotel with her," says Shirley, "and rushing out through a revolving door with the costumes while the marshal was coming in the other side. We had to get them out of Pennsylvania. So we took the costumes to the 30th Street station and gave them to a porter on the train. We didn't have a claim check. Nothing. Then we called a friend in New York and asked her to run over to Penn Station and meet the train."

Such monkeyshines rekindled in Josephine a certain *esprit de guerre*. Lawsuits held the promise of drama and intrigue.

One of Josephine's escorts was the Count de Vigne, a Beau Brummell with a villa in Haiti. She was frequently photographed with him as she left the theatre. Josephine suggested to Florence Dixon that since they were both the same size and approximately the same complexion, she should dash from the theatre on the arm of the Count. Florence was photographed from every angle. "Now," said Josephine, wringing her hands jubilantly, "if any of the papers publish those pictures, I'll show you how to sue them."

Though Josephine often sported an admirer on her arm as window dressing, that is all he was. Perhaps she could not get over her deep-seated hurt at never having achieved a trusting intimate relationship with a man. She offered several explanations. "Now that I am a symbol of motherhood, it would not be fitting for me to take lovers." When a Danish reporter interviewed her on the subject, mentioning that Maurice Chevalier had said he thought sex at his age was ugly, Josephine bristled: "I don't think anything in nature is ugly. I just don't have time for sex."

In fact, Josephine's preoccupation with money worries took up most of her time. Hoping to raise funds, she met with best-selling author Gerold Frank to discuss the possibility of doing her autobiography.

"I liked her very much," recalls Frank. "There was something very magical about Josephine. She was a wild creature, yet under control. She had this laser beam charm which can mesmerize 2000 people. Imagine what happens when she trains that laser beam on you."

During their initial talk Josephine dropped a few exciting stories to whet Frank's appetite. As usual, she was not bogged down by accuracy. In discussing her World War II activities, she said, "There I was, driving a truck for de Gaulle with a bullet in my stomach."

After they signed a letter of agreement and Gerold Frank's agent, Helen Straus, sent his proposal around to various publishing houses, Frank was shocked by the reaction. It turned out that this was not Josephine's first foray into American publishing. One editor told him, "She's been taking money on book advances for years."

Even though he had been taken for a ride, Gerold Frank never harbored animosity toward Josephine. "People who live on mountaintops make their own rules. These rules can bring them great fame and great power and satisfaction. When you think of where she began, it was a long voyage and she had to make detours."

The French have a word, *orgueilleux,* bursting with pride, that helps to account for Josephine's lack of accountability in her business dealings. Behind her conceit, seen again and again, was a hunger for revenge. By bamboozling managers, theatre owners, authors—anyone who drifted into her net—she was rebelling against a world she felt had cheated her from the very beginning.

Returning to France, Josephine called a press conference to dramatize her plight. Her creditors, drained of patience, had banded together and obtained a court order demanding that Josephine's household goods and personal possessions be put up for sale. The auction was imminent.

"I'm ruined," she wept. She also invited bankers, philanthropists and old friends to come to Les Milandes for a strategy session, at which it was decided that the commercial exploitation of the resort would be shelved for the time being and that the village would be put under the trusteeship of an international committee. This, to save the château.

Oscar Petersen, the Danish entertainer, sat in on several chaotic meetings and came away somewhat skeptical. "She was always surrounded by the children or by various people. This way she could always be performing."

Nonetheless, Josephine received support from the great and small. Brigitte Bardot and André Maurois mounted a nationwide television appeal that brought in $24,000. Empress Farah Diba of Iran sent a generous gift. Josephine also received hundreds of small contributions. Dozens of letters arrived each day at Les Milandes, many containing checks or ten-franc notes.

Because she had been able to raise so much cash, a bank in Switzerland now lent her enough money to stave off the auction.

Although many people came to her rescue, she was also widely criticized in newspapers all over Europe. One man in Denmark wrote to the *Berlingske Tidende*: "I, too, need $400,000. I don't have a castle or jewels or umpteen kids, but I need it because I'm broke. Is it necessary to live in a castle? Why doesn't Miss Baker just sell the whole thing and live in a decent house and bring up her kids like we all do?"

Josephine dismissed such criticism with a wave of the hand. "I'd never had children. I didn't know it costs so much. Food is important, atmosphere is important for the development of the brain."

Exhausted from the strain, Josephine suffered a heart attack on July 25, 1964. This proved to be a financial as well as physical setback. As bookkeeper Andrée Choqueteau remembers: "She was desperate. She called all over the world trying to get work but without much luck."

In 1965 Josephine made a quick trip to Fez, Morocco, to put the touch on King Hassan II. If one must borrow, monarchs make excellent creditors; they are rarely strapped and their position generally inhibits them from getting particular about repayment. Hassan—Allah bless him!—knows how to give with flair. Once he threw a sumptuous dinner for a covey of foreign diplomats who found gold coins embedded in their smoked salmon.

Hassan gave Josephine a check for $6000 and promised $20,000 annually. His munificence enabled Josephine to stop yet another auction of her property. Bailiffs were set to seize the château and sell it unless she settled $5000 of her debts by November 5.

The more Les Milandes decayed, the more determined Josephine became to establish a capital of brotherhood. In 1967 she invited a group of Danish architects to visit Les Milandes and develop a master plan for turning the château into an international school.

The head of the architects' group was a highly respected professional from Copenhagen named Anne Marie Rubin. It was clearly understood before the project was undertaken that Rubin would do this for a fee, not for charity. The group stayed a month and produced a highly detailed plan that required a great deal of work. Despite being wined and dined for the month, Rubin could not get Josephine to pay her. "Josephine was most unreliable when it came to the business side of things. She was a *master* at getting people to work for her for nothing"

No matter how rough things got for her, Josephine knew she had friends in high places, and so she never felt deserted. In 1966 she accepted an invitation from Fidel Castro to travel to Cuba for the 7th anniversary festivities of the Cuban revolution. She gave a speech and sang for the workers in the sugarcane fields. Castro agreed to pay for her transportation and lodging, as well as for that of several of her children. "We were petrified when Castro came to our villa in Cuba, because he had his armed bodyguards with him," Jari remembers.

The trip was followed by a five-hour intestinal operation in Neuilly, a suburb of Paris. "They took everything out but her heart and liver," says a friend. Still Josephine remained optimistic. Castro's generosity led her to believe that here was a man who would surely bail her out. She wrote a long plaintive letter to him explaining her disastrous financial condition and hinting broadly that a sizable check would be appreciated.

Castro replied promptly, saying in his letter, "I'm going to send you a present."

The next few weeks Josephine met the postman every day. "I just know he's going to save me," she told Andrée Choqueteau.

Finally Castro's present arrived—two dozen oranges and six grapefruit.

In 1966 Jo Bouillon returned from Buenos Aires to see if there was anything he could do to pull Les Milandes out of the hole. It was also the Christmas season and he wanted to be with the children.

Bouillon was not prepared to use any of his own money in support of the Rainbow Tribe. Choqueteau, Josephine's secretary during this period, recalls that every time Jo Bouillon spent money on the children, even if it was only ten francs, he would go to Merle Trijoulet, the accountant, and say, "Mark that down on my account."

As the situation became more and more drastic, and more and more of the staff were let go, the children felt their world crumbling around them. Because Josephine was forced to be away from the château so much, they had relied on the staff for the love and attention that parents usually provide.

Andrée Choqueteau wanted to stay on at Les Milandes but, because the job paid so little, she was forced to leave. Noël was crushed when he learned she was going. "He was just beginning to read when I was there. Every evening he came into my office and we read together. On my last day I was getting into my car when he opened the front door of the château.

"Madame Choqueteau, will you come back?"

"Of course," she said. "I'll come back and see you from time to time."

Noël started to cry, "But who will read with me at night?"

Even though the château was now in ramshackle condition, a trickle of tourists still stopped off at Les Milandes as they were touring the castles of the Dordogne. Josephine never failed to see them as potential donors to her cause.

On May 17, 1967, Americans Francis and Priscilla Hallowell remember coming across Josephine in her garden. She invited them in for a glass of champagne, very much *la grande chatelaine,* giving not the slightest indication of trouble.

She led them into the salon and produced a bottle that Francis Hallowell thought was "The best champagne I've ever tasted. And the way she poured it was like watching a performance. She had hands like butterfly wings. She chatted on about the Milandes and her hopes for a comeback. She was absolute utter charm."

It was late afternoon and the children began arriving from school. Josephine excused herself to speak to them in the hall. Twenty minutes later they paraded into the grand salon in a group. The Hallowells were struck by how well behaved they were. "They were all beautifully dressed and perhaps too well trained. They stood in line according to their ages," says Francis Hallowell. "Josephine went down the line, giving each name and country and patting each child. Then the youngest boy sang a song. And then she told them they could be excused."

After the Hallowells returned to the United States, they received a brochure about Les Milandes with a letter enclosed requesting a contribution.

Lack of funds did not stop Josephine from flying to New York in June 1968 for the funeral of Robert Kennedy at St. Patrick's Cathedral. She brought along five of her boys, outfitting them for the occasion in navy blue blazers, gray trousers and black shoes. "I had to come," said Josephine, "because he meant so much to me."

By the spring of 1969 Josephine had exhausted every possibility of saving her château. She was licked. Les Milandes was sold at auction for $320,000. Three years earlier the domain had been assessed at $1.6 million. The château was valued at $500,000 but went for $70,000. Josephine's personal property brought $52,000 on the auction block.

In the 1930s the *St. Louis Post-Dispatch* reported that Josephine was the richest black woman in the world. Now she was sixty-two years old, broke, homeless, without a husband, overweight, aging swiftly. And she had twelve children to support.

Josephine refused to give up her château without a fight. She sent the children to live with her friend Marie Spiers in Paris, who fed them from the daily proceeds of her small dress shop, then returned to Les Milandes and barricaded herself in the kitchen. She slept on an army cot and ate from tin cans. Jean Joli, a hotel owner who had bought Les Milandes as an invest-

The dream is shattered. Sixty-two years old, $400,000 in debt, Josephine sits crying on the back steps of her chateau, which had been seized by creditors. *AGIP, Robert Cohen*

ment, sent eight of his workers to forcibly eject her. Knowing that Joli's henchmen were due to arrive, she called the newspapers and television stations.

As they dragged Josephine from the kitchen, she grabbed the stove. In the ensuing scuffle, she kicked and scratched and bit. Finally she was thrown out the door into the rain.

For seven hours Josephine sat on the back steps of her castle, barefoot, wearing a housecoat and a frilly mobcap over her sparse gray hair, until an ambulance arrived and took her to Périgueux. There she was hospitalized for nervous exhaustion. She tried to be brave, telling a reporter for *Le Figaro:* "I'm not bitter. We can all live in a tent."

NINETEEN

"She was life itself, with all that life can bring of risk,
of folly, of beauty and of play."

—Florence Mothe

Five months after her expulsion from Les Milandes, despite
rumors that she was too old and weak to perform in the theatrical big time, Josephine was invited to be the guest star at the
1969 August ball of the Sporting Club of Monte Carlo.

While rehearsing for the show, Josephine became acquainted
with Princess Grace of Monaco, who was deeply moved by her
plight. The Princess admired Josephine. She had been at the
Stork Club the evening of Josephine's historic snub and she was
immensely impressed by her courage. "I wonder if I could have
done the same," Grace Kelly said later. She also applauded
Josephine's unflinching commitment to her Rainbow Tribe.

Princess Grace now arranged with the local chapter of the
Red Cross, of which she was president, to give Josephine a
down payment of $20,000 on a $100,000 house in Roquebrune,
a small town 5 kilometers east of Monte Carlo, near the
French-Italian border.

"Isn't it interesting that an American woman bailed her out,"
says Bobby Short. "The French are always quick to look the
other way if someone is in trouble. It's a strange kind of trait
they enjoy. But good old Gracie saved her—and with style."

Roquebrune-Cap-Martin is an exquisite cliffside village of
gardens, mansions and hibiscus trees nestled on the edge of the

Mediterranean between Monaco and Menton.

Josephine's villa, which she christened Maryvonne, rests above la Moyenne Corniche, one of the three ancient Roman roads that run along the Côte d'Azur. The picture window facing the sea offers a commanding view of the bay of Cap Martin and of Monaco. In the distance, on a promontory, sits the Grimaldi castle guarded by white-shod gendarmerie in candy-striped sentry boxes. Here Prince Rainier rules as one of the world's last absolute monarchs. Josephine could not fail to appreciate this irony. She said, "I'm not very far from Paradise."

Under the protective aegis of the Rainiers, Josephine enjoyed a privileged position, immune from the criticism of the press. Monaco is something of an autocracy, and the influence of the palace is felt along the Riviera. Reporters at *Nice-Matin* were instructed by their editors not to write anything unfavorable about La Bakaire.

Some of the shopkeepers did not recognize her at first since she went about town in plaid skirts and cardigans, without makeup. When she walked into the stationery store of Pierre Cazenave with her flock around her addressing her as "Maman," Cazenave looked from one racially dissimilar face to another. "*Mon Dieu,*" he thought. "This woman has certainly been around."

Maryvonne has four bedrooms, two baths, a spacious living room and an adequate kitchen. For Josephine and her children this was cramped quarters after the fifty rooms of Les Milandes.

Much to Josephine's sadness, her brood was growing up and away from her. There was no place in her master plan for the storm and stress of adolescence. She had a photograph of them as youngsters in the first floor hallway, which she often stopped and stared at for minutes on end. She told Marie Spiers, "Soon I'm going to be alone again."

Josephine could not understand why her children were not more grateful after all she had done for them. When she returned from a trip she would get all the children up to see her, but they appeared nonchalant and some were even hostile. There had been too many maids, nannies and teachers. Their distance put Josephine on the defensive. She felt guilty about Jo Bouillon's departure, as his absence deprived them of a father. In asking her children to love her, she exposed her vulnerability. Once, while taking Moïse to task for an act of delinquency that involved the police, he turned on her with: "I never asked you to adopt me."

At the same time, the loyalty of her children to each other was deeper and truer than the ties formed by most natural kin. "Them kids stuck together like glue," says Margaret, who lived nearby and still supervised their day-to-day lives.

One Sunday Josephine cooked a ragout for the noontime repast. Later in the day, while tidying the house, she discovered that one of the children had thrown the meal behind a radiator in an upstairs bedroom.

"Who did this?" Josephine bellowed. "Which one of you?" No matter how hard she pressed the issue, no child would point the finger at another. She applauded their integrity. "My experiment has been a great success," she told Marie Spiers. "They love each other."

Stellina, the baby, who went to elementary school with Princess Grace's daughter Stephanie, was still young enough to idolize Josephine uncritically. Once when Josephine was performing in a Copenhagen supper club, Stellina was sitting with friends in the audience. As the room dimmed and Josephine walked on stage under the spotlight, Stellina jumped up and ran down to the edge of the stage. "Mother!" she cried. "Oh, Mother!" Then, turning to the audience, she announced with pride, "That's my mother."

Although Josephine now wanted to spend more time with her children to try to become closer to them, most of her waking hours were taken up with mere survival. The auction of Les Milandes did not bring in enough money to wipe out her debts. She owed about $200,000 in taxes to the French government. She did not take the debt seriously, but they did.

Jacques Anslem, a dress manufacturer, was walking with Josephine down a street in Paris one day when suddenly she stopped dead in her tracks. "Jacques, I must make a phone call."

Jacques stood next to her as she pumped a token into a pay phone.

"Giscard d'Estaing, s'il vous plait. Josephine Baker ici."

"Ah, oui!"

The operator placed her call to Giscard d'Estaing, who was then Secretary of the Treasury.

"Allo, Giscard. Mon cher. How can you bother me about taxes when I have so many children? Stop sending me these collection notices. I have no intention of paying. Au revoir!"

About this time Marshal Tito offered Josephine a helping hand. He was her kind of Communist. This peasant's son and wartime guerilla leader who became the president of Yugoslavia luckily never succumbed to that dreary regard for thrift that turns so many comrades into party poopers. *Au contraire,* he relished luxury. Tito lived like a monarch with sumptuous palaces, a private island, his personal train and a bevy of servile toadies. Through his intercession, the town of Sibenik, on the Adriatic coastline, offered Josephine an island with a medieval fortress called "Saint Nicolas" to be used for her Universal Brotherhood School. Though pleased by the offer, Josephine knew that her school was now a distant dream.

She was still receiving offers to perform, but the big fish, the heavy-duty theatre owners and promoters, were not biting. At this critical juncture she turned to her "thirteenth child," Jean-Claude Baker, né Rouzaud. Though she never legally adopted him, Josephine created a bond with Jean-Claude which, in some respects, went deeper than the tenuous hold she had on her official children.

Blessed with Parisian good looks reminiscent of Louis Jordan and the manners of a diplomat, Jean-Claude was part of the aura Josephine created around herself. And in her last years, when he was in his twenties and she in her sixties, they traveled together.

With Jean-Claude, Josephine could play what she considered to be her truest role—Auntie Mame. She was his guardian angel in boa feathers who transported him out of his little French world, who walked with him along the beach in Rio de Janeiro, who shared tortillas with him in a mansion in

Josephine and her "thirteenth" child, Jean-Claude, at the April in
Paris ball in New York. They frequently traveled together. She was his
guardian angel in boa feathers who introduced him to everyone from
Liza Minnelli to Coco Chanel. Through Josephine, Jean-Claude understood Auntie Mame's immortal words, "Life is a banquet, and most
sons of bitches are starving to death."

Acapulco, who introduced him to everyone from Lisa Minnelli
to Coco Chanel. Through Josephine, Jean-Claude understood
the meaning of Mame's immortal words, "Life is a banquet, and
most sons of bitches are starving to death."

They met at the Hotel Scribe in the late 1950s. At the time
Josephine was staying in one of the drafty maids' rooms on the
top floor. The W.C. was down the hall and the walls were paper
thin. But from her tiny chamber she could look with delight
across the rooftops of Paris and contemplate the city beneath
her.

Jean-Claude, who was fourteen at the time of their meeting,
worked for the Hotel Scribe as a "chasseur," pushing the revolv-

ing door for the guests and carrying their packages.

Raised in Saint-Symphorien, a small village near Lyon, Jean-Claude was the son of a restaurateur who gambled, went broke and deserted his family. "We lived on charity," he says. "So I decided to escape to Paris."

Jean-Claude ran an errand for Josephine one day. She quickly realized that he was feeling lost.

"Where's your father? Where's your mother? What are you doing in Paris all alone?

After Jean-Claude told her the story, she put her arm around him, kissed him and said: "You'll never be alone again. I'm your mother now."

In the beginning Jean-Claude fed Josephine's need for unqualified adoration. "I worshipped her," he says. "My own mother went crazy when my father left. She couldn't pull herself together. Josephine seemed to me to be the ideal of what a mother should be, strong and independent."

Josephine sent Jean-Claude to hotel school in England so that he would learn a trade and to speak English. Subsequently she helped launch him as the owner of a cabaret in Berlin called Pimm's, a jet-set spot reminiscent of the transvestite bars of the 1920s. Thereafter Josephine called him Jean-Claude Berlin to distinguish him from her fourth son, Jean-Claude Bouillon, a French Canadian. When she was really down on her luck, she worked for Jean-Claude at Pimm's, sitting at the tables, egging customers on to buy more drinks. "If Josephine wasn't getting work, her self-confidence evaporated," says Jean-Claude. "When she got in those states, she'd take anything. When a theatre in Berlin expressed interest in having her perform, she told Jean-Claude, "We must find a woman singer to be the headliner." Josephine felt that a costar would bring her own following and help fill the house.

Since Jean-Claude was out in the world and had developed survival skills *sans pareil,* Josephine urged him to assume the role of older brother to her restless brood. He did so with enthusiasm, finding the children polite and appreciative, though some were prone to the vacant-eyed passivity so often found in the offspring of celebrities.

Seeing Josephine with her Rainbow Tribe made him acutely

aware of how desperately she was trying to be a good mother. She wanted them to see her not as a cranky workhorse but as an instrument of joy. "For fun, she would take all of us out to a restaurant together to eat and dance. Of course, it was always at the expense of someone else, but it was fabulous. Mostly she liked to go for walks, or to an amusement park or the theatre. Her favorite outing was the zoo. She loved to see the animals through the eyes of the children."

When in Roquebrune Jean-Claude sat at the head of the table and Josephine presided at the opposite end. One dinnertime she startled the children with the announcement that Jean-Claude was going to read a letter to them from her doctor. Then she put her head in her hands.

He read: "Dear Boys and Girls. You are being very mean to your mother. You are killing her. If you don't start being nice soon, she will die."

As soon as Jean-Claude finished, Josephine rose and waited a moment, as if she expected applause. Then she ran to her bedroom just off the dining room.

The younger children became frightened. Stellina started to cry. "Don't be silly," said one of the older boys. "It's an act. She's nutty. Leave her alone."

Josephine knew that if she was ever going to get out of debt she would have to have a smashing comeback. Yet even she had begun to think of herself as passée. "I'm too old to play Josephine Baker," she told friends.

But in the spring of 1972 Josephine had a visitor who thought otherwise. Jack Jordan, the charming black rapscallion who raised the money for her to participate in the March on Washington, stopped by to see her. Jordan had acted briefly as Josephine's promoter during some of her performances in the early 1960s; the liaison had left them both extremely wary of each other. Josephine hinted darkly about a "forged check" and other acts of larceny on Jordan's part, never proven. Still, she respected his chutzpah and his talent for producing money out of thin air.

Jordan suggested to Josephine that he line up a booking for her at Carnegie Hall.

Josephine could not believe that it was possible for her to make a comeback in the United States. "Nobody wants me," she insisted. "They've forgotten me."

At this point Margaret, ever mindful of Josephine's staggering bills, cut into the conversation: "I don't know what you're horsing around about. Go to New York and make some money."

Jordan stayed on the Côte d'Azur a few days while they discussed the details of her "comeback." The Josephine he saw now was softer, less self-righteous than the' woman he knew nine years earlier.

Together they made a sightseeing tour of Nice. Josephine carefully led him past a jewelry store on the rue Masséna that was displaying a pair of gold earrings she wanted. As Jordan wrote out a traveler's check for them, he kidded her about her powers as a courtesan.

Josephine laughed easily. "You know, Jack, I'm old now. But don't think I didn't know what to do with a man in bed."

Josephine's Carnegie Hall show in June 1973 turned out to be one of the high spots of her career. Jack Jordan's co-producer Howard Saunders, a highly successful advertising man who specialized in black promotions, was overjoyed at the opportunity to relaunch Josephine.

Saunders knew that the quickest way to pack Carnegie Hall was to appeal to the homosexual community. "Josephine's greatest fans were the gays," says Saunders. "I mean reputable gays. They love to watch artists like Marlene Dietrich, Judy Garland or Jo Baker camp it up, with their exaggerated gestures and their clothes. To a gay, they represent theatre pushed to its fullest expression."

Using the gay directory, he sent out flyers and he paid gays to talk up the show. He also launched a massive street campaign. "I got models from the Black Beauty Agency and dressed them in flesh-colored outfits and Nefertiti wigs. They walked up and down Madison Avenue, Park, Lexington, Third and all over Harlem. They passed out flyers, 'Black Legend Returns.' Five days I did that. It worked. It turned the town on."

The night of the opening, Bricktop, almost eighty and still a rascal, introduced Josephine to the packed house. Reminiscing about their shared youth in Paris, Bricktop said of Josephine, "She was a simple little girl—she's still a simple little girl." At that point Josephine strolled out in a skin-tight sequined net body stocking and a four-foot headdress of orange plumes.

The audience, a compendium of sartorial extravagance itself, stood and cheered. Each of Josephine's entrances was a revelation in sequins and feathers, set off by her jeweled microphone. The culmination of these creations was a stunning black-and-white outfit—the white, floor-length fur cape she threw to the ground and stepped on as a prelude to her haunting rendition of "J'ai Deux Amours."

Michael Clemmens, a former merchant seaman, stood in the crowded side aisle to get a closer look. He watched her with the practiced eye of a connoisseur. "I've seen her in Buenos Aires, Copenhagen and Stockholm. This is one of her best performances ever."

By the third night Josephine began to wonder if she was going to get all the money she was promised. As a precautionary measure, she had stipulated that Saunders and Jordan pay her share in cash to her trusted friend Bessie Buchanan. Still, there would be record sales and other spinoffs. One never knows, do one? Josephine decided the moment had arrived for a "strike."

Jimmy Hall, the barman at the Red Rooster in Harlem, had been hired by Josephine to do a walk-on in the show. He played a cigar-smoking dandy who passed back and forth behind her as she sang "Bill" from *Showboat*. When he arrived that evening, Saunders told him, "Josephine caught a cold from the air-conditioning in the limo. She can't talk, let alone sing."

Hall went ahead and applied his makeup, determined that the show would go on. "See, this was my first time on stage. So, before comin' to Carnegie Hall, I'd pass by the Russian Tea Room and get tanked up on vodka."

Emboldened by alcohol, he confronted Josephine. "Girl, what's wrong with you?"

"Jimmeee, I lost my voice," she whispered.

"Come on, Josephine. My makeup's runnin'. There ain't

nothin' wrong with you. I'll cook you some fried chicken after the show."

Josephine glowed like a Christmas tree. "Get the grease hot!"

Howard Saunders was right: She turned the town on. One laudatory review followed another. No one failed to wonder at her powers of professional resilience. John Wilson of *The New York Times* wrote: "There is about her, one eventually realized, something of the aura that Duke Ellington projects. It is not simply that they both have style and wit and a confident knowledge of who they are. It stems from basics—Miss Baker moves the way Ellington plays." And from William Raidy of *The Long Island Press:* "I'd just as soon see Miss Baker walk across the stage, headdress flying in the air and derriere almost poised, as watch Nureyev fly through the air."

During the Carnegie Hall run, Josephine went up to Harlem to have her hair done at Rose Morgan's beauty parlor. Rose, an ex-wife of Joe Louis, had made over a million dollars with a "conking" process for nappy hair. Josephine made a habit of asking rich people to be godparents to her brood. And though each child now had a slew of rich godparents, this did not stop Josephine from asking Rose to be godmother to all twelve.

Rose Morgan thought Josephine was kidding. She was stunned when she received a note from each child with a photograph and a flower pressed inside the stationery, but declined. "My goodness," she wrote Josephine, "a godmother must be responsible for the child. I employ ninety people in my salon and I have to look after all of them."

Knowing the Carnegie Hall show would not cover her debts, Josephine continued to go after money in whatever ways she could. Josephine had certainly mastered the first rule of fundraising: Don't look poor—it scares off the donors.

Through her friend the Count de Vigne, Josephine met George Broadfield, a controversial black economist with a mysterious employer whose name he refuses to divulge.

Broadfield invited Josephine and the Count for dinner. "It was like planning for the arrival of the head of state," he recalls. "The Count notified me two weeks before with specific instructions of what Miss Baker would want to eat."

"On the evening she was to arrive," Broadfield continued, "I was wild with excitement. The Count is back and forth on the phone, keeping me posted as she dresses and does her makeup. Finally he calls and says, 'The men are here for the installation of the jewels.'

"At last, the doorman calls me on the intercom: 'They are passing through the lobby.'

"Josephine walks into my apartment and says, 'Hello, my child.'

"She is wearing a fabulous mink coat. I help her remove it. She drops to the floor and sits Arab style on the carpet. She is wearing a saffron-colored dress with a décolletage. Now I realize what the 'installation' was all about. She has jewels planted on her bosom, each about three-sixteenths of an inch apart.

"She eats her pigs' feet. I keep watching the jewels. They move as she talks. I forget where the champagne is. She laughs. '*Pas mal* for a woman of sixty-seven. Hmm, baby?'

"*Pas mal du tout!* She is so spontaneous. Just like a child. She must be attended to all the time. Her sentences are unconnected, but I sense that she is leading up to something.

"'George, I'm told you are a genius.' And then she says, 'Oh, this food is heavenly!' And then her face changes momentarily. 'I've got a plan.'

"I reach for another glass of champagne."

Josephine explained to Broadfield that Doxiodus, the Greek architect, had designed a city for her children. "Now, George, I have no idea how much this is going to cost, but I was thinking that maybe you would like to serve as a committee member and give me, say, $10,000 as an opening contribution."

Broadfield abruptly changed the topic of conversation. Nonetheless, he felt guilty. "You become depressed because you can't do enough for Josephine. Empty your pockets. Lay the checkbook at her feet. Of course, Miss Baker knows how to take it all."

The Carnegie Hall show ran four nights and grossed over $120,000. On the last night Florence Dixon, substituting for Bessie as banker, stuffed $8000 in her girdle because Josephine was going to a party and did not want to carry money.

Saunders and Jordan quickly lined up a fall tour of major cities in the United States. They soon realized, however, that Josephine no longer considered herself stranded. As they were going over the contract with her, Josephine got up to leave. "I don't understand what you are talking about because my English isn't very good. But you know something? I listen when I hear the money. And it doesn't sound like the right money. Now, gentlemen, you keep on talking, and when you get finished you let me know what the outcome is. Goooood night!"

Josephine returned to Europe for the summer.

In July 1973, while in Copenhagen for a singing engagement, Josephine suffered a heart attack and a stroke that paralyzed part of her face and left her in a semiconscious state for days. When three of her boys—Brahim, Koffi and Noël—visited her hospital room, she did not recognize them.

The doctor ordered her to rest four months and to ease off for at least a year. But she insisted, "I can't. I have twelve children to raise." In just over a week she went back to working twelve hours a day.

A short time later Josephine made a pilgrimage to Lourdes, a town in Southwest France where in 1858 the Virgin Mary appeared to a peasant girl, Bernadette Soubirous. During this apparition the Virgin created a spring that she promised would have miraculous effects on people who were ill.

Thousands of invalids visit the shrine every year. Miraculous cures have been reported. Some believers leave their crutches, wheelchairs or arm splints as evidence of their recovery. Others bathe in the sacred waters of the grotto spring hoping a miracle will restore them to health.

Josephine believed in miracles. She knelt in the grotto and begged God to give her strength. "God, please don't take me now. I have too many things to accomplish. You can't take me now. Not now. Give me some more time. I have to survive."

What happened next, according to Josephine, was a miracle. "All of a sudden there was a fire under my feet," she told her friend Florence Dixon. "The fire rose and came through all my limbs, all over my body. I felt it in my hair and in my fingers. It only lasted for a few minutes. When I walked out of there I felt like the most beautiful well person."

In Catholicism Josephine found the paternal love that she had sorely missed while growing up. Religion provided intimacy without pain, a balm for her essential loneliness and a structure for her chaotic life. When she needed God she talked to Him, but she did not have to interrupt her schedule for Him. And, as far as Josephine was concerned, He did not make demands.

Josephine returned to the United States in the fall of 1973 for the seventeen-city tour arranged by Saunders and Jordan. This time she brought along Jean-Claude Baker to work as her master of ceremonies and traveling companion.

Soigné in his Yves Saint-Laurent suit, his English spiced with Gallic flavor, Jean-Claude greeted reporters and passed out press releases with the relaxed ease of a talk-show host. "This is my thirteenth child, ladies and gentlemen," Josephine would announce to the assembled newspapermen. "Don't let anyone tell you thirteen is an unlucky number, because I've never cried for my children but for joy."

Josephine looked her best in years. Her figure was slim and trim, appropriately displayed in a new wardrobe of youthful pantsuits dressed up by elegant fur hats. She hid the crow's-feet around her eyes with Martian-size sunglasses. When giving interviews, her voice was warm and velvety, unfailingly bright and joyful. She answered questions graciously and with charming good humor when they were silly.

"What food do you cook for your children in Monaco?" asked one reporter.

"Well, my dear, I go to the nearest forest and capture some monkeys," Josephine laughed. "Then I skin them and throw them in a big ole pot!"

In an elevator at the Ponchartrain Hotel in Detroit, Josephine stepped out before Jean-Claude. As he was leaving, he overheard a young man in his twenties nod to his friend as they watched Josephine sashay down the hall, "I'd like to fuck her."

"She's my mother," said Jean-Claude.

"Oh God, I'm sorry," said the man. "What can I say? She looks so wonderful."

Jean-Claude delivered the introduction to Josephine's show and floated on and off stage as she chatted in her purr-cat style between songs. He also aided with her famous on-stage costume changes. "And now my son Jean-Claude will help unbutton my dress for me so I can do a strip tease to help feed my children."

Traces of senility ran through her patter. Nobody was more aware of it than Josephine. "I'm an old lady now," she admitted to Jean-Claude. "It's embarrassing to have to do this." At the same time, she needed her audience desperately. The mass love of a full house was her obsessional narcotic. Yet there was always the fear she was losing her edge. Even when the crowd was with her, Josephine found it hard to believe. In Los Angeles she told a wildly enthusiastic opening-night audience for whom she could do no wrong: "Don't look too near. Don't look at me too much. I'm trying to help you hold on to your illusions. If I come near you, you're liable to lose them."

Offstage, Josephine's relationship to Jean-Claude lost its former innocence. It was Jean-Claude who witnessed her tantrums, was the target of her occasional cruelties, episodes often followed by equally inexplicable displays of kindness and generosity. "It was her crazy dieting that caused it," says Jean-Claude. "It's not possible to live with someone whose nerves were as frayed as hers."

Josephine was thirty pounds thinner than she had been when she toured the United States in 1964. For breakfast she drank lemon juice with sugar in hot water. Almost no lunch, just picking. After the show she gorged on a plate of spaghetti, washed down with beer.

Jean-Claude saw to it that she took the pills for her heart and that she did not overdo while running to cocktail parties, dinners and receptions. He was both nursemaid and policeman.

"In Los Angeles she called the consulates for every country listed in the phone book, hoping that they would buy tickets. We were invited everywhere."

Getting her from city to city was a nightmare. "She'd miss the plane," recalls Jean-Claude. "There would be a second one and then one after that. If she met a woman with a baby at the airline counter, she'd say, 'You take my seat, I'll get on the next flight.'"

Josephine became so dominating that she even wanted to control Jean-Claude's sex life. "She knew I was bisexual, but she only wanted me to be with men because they didn't represent any competition with her. She couldn't stand it if I brought a woman back to the hotel. She used to cruise for me just so I'd be with boys. One day I slept with a black girl in the suite next to her room. She almost killed me."

Most of the time Jean-Claude slept beside Josephine. Josephine needed him near her because she was afraid to be alone, frightened that she would die in the night. He saw the arrangement as simply an extension of their mother-son relationship. "In France, if a little boy gets good marks on his report card, he is allowed to sleep in the same bed with his mother as a treat."

The morning light was cruel to Josephine. "Sometimes I'd look at her on the pillow as she slept," recalls Jean-Claude. "Without her wig, practically bald, she looked so defenseless. Hardly breathing. I'd say to myself, 'Is she still alive?' All of a sudden, she'd bolt up in bed and look at me.

"'You thought I was dead, didn't you? Well, I'm not!'"

Before the opening in San Francisco, there was a break in the tour. "Four days!" Josephine said to Jack Jordan. "What am I going to do for four days?"

"You're going to rest and travel to the next destination."

"Oh, I see."

That night Josephine flew to Monte Carlo, picked up Stellina, then flew on to Israel. She wanted to help Golda Meir celebrate her country's twenty-fifth anniversary.

In Jerusalem, Josephine joined 450 international guests to nibble stuffed vine leaves under the stars, watch Nureyev dance and take part in a torchlight parade. During the day she made the pilgrimage to the Holy Sepulchre. Of all the guests who participated in the ceremony, none left a deeper impression than Josephine.

Making friends with the Arab porter who cleaned her room

at the Jerusalem Intercontinental, she accepted an invitation to visit his modest home in the West Bank village of Bethany. She noticed they were chilling their food on a block of ice, so she rushed to Jerusalem to buy them an electric refrigerator—a luxury few others in the village could afford.

Josephine returned to San Francisco from Israel hours after her performance was supposed to take place, standing up a packed house and costing her promoters thousands of dollars. When Saunders and Jordan tried to dock Josephine's pay, she was infuriated. She quit the tour, leaving them high and dry. As a precautionary measure, she asked Jean-Claude to fly her costumes out of the country under his baptismal name of Rouzaud. "I think it was her health," says Howard Saunders. "She knew she was going to die soon, and she'd be damned if she'd do it in the provinces."

A former friend of Josephine's said, "She carried gasoline and a torch, and she burned her bridges as she went along." This certainly applied to her dealings with Jean-Claude. When she met him he was a servant; when he tried to rise above that rank, she treated him with the hostility of a Charleston plantation owner confronted by a rebellious member of the household staff. "I was her slave," says Jean-Claude. "I can remember one morning when we were sitting in the Beverly Wilshire in Los Angeles and her dog left some ground meat in his dish. She said, 'Eat it, Jean-Claude.' When I refused, she said, 'I'm going to send you back home.' She thought about that for a moment and then said, 'Now, where will I send you?'"

Their relationship was based on a deal. Josephine had her "model child" while Jean-Claude received an apprenticeship in show business—and life—from the master. At the same time Jean-Claude was her employee and wanted his salary.

"How can you be so ungrateful?" Josephine asked him when he pressed the issue. "If you went to school, you would have to pay $10,000 for this experience. And the name. Do you know what it is to have my name?"

Ah, the name. There was the rub. "She made me feel it every day," he remembers with sadness.

As Jean-Claude outgrew his role of valet, it became obvious that he was no pisswilly. The trip to America represented a beginning to him. He wanted to carve his niche in the New World. To that end he began to talk more freely to the press. The columnist Suzy quoted him as saying that Josephine was thinking of marrying Robert Brady, an artist living in Mexico. "I never gave the interview," protests Jean-Claude. "Brady fed her the item to advance his career."

Fearing that he was becoming too assertive, Josephine dropped Jean-Claude, leaving him hurt and bewildered. "I saw her use everybody, but I never thought she would do it to me. I said to myself, But I am her son!" Still, he recognized that she was giving him the necessary push to make it on his own. Using $60,000 he saved from the profits of his Berlin nightclub, he launched *Téléfrance U.S.A.*, an award-winning French television program originating in New York, broadcast nationally via cable. Acting as host as well as producer of the show, Jean-Claude interviews luminaries such as Marlon Brando, Jeanne Moreau and François Truffaut. He also produces French documentaries, news programs and successful series such as *Madame Le Juge,* Her Ladyship the Judge, which starred Simone Signoret. With the backing of such sponsors as Revlon and Perrier, *Téléfrance U.S.A.* is now on firm financial footing—and so is Jean-Claude. "I would have been a success anyway," he says. "But I would have been a bourgeois. I would have seen life through a small window. She taught me to see through a big picture window."

Josephine returned to New York for a Christmas-week run at the Palace Theatre on Broadway, a booking arranged by Jean-Claude before his fall from grace. With Jean-Claude in exile, Josephine resurrected her nephew Richard Martin from St. Louis to run errands for her.

Rising ten stories over the entrance to the Palace was a giant billboard dominating Times Square. It advertised the appearance of Bette Midler, who had closed the week before. The only evidence of Josephine's show was her name in small aluminum letters on the marquee—and the picket line, hired by Saunders and Jordan, protesting her breach of their contract.

Dodson Rader, on assignment for *Esquire* magazine to do a nostalgia piece on Josephine, found her in the basement of the

Palace the morning of the opening. She struck him as a strange graft of youth and age pulled together by force of will and haute couture. But the skin was still lovely, "pale cocoa, the color of Chock Full o' Nuts coffee done light."

Josephine's memory was so poor that evening that Rader found watching her a painful experience. She forgot the words of her songs and she rambled incoherently: ". . . then I came back to New York and Billy Brice, no, not Billy . . . at the Follies in New York before the war, Bob Hope and . . . Brice . . ." She had forgotten Fanny Brice. Rader thought "she wants to stop now. She wants to throw it over. . . . Time for your travelin' shoes, sweet Josephine."

With the exception of a few generous reviews, the show was panned. Her memory lapses were beginning to attract wide attention. Dumping the newspapers in a wastebasket in her Waldorf suite, Josephine turned to Richard and said, "I'm going to go to one of those youth doctors in Switzerland and get shots for my brain."

After the Palace flop panic set in. She was physically and emotionally spent. Bette Midler had more people in the aisles at the Palace than Josephine had in the seats. Her luck was clearly running out.

Richard was beside himself with anxiety when Josephine invited twenty people to the Waldorf for a champagne and steak dinner. "Auntie, where are you going to get the money?" he pleaded.

"Richard, I have an image to maintain and I'm going to maintain it," she responded.

They made the rounds in New York, galas and receptions. Josephine always let it be known that she was a presence. "We were at a fancy-schmancy cocktail party at the St. Regis," recalls Richard. "John Lindsay was there and a lot of top models. So a photographer asked Auntie Jo if she would have her picture taken with them. She stood in back of the group. The others were forced to place their bodies in such a way that they framed her. Lindsay was just a prop."

By exhibiting herself here and there, Josephine was demonstrating that she was still a viable commodity. It worked.

The management of Raffles, an elegant little private club

behind discreet wooden doors at the Sherry-Netherland, wanted a hostess with a strong nostalgic pull. Raffles became Chez Joséphine Baker. Once more she was employed. "But the crunch was gone," lamented Anita Loos. "She sounded like a second-rate singer from St. Louis."

To cut costs, Josephine checked out of the Waldorf Astoria and moved into a suite at the Navarro on Central Park South, which she shared with her nephew. Here Josephine cooked soul food, greens and pork ribs; other nights she made Chinese dishes. "Noodles give you strength," she said.

She could not throw food away. In the mornings, if she could not finish her Danish pastry, Josephine would wrap them in napkins and save them for days, sprinkling them with water occasionally to try to keep them fresh.

Richard complained, "Auntie, we're going to get roaches." He got so sick of economy meals that he would sneak down to Rumpelmayer's to splurge on roast beef and wine.

In the intimacy of the hotel suite, Richard was aware of Josephine's haunting loneliness. "She wanted me around because I was family," says Richard. "She wanted to have the feeling of belonging. When I'd take my bath at night, she'd say, 'Richard, don't wash the tub. I'm going to bathe now.' It was as if sharing the grime in the bathtub gave us a bond."

After the Raffles booking, Josephine returned to Roquebrune and the bills. The butcher's fee was usually about $300 a month. The phone bill, her bête noire, often went as high as $800, sometimes per week! She paid it when she could; when she could not, they cut off her service. The children habitually charged items in stores in Roquebrune and Monte Carlo, so Josephine was never sure how much she owed the local merchants. Whenever she came into any money, she rolled up 20-franc notes in little sacks and distributed them to the shopkeepers like Christmas stocking stuffers. "If you pay everybody a little bit," she told her children, "they don't mind."

To save money, Josephine often hitchhiked up and down the Riviera in the course of doing her errands. In Nice she bought the children's clothing at Prisunic, the French equivalent of Woolworth's.

Arlette Sayac, a reporter and editor at *Nice-Matin*, once saw Josephine picking through piles of cheap clothes in Prisunic. "She looked like a vagrant, so tired, and her slip was hanging. At first I couldn't believe it was Josephine Baker."

In her desperation Josephine was reduced to approaching strangers for handouts. Once while singing in a cabaret near Roquebrune, she sat down at the table of Don Smith, a New York publicist.

"Are you rich?" she asked.

"No," he answered, looking at her curiously.

"You look rich," said Josephine, explaining, "I need money to feed my children."

Josephine still continued to spend extravagantly when she felt a situation merited the grand gesture. After taking tea on *La Belle Simone*, the yacht of William and Simone Levitt anchored in Monaco harbor, Josephine sent them a thank-you note accompanied by dozens of red roses.

As Josephine's memory grew worse, she decided to hire a secretary to help answer her enormous backlog of correspondence. Marie-Joli Gomi came to her through the Bic employment agency in Nice. A vivacious young woman with a dazzling smile, Marie-Joli arrived for her first day of work behind the wheel of a white Fiat.

Josephine ran out front of the villa and circled the car. *"Formidable!"* she cried. "Such style. I want one."

Later, when they sat down to begin work, Josephine said, "Now, I want to write a letter to Gianni Agnelli, the president of Fiat in Italy."

The letter began: "Dear Gianni. The Fiat is marvelous. Be a darling and send me one. . . ."

Agnelli responded promptly with the latest model. No charge, of course. Reflecting upon the incident, Marie-Joli says, "You know, if I had driven up in a Rolls Royce, she would have thought that was banal."

Marie-Joli followed Josephine about the house, upstairs, downstairs, in the kitchen, on the terrace, scratching notes on her steno pad as Josephine dictated lengthy epistles in a breathy cadence. "Her letters were like novels, they went on and on," says Marie-Joli. "She started on one subject, which would take seven or eight pages. Then she switched to another idea for six more. Sometimes she opened a letter in English, changed into French and then closed in Spanish. But what really confused me was when she started a letter to one person and ended it to somebody else."

"To whom should I address the envelope, Madame?"

"Oh, it doesn't matter. I changed my mind about what I want to say."

In the afternoons, when the younger children arrived home from school, Josephine insisted that they come up to her, kiss her on both cheeks and say, "Bonjour, Maman." But sometimes Josephine was so deep in her thoughts that she confused one child with another. Marie-Joli remembers the disheartened look on Noël's face when she said to him, "Excuse me. What did you say your name was?"

Josephine rented an office at the Continental Hotel in Monte Carlo where she kept her private papers. When she gave Mari-Joli a key to it, she warned her: "You must never let any of my children into that room. They will steal my love letters and sell them."

Despite having to live in an atmosphere of distrust, the children tried to help Josephine as best they could. They knew that much of her suspicion stemmed from fear and exhaustion. Jari chauffeured her around in the Fiat, Moïse accompanied her on business errands and Janot, who loved flowers, helped Margaret's husband Elmo keep up the garden. One Saturday when Josephine went over the bills with the children, she came across a letter from the local school asking for $60, but she misread it thinking they wanted $600. Akio tried to explain it to her, but she only became more bewildered. Finally she broke down and sobbed. "What's going to become of us?"

Just in time the Société des Bains-de-Mer, the guiding hand behind the gambling and entertainment interests in Monte Carlo, decided to organize a show around Josephine, a musical revue based on her life. The show was the brainchild of André Levasseur, a gifted set and costume designer and a veteran of many productions at the Paris Opéra and the Comédie Française. Levasseur adored Josephine. He decided that since she was rapidly approaching her half-century mark in French show

1974. Sporting Club of Monte Carlo. At sixty-seven, Josephine stars in musical revue based on her life. She sang over thirty songs and danced a rigorous Charleston. *Keystone*

business, the time had come to pull out all the stops.

Held in August 1974, Levasseur's production *Joséphine* was a great success. In song and dance it romanticized a life marked by desperate struggle. Josephine was *en pleine forme*. It was as if, in giving her all, she was saying "thank you" to Monaco for taking her to its heart.

Henri Astric, theatrical director of the Sporting Club of Monte Carlo—the place of her triumph—who has seen many top performers come and go, still becomes rapturous when the conversation turns to Josephine. "In her style, as the leading lady for a spectacular show, she is the number one who ever lived. She had fantastic appeal. In French we say '*elle dépasse la rampe.*' She went over the footlights. Pow! Did she ever. You had the feeling she was singing for you and only you. For everyone in the audience she was sitting on each one's lap."

The morning after the show opened, Josephine sat down with Marie-Joli and dictated notes to the "little people" who worked at the Sporting Club—the waitresses, the hat check girls, the kitchen help, even the washroom attendants—saying how much she appreciated their help. "I hand delivered them," says Marie-Joli, "and I will never forget the expressions on some of the faces when they opened the envelopes. One woman started to cry. She said, 'Of all the artists who have performed here, she is the first one to think of us. *C'est incroyable.*'"

Since the revue was so good, the producers decided to take it to Paris the following spring.

For Josephine, much was riding on the show. It was not just a question of getting ahead of the game financially. She wanted to make this final conquest of Paris, to take the city once more, just as she had done in 1925.

But there were many problems, and success was not assured. Her medical history was a big liability. Could a woman who had suffered a heart attack, who was pushing seventy, withstand the rigors of a major musical of which she was the star? The big music halls in Paris, the endroits of her former triumphs—the Folies-Bergère, the Casino de Paris and the Olympia—did not want to take the risk. No insurance company would cover her for such a gamble. If she dropped dead during the run of the show, the theatre could lose a fortune.   /

Roland Petit, director of the Casino de Paris, finally said he would be agreeable if Lisette Malidor, a young black headliner at the Casino, who was being hailed as the new Josephine Baker, could rehearse the show with Josephine and be prepared to go on as her double.

Josephine dismissed the idea as absurd. "Nobody can take my place."

The show was finally booked into the Bobino, a small music hall in Montparnasse that has presented the best singers in Paris for more than one hundred years. The Bobino is situated on the rue de la Gaieté, appropriately called "the street of joy." Here the cabarets, bars, luminous signs and player pianos give the street the atmosphere of a perpetual playground. The ever-lively Bobino is an authentic French theatre for students, workers, artists and small businessmen who drift in during an evening with the casualness of a movie crowd.

After Christmas Josephine moved to Paris to begin rehearsing the show. It had been fifty years since she first ventured down the broad avenues and ancient alleys of her adopted city. To the eyes of her youth it blazoned enchantment. Now, in her autumnal heyday, Paris still astonished her with its beauty and haunting charm. Joan of Arc still sat astride her golden horse in front of the Louvre; Napoleon rested in his tomb of red porphyry at the Invalides; the fishermen stood under the great elms on the stone banks of the Seine trying to catch a few *fritures* to take home to their families; and in the Place St. Sulpice the pigeons still perched on the statues of the bishops. "There is never any ending to Paris and the memory of each person who has lived in it differs from that of any other," wrote Hemingway in *A Moveable Feast.* "We always returned to it no matter who we were or how it was changed or with what difficulties, or ease, it could be reached. Paris was always worth it and you received return for whatever you brought to it."

Of all Josephine's extraordinary qualities, none was more amazing than the force of her artistic will. In the grueling process of rehearsing for the show, the "old lady" vanished.

Says technical director François Rosset: "Josephine was dancing with showgirls who were twenty and twenty-two years old, and yet there were moments when she appeared younger than they did. She had more staying power."

It became apparent to the cast that Josephine was radiantly happy and filled with goodwill toward everybody. "She returned to the person she had been before the tragedy of Les Milandes," says Jean-Louis Preslier, a performer in the show. "She was naïve and full of pep, always ready to help the new girls with their routines."

She could outlast anyone at the rehearsals, which ran until two and three in the morning. And she was usually the first one at the theatre the next day. "She'd call me at nine and say, 'Where's the piano player?'" Rosset remembers. The revue required Josephine to be onstage nearly all the time, singing over thirty songs and rigorously dancing, including—*bien sur!*—Le Charleston. To help her remember the songs, Rosset placed giant placards with key words on the floor of the stage.

At the dress rehearsal he noticed that Josephine was crying softly as she waited in the wings. "What's wrong?" he asked.

"I wish my kids could be here."

After several preliminary performances, the show officially opened on April 8, 1975.

As the curtain rose, Josephine sang the show's theme song, "Me Revoila Paris," lingering on the line "I will finish my life on the stage."

Much of her had changed. Much appeared the same. The brown eyes sparkled like the eyes of an Apache, but the skin around them was puffy and lined. To camouflage the ravages of time, Josephine wore inch-long lashes that rolled up and down like venetian blinds. To cover her sparse hair, she had a $2000 Alexandre wig. Her voice, however, was that of a much younger woman, having in it the echoes of Piaf and Dietrich, but very much her own. Only when she laughed, with the husky roughness of someone without any more tears to shed, did she reveal her age.

Trailing two white Russian wolfhounds down a scarlet staircase, racketing across the stage on a Harley-Davidson motorcycle, Josephine exuded her everlasting appetite for life. She still mugged, swaggered and strutted with the saucy abandon of a pigtailed kid on a St. Louis street corner.

In fact, when she sang in English, she still sounded like an American girl who just hit Broadway from the Middle West. There was a root-a-toot-toot bounce to her words and a guileless sincerity in her tone, particularly when she sang a number from *Shuffle Along:*

> *I'm just wild about Harry.*
> *Harry's wild about me.*
> *The heavenly blisses of his kisses,*
> *Fills me with ecstasy.*

> *He's sweet as chocolate candy,*
> *Sweet as the honey from the bee.*
> *For I'm just wild about Harry*
> *And he's just wild about,*
> *Cannot do without,*
> *He's just wild about meee.*

She ended the show in her special style: "Good night ladies and gentlemen, buona sera, buenos noches, shalom, shalom, ciao, ciao."

At the end of the performance, madly cheering Parisians rose to their feet and gave vent to a torrent of emotion. It was a response to memories of a time gone by, but most of all to the woman herself, the woman who had lived, survived and given them pleasure, to the indomitable spirit of Josephine.

As the crowd clapped, Josephine accepted the applause, pacing up and down the center aisle like a lashing panther. Preslier still shakes his head in wonderment when he thinks about that night. "When you see a woman of sixty-eight move like that, you ask yourself, Is it true?"

After the show a large segment of the crowd waited for her in front of the Bobino, hoping to catch one more glimpse. When she finally left the theatre at one o'clock, it was still impossible to move or to guide a car through the mob.

Once again Josephine brought La Ville Lumière to its feet. The show sold out twenty days in advance. The record from the performance was a smash hit. *"Ce n'est plus un comeback. C'est*

Josephine greets Sophia Loren and Carlo Ponti at a gala at the Hotel Bristol in Paris honoring her fifty years as a performer. *AGIP, Robert Cohen*

l'éternel retour," wrote the reviewer for *L'Express,* the French newsweekly.

Suddenly Paris was talking about Josephine again. A gala was given at the Hotel Bristol to honor her fifty years in show business. Princess Grace, Sophia Loren, Jeanne Moreau and Alain Delon turned out to see her. President Giscard d'Estaing congratulated her in a telegram ". . . in the name of a grateful France whose heart so often beat with yours."

Two nights later there was a party for the cast at a café near the Bobino. Josephine was drunk with success. After they cleared the table where Josephine was seated, she climbed on top of it and chanted, "I'm seventeen, I'm seventeen."

Jean-Louis Preslier tried to coax her back to terra firma. Finally, in exasperation, he said, "All right, Josephine, we believe you are seventeen. Let's not go all the way back to infancy."

By three in the morning most of the cast had gone home, but

As film star Jean-Claude Brialy looks on, Josephine cuts the cake at her gala, which took place five days before her death. French president Giscard d'Estaing sent a telegram "... in the name of a grateful France whose heart so often beat with yours." *AGIP, Robert Cohen*

Josephine stayed until the last, trying to get somebody to take her to Chez Michou, a cabaret where a beautiful black boy did an impersonation of her as a young girl, sporting a bone in his hair like a cannibal. Finding no takers, she returned to her apartment on the Avenue Paul Doumer.

The next morning she did not wake up. She lay in her flowered nightgown, surrounded by newspapers in which she was still making news. Josephine had suffered a cerebral hemorrhage during the night. She was now in a coma.

Lélia Scotto, Pepito's niece, who was staying with Josephine, called the doctor, who summoned an ambulance.

Josephine did not spend her final hours at a chic address. The Salpétrière Hospital, a short distance from the Gobelins district, was originally a hospital for prostitutes, beggars and criminal women. Today it is a home for the elderly and insane.

As the priest administered extreme unction, asking God to forgive Josephine's sins and take her soul to heaven, Princess Grace knelt by the side of the bed and prayed.

Margaret, who had flown up from Roquebrune, arrived just in time. Squeezing her sister's hand tightly, she said, "Tumpie, I made it."

At five o'clock in the morning on Friday, April 14, Josephine was pronounced dead.

While the corpse was still warm, Margaret bathed it herself. Later she said, "I felt like I was washing the body of Jesus."

With the help of two friends, Margaret dressed Josephine in the mousseline and toile dress she wore at her gala five days before. She put no makeup on Josephine because she thought she looked most beautiful with her face scrubbed, naked to the world. Not that anyone had a chance to see. As soon as Josephine's body was placed in a mahogany coffin, Margaret closed the lid. She would not share her sister with the paparazzi who hovered at the doors of the Salpétrière. "Nobody's takin' pictures of my dead sister," she told them.

Though the cerebral hemorrhage was given as the cause of her death, Henri Astric thought otherwise. "In my opinion, she died of joy."

News of Josephine's death reached the four corners of the globe. Even in Cambodia where the government had fallen and

April 15, 1975. The Madeleine. Josephine Baker received one of the greatest funerals Paris has ever known. A war recipient of the Légion d'Honneur and the Médaille de la Résistance, she is the only American woman to have received a twenty-one-gun salute in France. Following the service, dozens of floral arrangements—some so large they had to be carried by four men—were taken throughout Paris and placed on monuments of those killed during World War II. *Agence France-Presse*

the Americans had been evacuated, the anxious people listened to their radios, which gave a long obituary of Josephine. In Buenos Aires, Jo Bouillon prepared to fly back to Paris. Jean-Claude Baker in New York received a phone call from Air France saying that they had booked a reservation for him upon hearing the news. In Harlem, Jimmy Hall draped the Red Rooster bar in black. And in Chicago, Bricktop, now eighty-two, was holding court at the Tango Club, where she was about to open in a new show. Sitting on a banquette, drinking with a group of journalists, Bricktop sighed, "She's gone, God bless her."

Of the twelve children, only two, Mara and Jari, attended Josephine's majestic funeral at the Madeleine. The rest waited in seclusion at the villa in Roquebrune. A second, more private funeral was scheduled to take place in Monaco following the national service in Paris.

Princess Grace arranged with her chapter of the Red Cross to supply Josephine's children proper clothes for the Monaco funeral. She also paid for the burial and exercised her authority to prevent the service from disintegrating into the circus atmosphere of the one in Paris where, when the Mass ended, crowds descended and plucked flowers from the altar.

Josephine's boys acted as pallbearers, carrying the casket up the small hill to the Monaco cemetery. Then, as the priest intoned the prayers for the dead, they joined the rest of the family, standing in two solid rows with Jo Bouillon holding the hand of Stellina, who used her free hand to wipe her tears.

The children now conveyed the uncontrived solidity of a true family. However contradictory and complex their feelings had been about Josephine, they were stunned by her death. Despite her long absences, she was the shaping force in their lives.

As the mourners listened in silence to the final blessing, Jean-Claude Baker surveyed the scene with the shrewd eye of a showman. Here was Princess Grace choked with emotion, children clutching rosary beads, Josephine's comrades from the war standing at full attention. Then he looked at the coffin and pictured Josephine inside. He could not imagine her face immobile, her body stiff. She was always in the process of taking off, of practicing her songs like an incantation, an affirmation of her vitality. Now the restless life was stilled.

As he bent his head, a vision crossed his mind of Josephine in the coffin. He did not see a crone. Instead, he imagined her as a young girl, as she first appeared in Paris on her opening night, naked except for the hot-pink feather. He smiled to himself at the irony of it all. "Here she was, the main attraction. It was the best show she ever had. And yet she could do nothing. She had to shut up and watch the program. I thought, 'You're not dead, Josephine. You can't be dead. Let's have fun.'"

Josephine's body was placed in a mausoleum for six months until a suitable plot was found in the principality's crowded cemetery; in the postage stamp fiefdom of Monaco, space is tight even in the grave. Though a long, long way from the banks of the Mississippi River, the cemetery of Monaco is an appropriate final resting place for Josephine, whose hunger for life and beauty and her need of people was insatiable.

Her plot is situated in the middle of an aisle, embellished by a simple black African granite marker and surrounded by the lush foliage of the Mediterranean coast. The olive trees, mimosa and cyclamen bushes suit a pantheist like Josephine.

Many surrounding headstones carry pictures of the deceased, photographs mounted on weather-resistant tin— smiling children, dignified grandmothers, soldiers in uniform—giving the cemetery an ironic vibrancy of life.

The ragamuffin from St. Louis, who dreamed of castles and kings, who hoisted herself up and out of the cruel confines of American racial prejudice, had now come to rest.

And so in this cliff-bound enclave, screened by the Alps from the cold north winds, Josephine lies among the same bouillabaisse of humanity with whom she surrounded herself—the corner grocer and the policeman as well as dowager empresses and itinerant swindlers. What could be more fitting for Josephine, who hopscotched from one perilous crisis to the next, to finish her days in a gambler's paradise.

A Note on the Rainbow Tribe

Josephine did not do a bad job with her children. Those old enough to choose have opted for simple lives, far away from the spotlight, where the rewards come from the small joys of harmonious days rather than the ephemeral thrill of hooking the brass ring.

The older ones, now in their twenties, live ordinary lives: Moïse is a waiter, Janot a florist, Koffi a baker, Luis an insurance salesman, Marianne a secretary, Jari a hotel manager. Akio works for Jo Bouillon in his restaurant in Buenos Aires. The younger children will be the responsibility of their father until they come of age.

Bibliography

Abtey, Jacques. *La Guerre Secret de Joséphine Baker*. Paris: Siboney, 1948.

Baker, Joséphine, and Bouillon, Jo. *Joséphine*. Avec la collaboration de Jacqueline Cartier. Paris: Editions Robert Laffont-Opéra Mundi, 1976.

Baker, Joséphine, and Sauvage, Marcel. *Les Mémoires de Joséphine Baker*. Kra, 1927.

Baker, Joséphine, and Sauvage, Marcel. *Les Mémoires de Joséphine Baker*. Kra, 1947.

Baker, Joséphine, and Sauvage, Marcel. *Voyages et Adventures de Joséphine Baker*. Kra, 1931.

Baker, Joséphine, and Rivollet, André. *Une Vie de Toutes les Couleurs*. Grenoble: B. Arthaud, 1935.

Blesh, Rudi, and Janis, Harriet. *They All Played Ragtime*. New York: Oak Publications, 1971.

Boyle, Kay, and McAlmon, Robert. *Being Geniuses Together 1920–1930*. New York: Doubleday & Company, 1968.

Charles, Jacques. *Cent Ans de Music-Hall*. Geneva, Paris: Editions Jeheber, 1956.

Chevalier, Maurice. *The Man in the Straw Hat*. New York: Thomas Y. Crowell, 1949.

Chevalier, Maurice. *With Love*. Boston: Little, Brown & Company, 1960.

Crawford, Kenneth G. *Report on North Africa*. New York, Toronto: Farrar & Rinehart, Inc., 1943.

Crespelle, Jean-Paul. Montparnasse, *A La Grande Epoque 1905–1930*. Paris: Librairie Hachette, 1976.

Crespelle, Jean-Paul. *La Folle Epoque des Ballets Russes au Surrealisme*. Paris: Librairie Hachette, 1968.

Damase, Jacques. *Les Folies du Music-Hall*. Paris: Editions Spectacles, 1960.

Derval, Paul. *Folies-Bergère*. New York: E. P. Dutton & Co., Inc., 1955.

Feschotte, Jacques. *Histoire du Music-Hall*. Paris: Presses Universitaires de France, 1965.

Flanner, Janet. *An American in Paris*. New York: Simon and Schuster, 1940.

331

Flanner, Janet. *Paris Was Yesterday.* New York: The Viking Press, 1972.

Friedrich, Otto. *Before the Deluge: A Portrait of Berlin in the 1920's.* New York: Harper & Row, 1972.

Gheusi, P. B. *Cinquante Ans de Paris, Mémoires d'un Témoin 1889–1938.* Paris: Librairie Plon, 1939.

Guilleminault, Gilbert. *Le Roman Vrai des Années Folles 1918–1930.* Paris: Denoël. 1975.

Halimi, Andre. *Chantons Sous l'Occupation.* Paris: Olivier Orban, 1976.

Huddleston, Sisley. *Paris, Salons, Cafés, Studios.* Philadelphia: J. B. Lippincott, 1928.

Hughes, Langston, and Meltzer, Milton. *Black Magic: A Pictorial History of Black Entertainers in America.* New York: Bonanza Books, 1968.

Hughes, Langston. *The Big Sea.* New York: Hill and Wang, 1940.

Jackson, Stanley. *Inside Monte Carlo.* New York: Stein & Day, 1975.

Johnson, James Weldon. *Black Manhattan.* New York: Atheneum, 1930.

Kessler, Harry. *In the Twenties: The Diaries of Count Harry Kessler.* New York: Harcourt Brace Jovanovich, Inc., 1971.

Klurfeld, Herman. *Winchell, His Life and Times.* New York: Praeger Publishing Company, 1976.

Lanoux, Armand. *Paris in the Twenties.* New York: Golden Griffin Books, Essential Encyclopedia Arts, Inc., 1960.

Mann, Mary. *Evita, The Woman with the Whip.* New York: Dodd, Mead & Company, Inc., 1952.

Mauley, Raymond. *Sidney Bechet, Notre Ami.* Paris: La Table Ronde, 1959.

Miller, Douglas T., and Nowak, Marion. *The Fifties: The Way We Really Were.* Garden City, New York: Doubleday & Company, 1977.

Mistinguett. *Toute Ma Vie, de 1924 à Nos Jours.* Paris: René Julliard, 1954.

Osofsky, Gilbert. *Harlem: The Making of a Ghetto Negro, New York 1890–1930.* New York: Harper Torchbooks, 1931.

Otéro, Caroline. *Le Roman de la Belle Otero: Sa vie intime, ses amours, ses succes racontés par elle-même.* Paris: Editions "Le Calame," 1926.

Papich, Stephen. *Remembering Josephine.* Indianapolis, New York: The Bobbs-Merrill Company, Inc., 1976.

Prasteau, Jean. *La Merveilleuse Adventure du Casino de Paris.* Paris: Denoël, 1975.

Quarles, Benjamin. *The Negro in the Making of America.* New York: The Macmillan Company, 1964.

Rudwick, Elliot M. *Race Riot At East St. Louis, July 2, 1917.* Cleveland, New York: The World Publishing Company, 1966.

Skinner, Cornelia Otis. *Elegant Wits and Grand Horizontals.* Boston: Houghton Mifflin Company, 1962.

Stagg, Jerry. *The Brothers Shubert.* New York: Random House, 1968.

Stearns, Marshall. *The Story of Jazz.* New York: Oxford University Press, Inc., 1956.

Tomkins, Calvin. *Living Well is the Best Revenge.* New York: The Viking Press, 1962.

Veronesi, Giula. *Style 1925, Triomphe et Chute des "Arts-Deco."* Lausanne: Editions Anthony Krafft, 1968.

Woon, Basil. *The Paris That's Not in the Guidebooks.* New York: Brentano's, 1926.

Index